ON MEASURING DEMOCRACY

ON MEASURING DEMOCRACY

Its Consequences and Concomitants

Edited by
Alex Inkeles

Transaction Publishers
New Brunswick (U.S.A.) and London (U.K.)

Library of Congress Catalog Number: 90-19832
ISBN: 0-88738-881-7
Printed in the United States of America

Library of Congress Cataloging-in-Publication Data
On measuring democracy: its consequences and concomitants/edited
  by Alex Inkeles.
      p.   cm.
    ISBN 0-88738-881-7
    1. Democracy—Congresses.   2. Comparative government—
    Congresses.
  I. Inkeles, Alex, 1920–
  JC421.05 1991
  321.8—dc20   90-19832
                                                          CIP

Contents

Introduction

We here present the papers prepared for a Conference on Measuring Democracy held at the Hoover Institution of Stanford University on May 27 and 28, 1988. The conference was part of a larger ongoing program of research on democratic societies being conducted at the Hoover Institution. That larger project includes case studies, broad descriptive surveys and systematic analyses designed to test hypotheses and develop generalizations. For example, we are attempting to ascertain the correctness of the common assumption that democratic nations enjoy less rapid economic growth, and of the equally common belief that, whatever their growth rates, the more democratic systems offer less income equality than do nondemocratic societies.

It is obvious that to make such tests requires that we have good measures, and have them available over time. This in turn leads to the question: "What is a good measure of democracy, and where is it to be found?" Our initial search for appropriate measures made it evident that there were a number available, all pressing a claim for their virtues. But, perhaps inevitably, there seemed to be considerable disagreement among those attempting the measurement as to both theoretical and methodological issues. We felt it would be useful, therefore, to bring together some of the leaders in the measurement effort to review their experience, confront their disagreements, attempt some assessment of the state of the art, and perhaps find some common ground for future work.

With the aid of a grant from the MacArthur Foundation we were able to bring together more than a dozen social scientists interested in efforts to measure the properties of political systems, and they prepared the nine formal papers included in this volume. All of the authors were requested to address themselves, so far as they could, to seven issues.

1. What was the intellectual, and especially theoretic, concern which led them into the particular measurement effort they undertook?
2. What specific conceptualization of democracy did they develop or adopt?

Alex Inkeles received his Ph.D. from Columbia University in 1949 and taught at Harvard University from 1948 to 1970. Currently professor of sociology, and senior fellow, Hoover Institution on War, Revolution and Peace, Stanford University, he has been elected to the National Academy of Sciences, American Academy of Arts and Sciences, and American Philosophical Society. He has published more than 115 articles in sociology and social psychology. Of his six books, the most recent is *Exploring Individual Modernity*, 1983. He is currently studying convergence and divergent trends in the social organizations and popular attitudes and values within sets of industrial and industrializing countries.

3. Could they describe and evaluate the precise indicators they used to represent the concepts they had developed?
4. What information could they provide concerning the reliability and validity of the measures they used?
5. What has been the experience of using the measure; in particular what seems to be its power, what conclusions has it led to, what difficulties and limitations become apparent through its use?
6. What emerges from critical and especially comparative analysis of the measure, especially as such analysis highlighted theoretical, conceptual, and methodological similarities and contrasts?
7. Finally, what suggestions could be made leading to improvement of the measure and extension of its utility in further systematic research?

All these issues certainly were not touched on in all the papers submitted. Indeed, in some cases the authors dealt with measures still in process of elaboration or just recently developed, and so they could not report on actual experience in working with their measure. But in the set of papers as a whole, each of the seven issues is dealt with, some in considerable depth.

Another source of variation, one we did not attempt to censor, arose from the fact that some authors focused quite explicitly and more or less exclusively on the democratic polity as such, whereas others concentrated more on what might be thought of as the consequences and concomitants of democracy. Some of these scholars are studying phenomena relevant to the analysis of *any* political system, and that means, of course, that they are also germane to the study of democracies. Examples of such attributes or any political system include the capacity to function effectively in achieving the government's will, the regularity and irregularity of the process of periodically replacing the executive, and the propensity to go to war. Although in all cases the papers we present have in common their concern with the promise, the challenge and the vicissitudes of attempting precise measurement, we have deemed it appropriate to acknowledge the distinction that arose spontaneously, and to group the papers in two sets. The first focused more on measuring democratic political systems as such, and the second was concerned more with the consequences and concomitants.

Since our Conference did not attempt to reach any formal consensus, there remains the question: "What did all this lead to?" The answer, in part, lies in the papers themselves, but most will appreciate being presented with some main conclusions, if such can safely be drawn. It falls to me, as the convener of the Conference and the editor of this volume, to attempt a summary, with the understanding that these conclusions formally represent only the position I personally reached. None of the other participants should be assumed to agree with me, although I rather believe the great majority would do so with regard to most of the points I make here.

1. Democracy should be recognized as only one specific form of political system, or regime type, important in the contemporary era. Autocracy in

general, and totalitarianism in particular, are identified as polar opposites of democracy, but a number of variant forms fall in between. The problem of defining and measuring democracy is therefore only a particular case of the general problem of defining and measuring political systems.

2. As one moves from one conceptualization of democracy to another, the language used may be different, even distinctive, but the essence of what is expressed is notably similar. The definitions offered generally distinguish two components of a democratic system, one treating of *political rights* and *political structures*, the other of *civic rights* or *civil liberties*. In democracies the governors, those who wield political power, are selected by the governed, are accountable to them, and can be replaced by orderly procedures whereby the governed express their preferences as to who shall rule and how. In other words, ordinary people have meaningful political rights and mechanisms exist to make the implementation of those rights effective. To ensure the meaningfulness and effectiveness of their *political* rights citizens and organizations must be assured certain basic *civil* rights, such as freedom of communication in speech and writing, freedom of assembly and of petition, freedom to form associations and engage in peaceful protest, and freedom from arbitrary arrest and lawless punishment. The political structures are important in their own right, but without significant opportunity to exercise such civil liberties there can be no effective exercise of the political rights generally placed at the core of any definition of democracy.

3. The exact *indicators* used to represent the conceptualized dimensions of a democratic system vary considerably, but they are actually drawn from a limited pool of commonly utilized measures, and in various ways they all express the underlying dimensions of participation in political contestation and of guarantees of civil freedoms of expression. Thus, to measure political rights, Bollen considers only three issues: "the fairness of elections, whether the chief executive came to office via an election, and the effectiveness and elective/non-elective nature of the national legislative body." Coppedge and Reinicke, working within the framework of the conception of democracy elaborated by Robert Dahl, also limited themselves to three questions: 1) whether elections present voters a meaningful choice; 2) whether the outcome is affected by significant fraud; and 3) whether all, some, or no political organizations are banned.

4. The experience of working with indicators also helps to identify characteristics of political systems presumed by some theory to identify democracies but which fail to prove serviceable in measurement efforts. Outstanding among these is voter turnout, or percent voting, which, as emphasized by Bollen, is seriously flawed as an indicator on both theoretical and methodological grounds. In addition, many distinctions intended to give a more fine-grained differentiation of regimes fail to prove useful. Thus, Coppedge and Reinicke found that the distinction between no election at all and a sham "approval" election had no practical significance in constructing a scale of polyarchy.

5. Although tests of scale reliability are not applied as regularly as they

should be, it seems clear that the indicators most commonly selected to measure democratic systems generally form a notably coherent syndrome, achieving high reliability as measurement scales. Important as the distinction between political rights and civil liberties may be on theoretical grounds, we discover that in the real world they are so intimately linked as to be almost perfect substitutes for each other. When measured separately they correlate at .90 and above. When incorporated in a single scale, their being combined adds significantly to the scales' reliability. In this statistical sense democracy, properly measured, is clearly a decidedly unidimensional phenomenon.

6. A testimonial to the robustness of the underlying common form and structure of democratic systems is found in the high degree of agreement produced by the classification of nations as democratic or not, even when democracy is measured in somewhat different ways by different analysts. This is, perhaps, another way of saying that democracy is a distinctive and highly coherent syndrome of characteristics such that anyone measuring only a few of the salient characteristics will classify nations in much the same way as will another analyst who also measures only a few qualities but uses a different subset of characteristics, so long as both have selected their indicators from the same larger pool of validated measures. Far from being like the elephant confronting the blind sages, democracy is more like a ball of wax. Thus Coppedge and Reinicke, following a quite independent theoretical model, end up with a scale of polyarchy that correlates .94 with Gastil's civil liberties measure for some 170 countries in 1985. Gurr's measure performs similarly in relation to Bollen's. He considers three, mainly political, features such as competitiveness of political participation, openness of executive recruitment, and constraints on the chief executive, and did not weigh in any of the civil-liberties dimensions. Yet, by our calculations, his ratings of 118 countries circa 1965 correlate .83 with Bollen's measure, and it correlates .89 with a score combining Gastil's separate measures of political and civil liberties for 133 countries as rated for the year 1985.

7. Finally, our Conference found that democracy must be valued as an end in itself, rather than being seen mainly as a means to some other goal such as rapid economic growth or greater equality of income distribution. It may well generate both, but that seems neither a certain nor a distinctive feature of such systems. Moreover we cannot, on the available evidence, make indisputable claims to the effect that democratic systems are more effective in carrying out the will of government or that democracies are less often at war than other states. What is unmistakable is that democratic systems give people a greater sense of freedom and, I would argue, more *actual* freedom, to influence the course of public events, express themselves, and realize their individual human potential.

ALEX INKELES

I
Measuring Democratic Political Systems

1

Political Democracy: Conceptual and Measurement Traps

Kenneth A. Bollen

The movement toward democratic political systems in many nations in the 1980s has renewed interest in measurement of political democracy. This paper calls attention to the problems that surround both the definition and measurement of political democracy. The main conceptual problems are the failure to develop an adequate theoretical definition of this concept, the confounding of the concept with others, and treating democracy as a binary rather than a continuous concept. Four problems of measurement are: invalid indicators, subjective indicators, ordinal or dichotomous measures, and the failure to test reliability or validity. The paper offers several suggestions to improve measurement as well as a warning about the danger of repeating past errors.

In the late 1950s and early 1960s a record number of countries became independent. A surprisingly large group began with relatively democratic political systems (e.g., Somalia, Sierra Leone, and Jamaica). Accompanying this were the first major efforts at developing cross-national measures of national political democracy. Lerner (1958), Lipset (1959), Coleman (1960), Cutright (1963), and Banks and Textor (1963) are only a few of the many who provided indices or indicators of democracy. As democracies collapsed and authoritarian regimes rose, the 1970s saw a decline in social science interest in measuring democracy. Important work was done during this period (e.g., Banks 1971; Dahl 1971; Gastil 1978), but the volume of studies declined. And much of this work developed cross-national measures of political democracy for the 1960s rather than the 1970s.[1] Political democracy indicators received some attention in the early 1980s (e.g., Bollen 1980) but here again the indices often referred to the 1960s.

Kenneth A. Bollen is a professor of sociology at the University of North Carolina at Chapel Hill. His major research interests are in international development and statistics. He is the author of *Structural Equations with Latent Variables* (1989), published in John Wiley's Series in Probability and Mathematical Statistics.

Redemocratization in the 1980s in Argentina, Brazil, the Philippines, and elsewhere has sparked renewed interest in empirical measures. I suspect that we will see at least as much attention to measuring democracy in the 1990s as we saw during the 1960s and certainly more than has been true during most of the 1970s and the early 1980s.

The measurement of political democracy in cross-national research is the focus of this article. An examination of the efforts to quantify political democracy does not reveal a smooth evolution toward clear theoretical definitions and finely calibrated instruments. Instead, we see advances as well as backsliding. Consider the theoretical definitions that should accompany the presentation of new measures. Studies such as Dahl's (1971) are exemplary in the attention they give to defining political democracy while others, even recent work, do not provide a definition or do not have a sharp line separating their theoretical from their operational definitions. Nor is a trend toward improved calibration of measures evident. Ironically, some of the early studies by Lerner (1958) and Cutright (1963) have measures with more precise gradations than do several more recent studies that classify political democracy as "present" or "absent" in each year (e.g., Hewitt 1977; Muller 1988). Another sign of measurement advancement is understanding the boundaries of a concept and using measures that do not confuse one concept with another. Here, too, progress is not obvious. Voter turnout and political stability are two examples of concepts that are confounded with political democracy. This occurs in early works (e.g., Lerner 1958; Cutright 1963) as well as in recent studies (e.g., Hewitt 1977; Muller 1988).

The history of research in this area suggests that the renewed interest in measuring political democracy is no guarantee that we will escape the errors made in earlier measurement efforts. Those researchers new to this area may dismiss this warning, believing that virtually all social science data contain errors and that such errors have a trivial impact. I do not doubt that measurement error is present in most variables, but this ignores the degree of measurement error and whether it is systematic or random. It is my contention that, indicators of political democracy contain both types of error and the proportion of error is sizable.

Does it matter? Yes. Consider the monitoring of the worldwide trends in political democracy. The U.S. State Department, Amnesty International, and many other organizations and scholars are committed to assessing human rights in countries. An important sector of human rights are political rights and liberties that are closely tied to political democracy. If we were to follow the conventions established with some measures of political democracy, these monitoring efforts would be undermined. For instance, Lerner (1958) used voter turnout to gauge degrees of political democracy and this practice has continued (e.g., Smith 1969; Coulter 1975; Vanhanen 1979). Yet, when we contemplate that in some countries voters are legally obligated to vote, that high turnouts can occur in elections with no choice or under conditions of fraud, and that turnout is affected by many things, ranging from voter satisfaction or apathy to whether it rains on the election day, we see that voter turnout reflects factors that have little to do with measuring political democracy. Monitoring efforts relying on voter turnout are seriously compromised. Add to this that policy decisions ranging from foreign aid and investments to the imposition of sanctions on foreign governments are influenced by human rights reports and measures, and it is easy to see that flawed measures have potentially serious policy repercussions.

Academic research has not escaped the negative consequences of faulty political democracy measures. An example is the research on the relation between political democracy and income inequality. For more than two decades quantitative cross-national studies have presented conflicting evidence on the impact of political democracy on income inequality (e.g., Cutright 1967; Jackman 1974; Bollen and Jackman 1985; Muller 1988). At the center of the controversy is the measurement of political democracy (Bollen and Jackman 1985; 1989). Thus, measurement error in indicators matters for monitoring trends in political democracy, for policy decisions, and for scholarly research.

To call attention to common problems that surround the definition and measurement of political democracy, I will draw upon my earlier research (Bollen 1980; Bollen and Grandjean 1981; Bollen 1986; Bollen and Jackman 1989), providing new illustrations of points made in these studies and elaborating definitional issues growing out of this work. A consideration of the definitional and conceptual issues, and of measurement problems besetting political democracy is followed by recommendations for future research.

Conceptual Issues

The starting point in evaluating the validity of political democracy measures is the theoretical definition of the concept. Clearly, providing a definition of political democracy that everyone accepts is impossible. I will settle for the less ambitious goal of providing a working definition of political democracy and contrasting it with other definitions.

I define political democracy as the extent to which the political power of the elites is minimized and that of the nonelites is maximized (Bollen 1980:372). By political power I am referring to the ability to control the national governing system. The elites are those members of a society who hold a disproportionate amount of the political power. These include the members of the executive, judicial, and legislative branches of the government as well as leaders of political parties, local governments, businesses, labor unions, professional associations, or religious bodies. Like Mosca (1939), Michels (1962), Mills (1956), and many others, I recognize the existence of elites. However, unlike them, I do not conclude that the presence of elites means that their relative power compared to the nonelites is everywhere the same. Indeed, it is the relative balance of power between elites and nonelites that determines the degree of political democracy. Where the nonelites have little control over the elites, political democracy is low. When the elites are accountable to the nonelites, political democracy is higher.

The minimization of elite political power and the maximization of nonelite power remain fairly abstract ideas. How do we determine the elites and nonelites in each society. Even if we can determine these groups, how do we measure their relative political power? Until someone finds a direct measure of political power, these goals remain elusive. However, we can indirectly gauge the relative political power of elites and nonelites. As I have argued elsewhere (Bollen 1980; 1986), political rights and political liberties reflect the political power of these two groups. Political rights and liberties are two dimensions of political democracy:[2]

> Political rights exist to the extent that the national government is accountable to the
> general population and each individual is entitled to participate in the government
> directly or through representatives. Political liberties exist to the extent that the
> people of a country have the freedom to express any political opinions in any media
> and the freedom to form or to participate in any political group. (Bollen 1986:568)

Political rights are typically assessed by examining characteristics of the electoral system. Leaders selected by elections, equal weighting of votes, the extent of the franchise, the openness of the candidate selection process, the fairness of elections, the representativeness of office holders, and the timeliness of elections, are specific examples of political rights. The higher the level of political democracy in a country, the more we expect these rights to be present.

Political liberties refer to the freedom that the population has in the political system. Here I refer to characteristics such as the freedom of the media, the freedom of individuals or political groups to oppose government policies or officials, and the absence of political censorship.

Differences in political rights and liberties correspond to differences in the relative political power of the elites versus the nonelites. If a country's standing on political rights or liberties is low, this suggests that the elites in that society have greater political power over the nonelites than in a society where these rights and liberties are high. Hence, political rights and political liberties provide evidence on political democracy.

How does this definition compare to others? These two dimensions encompass many of the more specific characteristics of political democracy laid out by others. To illustrate this I will consider Dahl's (1971) definition. He (1971:3) proposed that political democracies must have eight "institutional guarantees": (1) freedom to join and form organizations, (2) freedom of expression, (3) right to vote, (4) eligibility for public office, (5) right of political leaders to compete for support and votes, (6) alternative sources of information, (7) free and fair elections, and (8) institutions for making government policies depend on votes and other expressions of preference. Table 1 classifies Dahl's eight "requirements for a democracy" under either the political rights or political liberties dimension, demonstrating that Dahl's requirements are encompassed by my definition.

Interestingly, Dahl (1974:4) also argued that two dimensions run through these items, but his dimensions differ from mine. Instead he sees these as public contestation and inclusiveness (participation). Public contestation is "the extent to which the eight institutional conditions are openly available, publicly employed, and fully guaranteed to at least some members of the political system . . ." while inclusiveness is "the proportion of the population entitled to participate on a more or less equal plane in controlling and contesting the conduct of government: to participate,

TABLE 1
Classification of Dahl's (1971, p. 3) Eight "Requirements for a
Democracy" into Political Rights or Political Liberties

Dimension of Political Democracy	
Political Rights	**Political Liberties**
	1. freedom to form and join organizations
	2. freedom of expression
3. right to vote	
4. eligibility for public office	
5. right of leaders to compete for votes	
	6. alternative sources of information
7. free and fair elections	
8. institutions for making government policies depend on votes & other expressions of preferences	

so to speak, in the system of public contestation'' (Dahl 1971:4). Dahl states that the eight criteria of democracy in Table 1 indicate the first dimension, public contestation, and suggests that by measuring the "breadth" of these we can assess inclusiveness:

> The right to vote in free and fair elections, for example, partakes of both dimensions. When a regime grants this right to some of its citizens, it moves toward greater public contestation. But the larger the proportion of citizens who enjoy the right, the more inclusive the regime. (Dahl 1971:4)

If each characteristic in Table 1 measures both public contestation and inclusiveness, then it is difficult to know how we can track each dimension separately. Dahl suggests that public contestation exists when at least some unspecified portion of the population satisfies the eight criteria. But he also refers to the extent of public contestation, suggesting that we can discriminate degrees of it. I am not certain how the degree of public contestation differs from the degree of inclusiveness. Perhaps to overcome this ambiguity, the measurement of inclusivenss which is presented in the appendix of Dahl (1971) relies exclusively on the extent of the franchise, while public contestation includes the remaining "institutional guarantees." In brief, I largely agree with Dahl's list of criteria for political democracy, but I view political rights and political liberties as the two dimensions that underlie them.

Other suggested definitions or requirements for political democracy emphasize one dimension to the exclusion of the other. Downs (1957:23-24) states that a democracy must have periodic elections decided by majority rule with a one-person one-vote, standard. According to Schumpeter (1950:269), a political democracy is "that institutional arrangement for arriving at political decisions in which individuals acquire the power to decide by means of a competitive struggle for the people's vote." Lipset (1959:71) defines political democracy as "a political system which provides regular constitutional opportunities for changing governing officials . . . permits the largest possible part of the population to influence decisions through their ability to choose among alternative contenders for political office.'' All three emphasize the political rights dimension of political democracy. They do not explicitly include the political liberties dimension. An examination of additional definitions and lists of criteria for democracy would reveal that most could be classified under one or both dimensions that I have identified.

What is the relation between these dimensions? Conceptually, I view political rights and political liberties as aspects of political democracy. I could imagine these as moving in response to changes in democracy. For instance, if democracy declines in a nation, I would expect this to lead to declines in political liberties and rights. On the other hand, a good case could be made that these two dimensions mutually reinforce one another. That is, it is difficult for a system to maintain political liberties without political rights being in place and vice versa. This suggests a positive feedback relation linking the two dimensions. It is not known which, if either, of these relations is valid.

In sum, I have defined political democracy to be the extent to which the political power of the elite is minimized and that of the nonelite is maximized. Political rights and political liberties are two major dimensions of the concept and these encompass most of the traits usually attributed to democratic systems.

Almost as important as defining what is political democracy is describing what it is not. This raises the second conceptual problem: the confounding of other concepts with political democracy. The many connotations of democracy have led it to be associated with a variety of phenomena. Perhaps the most prevalent practice of confounding concepts is combining political democracy with stability. It is common to find researchers referring to the concept of ''stable democracy'' or the ''democratic experience'' of a country (e.g., Lipset 1959; Hewitt 1977). As a short-hand expression to describe countries that have experienced both high levels of stability and high levels of political democracy, this can be helpful in nonquantitative work. But, in quantitative empirical research it has led to extensive confusion. The difficulty is that two concepts are being treated as one. Imagine an analogous situation where a medical study seeks to determine if ''big'' people have higher blood pressure than ''small'' people. The term big could refer to at least two concepts: height or weight. Suppose that weight has a far greater impact on blood pressure than height. By forcing these correlated but separate concepts together we can be led astray and might miss this. Similar arguments can be made for ''democratic stability.'' Political democracies can be stable (e.g., U.K.) or unstable (e.g., Argentina) as can authoritarian regimes. Unfortunately, an all too frequent practice is to conceptually confuse political democracy and stability and then to measure them with a single index (see, e.g., Hewitt 1977; Muller 1988). The cost is that we cannot know whether democracy or stability is responsible for any relations found. Distinct concepts should be treated distinctly (see Bollen and Jackman 1989).

Another common practice is to confuse political democracy with social or economic democracy. The distribution of wealth, work place ''democracy,'' or the health of the population are not part of the concept. These are important in their own right and should not be confounded with national levels of political democracy. Dahl (1971), Gastil (1987), and others make clear that their object of study is political not social democracy. All of us would be prudent to do likewise.

The concept of a multiparty political system also is sometimes mixed with political democracy (Cutright 1963; Cutright and Wiley 1969; Vanhanen 1979). In the extreme case, researchers believe that political democracies are systems that must have a particular type of party representation in the major legislative bodies and that shifts in political democracy can be judged by shifts in the party percentages. Having a multiparty system does not guarantee political rights and liberties. Although in practice most nations that are politically democratic give rise to multiple parties, it is theoretically possible for a one-party system to respect political rights and political liberties. Banning or restricting political parties is another matter. This indicates lower political liberties than if all parties are free. In short, the number of political parties gives hints about the degree of political democracy but having multiple parties is not the same as being highly democratic.

A third conceptual issue is whether political democracy is a dichotomous or continuous concept. It is easy to confuse treating a *concept as dichotomous* with measuring a continuous concept with a *dichotomous indicator*. Here my remarks are restricted to the former issue while I tackle the latter in the next section. The practice of treating continuous concepts as if they were dichotomies or were divisible into several categories is widespread. In development studies we have industrialized and nonindustrialized, capitalist and socialist, and militaristic and nonmilitaristic countries. Though these may be convenient short-hand references to the relative positions of countries, some forget that the underlying concept is continuous. A reminder comes when we attempt to classify countries into categories. For instance, are Argentina, Spain, Greece, or South Korea industrialized or nonindustrialized? The problem is that industrialization varies in degrees, and, if we see it as a binary concept, we will find countries near a cutoff point hard to place.

The same argument applies to political democracy. The concept of political democracy is continuous. We talk and think about the degree to which democracy is present. For example, Sweden has greater political democracy than Mexico, Mexico has more democracy than Chile. Unfortunately, some authors treat political democracy as present or absent. Hewitt (1977:456-457) argues that political democracy exists only when (1) the executive is elected and responsible to an elected assembly, (2) there is universal manhood suffrage, and (3) elections are fair as indicated by a secret ballot. An examination of these criteria reveals several problems. For instance, the fairness of elections is a matter of degree. Is a country with widespread fraud the same as one with minor irregularities? Even ignoring the questionable practice of restricting the franchise criterion only to men, suffrage is a continuous variable. Is there no difference in the degree of political democracy, if 95 percent of men are eligible in one country versus 20 percent in another? In Hewitt's categorical approach to political democracy, there is not.[3]

I believe that we unnecessarily compromise the concept of political democracy by considering it a dichotomous phenomenon. This leads to a crude lumping of countries into the same category when in reality they have very different degrees of political democracy. In short, I hope that the new efforts at analyzing political democracy recognize its continuous nature. Whether we must measure this continuous concept with dichotomies or ordinal variables is a distinct issue.

Measures of Political Democracy

In the last section I restricted my comments to the meaning of political democracy. In this section I turn to its empirical indicators. I briefly describe the measures that I have employed and their relation to the political rights and political liberties dimensions. Then, I examine other indicators that are part of political democracy indices. I highlight four problems of measurement: (1) invalid indicators, (2) subjective indicators, (3) dichotomous or ordinal measures, and (4) the failure to test reliability or validity.

In my work I use three indicators each for the political liberties and for the political rights dimensions to measure political democracy. The indicators of political liberties are subjective ratings of press freedom, the freedom that political parties have to organize and oppose the government, and the extent of government sanctions imposed on individuals or groups. The three measures of political rights are the fairness of elections, whether the chief executive came to office via an election, and the effectiveness and elective/nonelective nature of the national legislative body. Banks (1971), Nixon (1965; 1960), and Taylor and Hudson (1972) are the primary sources for these indicators. The six variables are combined into a single index. The appendix lists values of the index for 1965 and 1960 for 123 and 113 countries, respectively. Further details are in Bollen (1980). A confirmatory factor analysis of the indicators revealed moderate to high degrees of reliability and validity with evidence of correlated measurement errors for variables originating in the same data source. The correlated errors suggests that systematic biases occur for variables that are rated by the same judge(s). In Bollen and Grandjean (1981) we found that political liberties and political rights were nearly perfectly correlated once the effects of measurement error were removed.

I believe that the indicators I have selected correspond fairly closely to the liberty and rights facets of political democracy. Other variables sometimes used in democracy indices seem somewhat removed from these dimensions. For instance, Lerner (1958), Vanhanen (1979), and others have employed voter turnout statistics. As I have argued in the introduction to this article and elsewhere (Bollen 1980:373-374; Bollen 1986:571), turnout figures are influenced by many other factors, some of which are only marginally related to political rights and political liberties. Voter turnout may be a better measure of political participation, a concept that should be studied in its own right.

Political party composition of the legislative bodies also finds its way into measures of political democracy. Cutright's (1963) and Cutright and Wiley's (1969) operational definition relies heavily on the party composition of a nation's governing body: "The highest scores are assigned to nations with balanced multiparty parliaments in which the chief executive is selected by parliament or direct election, and where a large proportion of the population has been extended suffrage"(Cutright and

Wiley 1969:24). Vanhanen (1979:28) provides another more recent example. One component of his democracy index is "the smaller parties' share of the votes cast in parliamentary or presidential elections or both . . . calculated by subtracting the percentage of the votes won by the largest party from 100." I like the relatively objective nature of the party composition measures but I question their validity. This returns to the issue of confounding a multiparty system with political democracy examined in the last section. We can have legislative bodies with two parties but they could be powerless or other political parties may be banned. Also, the objective percentages may have little correspondence to real differences in political democracy. For instance, with Vanhanen's approach a shift from 30 percent to 40 percent would be a 10 percent increase in "democracy" while political rights and political liberties might stay the same. It may be possible to develop more sophisticated models to relate party composition to more valid measures of political democracy. This would allow a way of translating changes in party composition to changes in political democracy, but at this date the knowledge does not exist.

Another source of invalid measures is the practice of combining political democracy and stability. The measure may be called democratic stability, years of democracy, or democratic experience. What they have in common is that they measure two concepts—democracy and stability—in a single index over a period of years. Examples include the measures by Lipset (1959, 1981), Cutright (1963), Cutright and Wiley (1969), Coulter (1975), Hewitt (1977), Vanhanen (1979), and Muller (1988).

Lipset (1959) provides an early example. He classified European and Latin American countries according to whether they were democratic or not, using the procedure described below:

> The main criteria . . . to locate European democracies are the uninterrupted continuation of political democracy since WWI and the absence over the past 25 years of a major political movement opposed to the democratic "rules of the game." The somewhat less stringent criterion employed in Latin America is whether a given country has had a history of more or less free elections for most of the post-WWI period. Where in Europe we look for stable democracies, in South America we look for countries which have not had fairly constant dictatorial rule. (Lipset, 1959:74)

So for Lipset's measure as well as many others, stability is combined with political democracy.

We can classify stable democracy measures into those that treat political democracy as a dichotomous variable and those that use continuous measures in each year. Muller (1988) provides an example of the first approach. Muller (1988:54-56) lists criteria that a country must satisfy to be a democracy and then adds up the years for which these criteria are satisfied. The combination of using a dichotomous coding for political democracy and counting the years that democracy is "present" can be misleading. Consider a hypothetical example of three countries, A, B, and C in Table 2. Suppose that for a five-year period we know their degrees of political democracy on a 100-point scale. Assume a country that scores 75 or more satisfies Muller's criteria of democracy. Each year that a country does so it has one year of democracy. The years of democracy are determined by summing the number of

TABLE 2
Hypothetical Example of Three Countries' Scores
On "Years of Democracy"

| Country | year | | | | | "years of democracy" |
	1	2	3	4	5	
A	70	70	70	70	70	0
B	100	80	75	90	60	4
C	10	15	15	10	10	0

years in which political democracy is greater than 74. This measure scores countries A and C as having no years of democracy even though A had a substantially higher degree of political democracy than C over all five years.Country B receives four years of democracy despite its large fluctuations over the period. Such an approach suffers at least two problems. One is that it treats a continuous concept as if it were discrete and misses important substantive differences in political democracy between countries. Second, it aggregates values over a period of years and ignores temporal fluctuations that could have important effects.

The continuous nature of political democracy enters stable democracy measures such as Cutright's (1963), Cutright and Wiley's (1969), and Vanhanen's (1979). However, these too suffer from aggregating over a period of years. To illustrate the technique, consider again three hypothetical countries over a five-year period in Table 3. "Democratic stability" is the average value for the five-year period. All three countries have scores of 50. Much is lost due to this averaging. For instance, country A was the only one to stay at 50 throughout the period. Country B bounced from one extreme to the other. Its average was 50 though it never was close to this level. Country C had a clear democratization trend that is not visible from the period measure of 50.

An additional complication for these period measures is they tend to tie a nation's age to political democracy. Measures like Muller's (1988) extend over many decades. Only the years since independence are counted, which means that the developing societies that are more recently independent will automatically score lower on such measures. Even if a country experienced limited forms of democratic self-government under colonial rule, this would count the same as a colony under centralized and rigid authoritarian rule. Thus, the measure penalizes a country for its age rather than its degree of political democracy.

A problem with these democratic experience or stability measures is that stability and democracy do not have identical causes and consequences. If an association is (or is not) found, we do not know which component is responsible. Jackman (1974) argued that building stability into democracy indices has misled investigations of the relation between political democracy and income inequality. He argued that measures that include stability, such as Cutright's (1963), assign to political democracy effects that are in fact due to political stability. The same problem has reappeared in more recent work by Muller (1988) where his measure combines political democracy with political stability (Bollen and Jackman 1989).

The stability component also affects hypotheses about the timing of development

TABLE 3
Hypothetical Example of Three Countries' Scores
For "Democratic Stability"

Country	1	2	3	4	5	"democratic stability"
				year		
A	50	50	50	50	50	50
B	95	20	20	20	95	50
C	30	40	50	60	70	50

and political democracy. Social scientists such as De Schweinitz (1964) and Moore (1966) have hypothesized that those countries industrializing first (e.g., nations in the West) faced conditions that were far more favorable for political democracy than those industrializing later and that this is true even net of a nation's level of industrialization. In Bollen (1979; 1980:382-384), I demonstrated that measures that combine stability with political democracy, such as Cutright's (1963), support this hypothesis while measures that do not include stability show a null relation. The implication is that confounding stability with political democracy can frustrate our attempts to understand the determinants of political democracy.

Furthermore, it is obvious that we cannot monitor annual changes in political democracy with measures that refer to decades or more. I hope that new measures of political democracy follow the examples of Banks (1971) and Gastil (1987) in providing annual measures rather than periodic ones. With annual measures, models of the causes and consequences of political democracy could allow lagged influences and effects of democracy that extend beyond a single year. We could, for instance, study the impact of political democracy lagged one, two, three, etc. years before income inequality data to assess if any lagged effects exist, and we could determine the optimal lag. Obviously with period measures this is not possible. Also worth remembering is that we can aggregate annual measures to create period ones. But with the period measures we cannot recover the annual ones. Thus, annual measures offer us a better opportunity to study the history of political democracy and its various ebbs and flows.

The subjective nature of many indicators of political democracy is another issue of validity whether or not annual measures are developed. Indeed nonsubjective indicators besides party composition and voter turnout are rare. These two are less subjective but as I discussed earlier there are good reasons to question their validity. Ratings of the "freedom of the press," "fairness of elections," "restrictions on political parties," and so on are more appropriate as measures of political freedoms or political rights, but invalidity enters these subjective measures in at least two ways. One is that the judges cannot have first-hand knowledge of the political rights and liberties of all countries. The result is that they must rely on secondary sources for information. Often these are U.S. or Western European publications. The secondary sources contain only a subset of all the information on political rights and political liberties in a country. Many factors act to filter the knowledge that enters these secondary publications. Some factors lead to an overly optimistic perspective on rights and liberties while others can underestimate them. The openness of a country, for instance, might lead to more reporting of human rights violations in the secondary sources than is true for a country with an identical record but with a government that tightly controls the flow of information. The net effect of this filtering process is hard to predict; however the potential for bias in the secondary sources is high.

A second origin of error in ratings follows from the processing of the information by the judge. A variety of personal factors could unconsciously affect a judge's ratings. These include the relation of the country being rated to the judge's home country, the political orientation of the judge, or any personal stakes in the rating. I provide more detail on the likely biases in subjective measures in Bollen (1986). This is an issue that has received surprisingly little attention.

Closely related to the subjective nature of the ratings is the use of ordinal or dichotomous scales. As I have noted, political democracy, rights, and liberties are continuous concepts. When we measure them with binary or ordinal variables we can introduce substantial measurement error. Given the incomplete information on rights and liberties in countries, subjective raters are necessarily limited in the fineness of their ratings. Although I recognize these limits, I believe that we can do better than dichotomous or three-point scales. We could benefit from experiments to determine how many scale points experts can form before the errors of judgments overwhelm the benefits of more categories. We could further increase the number of scale points by combining the ratings of several experts making independent ratings for the same characteristics such as is done in the Fitzgibbon-Johnson democracy indicators for Latin America (Johnson 1976). Experiments with magnitude scaling techniques also may be fruitful in better approximating continuous indicators (Bollen 1986:590).

I recommend increasing the number of rating points for two reasons. One is to enable us to say more about the relative level of political democracy between countries or the democratization trends within countries. Dichotomous or trichotomous indicators are too crude. Second, the error introduced by analyzing ordinal indicators as if they were continuous generally is less, the greater is the number of categories. For instance, K. Barb and I found that the correlations between ordinal variables with six or more categories were very close to the correlations between the continuous versions of these variables. This was less true when the ordinal measures had only two or three categories (Bollen and Barb 1981).

We have statistical methodologies that can handle ordinal versions of continuous indicators (e.g., Muthen 1984). Their biggest disadvantages are that they are computer intensive and they make distributional assumptions that are not always applicable.[4] Procedures for categorical variables that assume the concept as well as the indicator are categorical are not appropriate since the concept is continuous. Techniques that ignore the measurement error in indicators fail to meet our needs. So, some statistical procedures may improve the analysis of ordinal indicators with few categories. But, the payoff would be far greater if we developed indicators of political democracy that better approximated continuous measures.

The last measurement problem is the failure to assess the reliability and validity of indicators. In 1980 I could not find any researchers who published a reliability estimate for their democracy index (Bollen 1980:379-380). The situation was only marginally better in a recent American Association for the Advancement of Science review of such measures (Bollen 1986:587-89). There is a considerable literature on reliability and confirmatory factor analysis that explains ways of estimating reliability. Having multiple indicators of each dimension of political democracy facilitates this task. It should be standard practice to report reliability estimates for indices or indicators. Validity tests of measures also would help to advance efforts to measure political democracy.

Conclusions

Measures of political democracy suffer both conceptual and measurement problems. The main conceptual problems are the failure to develop an adequate theoretical definition of political democracy, the confounding of this concept with others, and treating democracy as a binary rather than as a continuous concept. Four problems of measurement are invalid indicators, subjective indicators, ordinal or dichotomous indicators, and the failure to test reliability or validity.

Rather than reviewing each of these points, I will make some suggestions for future measurement efforts. First, I believe that if we follow six conventional standards of measurement (Bollen 1989: ch. 6), we can avoid several of the problems I described earlier. These standards are to:

(1) provide a theoretical definition of political democracy,
(2) identify its major dimensions,
(3) measure each dimension with several indicators,
(4) explain how the indicators were created and how to replicate them,[5]
(5) specify the relation between each dimension and the indicators, and,
(6) report estimates of reliability and validity.

These should come as no surprise but I believe that such a checklist is useful.

The list highlights the importance of a theoretical definition of political democracy. Satisfying the other standards depends on it. Part of our agenda should be to build a consensus around a working definition that clearly identifies and defines its major dimensions. Perhaps by modifying existing defintions we can obtain one that satisfies most researchers.

With agreement on the major dimensions and the meaning of political democracy, we could move toward developing operational definitions of each dimension. For instance, political rights indicators might include the representativeness of members of the legislative body. Minority, female, regional, and socioeconomic representativeness could be evaluated by comparing the composition of the government body to the general population. These could be objective variables with possibly high validity. New indicators on the ease of voter registration, voting fraud or vote buying, the influences on government decisions by big businesses, large landowners, trade unions, and political parties, and the role of the general population in selecting candidates would further diversify our political rights indicators. Political liberties indicators might provide more detailed information on the self-censorship of the major media, the day-to-day control over political news by censors, the harassment of nonviolent antigovernment movements, and the obstacles placed on small political parties.

Although the information to construct such measures is not available for all countries, it may be possible to intensively study a smaller group of nations (e.g., twenty). We could then compare refined measures to the more general ones that are more readily available. The comparison might suggest revisions in the worldwide measures.

In sum, we can advance the measurement of political democracy by clarifying the meaning of political democracy, being more selective in indicators, and experimenting with new measures. Alternatively, we can repeat the errors that plagued past efforts by ignoring the lessons they have taught.

Appendix

Below I list the values for the political democracy indices for 1965 and 1960. Each index is the average of six indicators. The possible range for the indices is from 0 to 100. The reliability estimates for the 1965 and 1960 indices are .88 and .89, respectively. Readers should not overinterpret minor differences in the scores since such differences could be due to random measurement error. See Bollen (1980) for a discussion of the construction, merits, and limitations of the scales.

Political Democracy

Country	1965	1960
Afghanistan	23.2	14.4
Albania	18.2	20.4
Algeria	27.2	—
Angola	12.0	—
Argentina	52.6	62.7
Australia	99.9	100.0
Austria	97.1	97.2
Barbados	99.6	—
Belgium	99.9	99.7
Benin	24.7	55.4
Bolivia	36.2	59.8
Brazil	60.9	90.5
Bulgaria	37.5	23.0
Burkina Faso	7.2	13.5
Burma	—	63.4
Burundi	58.0	30.8
Cambodia	36.3	38.6
Cameroon	56.0	73.5
Canada	99.5	99.9
Central African Republic	34.2	64.8
Chad	47.6	57.8
Chile	97.0	99.7

Political Democracy

Country	1965	1960
China	16.4	22.6
Colombia	71.4	69.7
Congo	45.8	71.1
Costa Rica	90.1	91.3
Cuba	5.2	13.9
Cyprus	87.0	85.7
Czechoslovakia	20.5	22.3
Denmark	99.9	99.9
Dominican Republic	38.8	20.6
Ecuador	44.6	84.3
Egypt	38.7	37.0
El Salvador	72.1	53.5
Ethiopia	12.5	31.0
Finland	97.3	97.3
France	90.8	89.7
Gabon	44.7	63.4
Germany (E)	18.1	19.6
Germany (W)	88.6	88.0
Ghana	23.7	57.4
Greece	82.8	88.0
Guatemala	39.5	69.8
Guinea	37.3	—
Guyana	53.1	—
Haiti	20.7	34.9
Honduras	50.0	70.1
Hungary	11.6	28.0
Iceland	100.0	100.0
India	91.2	93.6
Indonesia	9.8	20.3
Iran	45.0	34.9
Iraq	11.4	15.5
Ireland	97.2	94.8
Israel	96.8	94.6
Italy	96.8	97.0
Ivory Coast	45.6	43.1
Jamaica	90.1	91.0
Japan	99.8	99.3
Jordan	30.8	31.9
Kenya	58.2	71.1
Korea (N)	21.0	21.0
Korea (S)	53.0	51.7
Laos	42.8	56.6
Lebanon	74.0	84.0
Liberia	45.6	47.2

Political Democracy

Country	1965	1960
Libya	34.4	31.0
Luxembourg	97.7	100.0
Madagascar	83.0	91.7
Malawi	57.9	—
Malaysia	80.3	83.5
Mali	37.2	53.0
Mauritania	59.1	66.8
Mexico	74.5	80.1
Mongolia	16.2	22.1
Morocco	32.2	40.6
Mozambique	11.8	—
Nepal	29.2	39.7
Netherlands	99.7	99.9
New Zealand	100.0	100.0
Nicaragua	55.4	48.7
Niger	16.0	56.8
Nigeria	49.5	86.5
Norway	99.9	99.9
Pakistan	62.5	40.0
Panama	76.9	75.4
Paraguay	44.7	39.1
Peru	87.0	83.4
Philippines	92.6	93.0
Poland	22.1	23.8
Portugal	39.0	41.6
Romania	20.9	20.3
Rwanda	29.9	30.8
Saudi Arabia	9.7	12.0
Senegal	53.7	49.4
Sierra Leone	74.6	93.9
Singapore	76.9	81.2
Somalia	77.0	85.7
South Africa	58.9	64.7
Spain	10.4	10.7
Sri Lanka	85.9	94.0
Sudan	37.9	25.2
Sweden	99.9	99.9
Switzerland	99.7	99.6
Syria	19.9	39.3
Taiwan	22.8	—
Tanzania	63.3	—
Thailand	17.3	33.1
Togo	45.5	—
Trinidad & Tabago	84.7	94.0
Tunisia	63.6	83.7

Political Democracy

Country	1965	1960
Turkey	76.4	59.1
Uganda	68.9	76.7
United Kingdom	99.1	99.3
United States	92.4	94.6
Uruguay	99.6	99.8
USSR	18.2	20.4
Venezuela	73.4	72.5
Vietnam (N)	33.1	31.2
Vietnam (S)	12.4	54.6
Yemen (N)	6.5	11.9
Yugoslavia	50.8	42.6
Zaire	38.5	50.0
Zambia	67.4	—

Note: "—" means data are missing

Notes

An earlier version of this paper was presented at "The Measurement of Democracy" conference held at the Hoover Institution, Stanford University, May 1988. I wish to thank Alex Inkeles and the other members of the conference and Barbara Entwisle for their helpful comments. Partial support for this paper was provided by NSF Grant No. SES-8908361 and a University Faculty Research Grant from the University of North Carolina.

1. Gastil (1978) is an important exception since his indicators referred to the 1970s.
2. In Bollen (1980) and Bollen and Grandjean (1981), I refer to the political rights dimension as "popular sovereignty." Only the term has changed, not its meaning.
3. The binary conception of political democracy has reappeared in recent work by Muller (1988). See Bollen and Jackman (1989) for further discussion.
4. Muthen's (1984) method assumes that the continuous indicators which underlie the ordinal variables are multi-normally distributed, conditionally upon the exogenous variables of a model. In Bollen (1989:ch. 9), I compared the results of a confirmatory factor analysis of political democracy indicators (ignoring the ordinal nature of the indicators) to those from Muthen's method. The results were very close.
5. This standard is more appropriate when documentation on the indicators is not available elsewhere.

References

BANKS, ARTHUR S.
    1971   Cross-polity time-series data. Cambridge, MA: The MIT Press.
BANKS, ARTHUR S. and R. B. TEXTOR
    1963   A cross-polity survey. Cambridge: The MIT Press.
BOLLEN, KENNETH A.
    1979   Political democracy and the timing of development. American Sociological Review 44:572–587.
    1980   Issues in the comparative measurement of political democracy. American Sociological Review 45:370–390.
    1986   Political rights and political liberties in nations: An evaluation of human rights measures, 1950 to 1984. Human Rights Quarterly 8:567–591.
    1989   Structural equations with latent variables. New York: Wiley.
BOLLEN, KENNETH A. and KENNEY H. BARB
    1981   Pearson's R and coarsely categorized measures. American Sociological Review 46:232–239.
BOLLEN, KENNETH A. and BURKE GRANDJEAN
    1981   The Dimensions of democracy: Further issues in the measurement and effects of political democracy. American Sociological Review 46:651–659.
AFRICAN AMERICANBOLLEN, KENNETH A. and ROBERT W. JACKMAN
    1985   Political democracy and the size distribution of income. American Sociological Review 50:438–457.
    1989   Democracy, stability, and dichotomies. American Sociological Review. 54:612–621.
COLEMAN, J. S.
    1960   Conclusion: The political systems of the developing areas. In The Politics of Developing Areas, edited by G. A. Almond and J. S. Coleman. Princeton: Princeton University Press.

COULTER, PHILIP
    1975   *Social mobilization and liberal democracy*. Lexington: Lexington Books.
CUTRIGHT, PHILLIPS
    1963   National political development: Its measures and analysis. *American Sociological Review* 28:253–64.
    1967   Inequality: A cross-national analysis. *American Sociological Review* 32:562–578.
CUTRIGHT, PHILLIPS and JAMES A. WILEY
    1969   Modernization and political representation, 1927–1966. *Studies in Comparative International Development* 5:(2)23–41.
DAHL, ROBERT A.
    1971   *Polyarchy: participation and opposition*. New Haven: Yale.
DE SCHWEINITZ, KARL
    1964   *Industrialization and democracy*. Glencoe, IL: Free Press.
DOWNS, ANTHONY
    1957   *An economic theory of democracy*. New York: Harper & Brothers.
GASTIL, RAYMOND D.
    1978   *Freedom in the world: Political rights and civil liberties 1978*. New York: Freedom House.
    1987   *Freedom in the world: Political rights and civil liberties 1986–1987*. Westport, CT: Greenwood Press.
HEWITT, CHRISTOPHER
    1977   The effect of political democracy and social democracy on equality in industrial societies: A cross-national comparison. *American Sociological Review* 42:450–464.
JACKMAN, ROBERT W.
    1974   Political democracy and social equality: A comparative analysis. *American Sociological Review* 39:29–45.
JOHNSON, KENNETH F.
    1976   Measuring the scholarly image of Latin America democracy, 1945–1970. In *Statistical Abstract of Latin America*. Vol. 17, edited by James W. Wilkie. Los Angeles:UCLA Latin American Center.
LERNER, DANIEL
    1958   *The passing of traditional society*. Glencoe: Free Press.
LIPSET, SEYMOUR MARTIN
    1959   Some social requisites of democracy. *American Political Science Review* 53:69–105.
    1981   *Political man*. Baltimore: Johns Hopkins.
MICHELS, ROBERT
    1962   *Political parties*. New York: Free Press.
MILLS, C. W.
    1956   *The power elite*. New York: Oxford University Press.
MOORE, BARRINGTON, JR.
    1966   *Social origins of dictatorship and democracy*. Boston:Beacon.
MOSCA, G.
    1939   *The ruling class*. New York: McGraw-Hill.
MULLER, EDWARD N.
    1988   Democracy, economic development, and income inequality. *American Sociological Review* 53:50–68.
MUTHEN, BENGT
    1984   A general structural equation model with dichotomous, ordered categorical, and continuous latent indicators. *Psychometrika* 49:115–132.
NIXON, RAYMOND B.
    1960   Factors related to freedom in national press systems. *Journalism Quarterly* 37:13–28.
    1965   Freedom in the world's press: A fresh appraisal with new data. *Journalism Quarterly* 42:3–15, 118–119.
SCHUMPETER, JOSEPH A.
    1950   *Capitalism, socialism, and democracy*. New York: Harper & Row.
SMITH, ARTHUR K.
    1969   Socioeconomic development and political democracy. *Midwest Journal of Political Science* 13:95–125.
TAYLOR, CHARLES LEWIS and MICHAEL C. HUDSON
    1972   *World handbook of political and social indicators*, 2d ed. New Haven:Yale University Press.
VANHANEN, TATU
    1979   *Power and the means to power*. Ann Arbor, MI: University Microfilms International.

2

The Comparative Survey of Freedom: Experiences and Suggestions

Raymond Duncan Gastil

The article describes the Comparative Survey of Freedom, produced from 1975 to 1989 in article form, and from 1978 to 1989 in book form as well. The survey rates annually all independent states and dependent territories. It is a loose, intuitive rating system for levels of freedom or democracy, as defined by the traditional political rights and civil liberties of the Western democracies. The checklists used for political rights and civil liberties are discussed point by point. Although open to criticism, the ratings are quite similar to those produced by other analysts from different perspectives during this time period. Unlike other studies, the survey's regular production provides a useful and consistent time series. Democracy is a moving target. Extensions of the survey in time or levels of discrimination would force the investigator to address a variety of new and difficult problems in comparability that are not faced by the survey in its present form.

The Comparative Survey of Freedom has been published by Freedom House since 1973 (Gastil 1973). At first it was published annually, or even semiannually, in the organization's bimonthly. Since 1978 it has also appeared as part of an annual volume devoted to the survey and related topics (Gastil 1978–89). The original intention was to produce, with relatively few manhours, an orienting discussion of variation in levels of freedom. Later, when it became the full-time activity

After receiving a degree in social science and Middle Eastern Studies at Harvard University, Dr. Gastil taught anthropology and honors social science at the University of Oregon. For seven years he analyzed national security and other policy issues at Hudson Institute. Basic research at Battelle Seattle Research Center led to the publication of *Cultural Regions of the United States*, and *Social Humanities: Toward an Integrative Discipline of Science and Values*, as well as numerous scholarly articles. From 1977 to 1989, Dr. Gastil was director of the Comparative Survey of Freedom at Freedom House. In this capacity he wrote and produced an annual yearbook entitled *Freedom in the World: Political Rights and Civil Liberties*, and held conferences on supporting liberalization in the Soviet Union, Muslim Central Asia, China, and Eastern Europe, as well as on the problem of political participation in the United States.

of the author, the survey's goals became somewhat more serious without abandoning much of the flavor of its beginnings. Although the survey has always been highly personal, most attempts to rate democracies or levels of freedom in the 1970s or 1980s have come up with similar results. The survey has been criticized for its right-wing bias, but generally such criticism is based on opinions about Freedom House rather than detailed examination of survey ratings. Perhaps the survey's strongest claim to "scientific" status results from the author's determination not to let current international opinion, the interests of American foreign policy, Freedom House, or personal prejudices affect survey ratings.[1]

The survey's origins are reflected in the use of "freedom" rather than democracy as the criterion for the rating system. Although freedom has always been understood primarily by comparison with modern political democracy, it was years before its author understood that the survey was essentially a survey of democracy. This is one reason why the survey has been less concerned with institutional arrangements and laws and more concerned with actual behavior than most discussions of democratic freedoms. This origin may also explain why the author still looks for democratic systems with limited freedoms, or extensive freedoms without a democratic system.

With little or no staff support, the author has carried out most of the research and ratings. Lack of a research staff is not as overwhelming a fault as it might appear. By working alone the author has not had to integrate the judgments of a variety of people. The hunches and impressions that are so important in a survey of this kind would be almost impossible to keep on the same wave lengths if one had an Asianist, Africanist, and Latin Americanist to satisfy before the ratings were finalized for each year.

With more adequate resources, the survey could be made less superficial. However, the few times that the monograph or journal literature has actually been researched, remarkably little has been found that affected the ratings. By their nature, academic studies of countries are likely to be more theoretically oriented than the ordinary data sources of the survey. Often, information in serious works is offered as evidence for or against a thesis. Of course, all information is presented by someone to make a point, but when the purposes are nontheoretical and journalistic they are less likely to be consistently slanted in a way deleterious to the survey effort.[2]

Detailed comparative literature on political systems and behavior opens up problems that the relatively superficial survey has not addressed. For example, let us consider variations within the 1-1 countries (see pp. 42–46), a group that includes most of the traditional Western democracies. Examining in detail the literature on the United States, Great Britain, Sweden, Switzerland, or Japan, raises many doubts as to the degree to which political competition is really open and fair, or "meaningful." Although the media appear "fair," are they not constrained by an unspoken consensus representing powerful economic and bureaucratic forces in the society that makes effective criticism and mobilization for change impossible? Similarly, how do we compare party systems? In most party systems, the choice of candidates is made from the top down, with little more than ratification at local levels. The United States has been the only major democracy with a primary system. Yet in our system, the advantages for incumbents in the House of Representatives are such that only flagrant public abuses or incompetence makes possible an effective challenge. Our ineffective party system and lack of party discipline means that most senators and representatives cannot be held responsible by the voters for the success or failure of successive governments. To weigh such criticisms and differences in a more detailed survey with more rating levels would require more than marginal growth in the present resources of the survey.

Given the rough-cut of the survey, traditional democracies are differentiated only when easily discernible differences are discovered. France is rated down on its civil liberties for such traits as a relatively coercive police system affecting political expression (for example, the practice of preventing the publication of works criticizing favored foreign powers, or direct or indirect bias in television broadcasting). Post-World War II restrictions in a number of European countries against promoting Fascist or Nazi ideologies, such as that in West Germany, may affect the rating of these countries. These adjustments seem reasonable because such restrictions are comparable to those controls on discussion often reported from other parts of the world. To judge such restrictions requires no special analysis of hidden forces, or the acceptance of any very complex theories about what gives greater or lesser freedom to a society.

On the other hand, it is important not to always remain on a level of profound ignorance. Reading and experience over the years convinced the author that in the first surveys he was too impressed with the surface, and not sufficiently attuned to the extent of oligarchical domination that could exist in spite of an apparently open electoral system, for example in Latin America. He should have known this from the analysis of the "traditional" pattern of politics in the American South as described by Daniel Elazar (Elazar 1972, 1970). In recent years, therefore, the author has assumed that poor societies with a great gap between classes have a lower democratic performance—unless there is evidence that the assumption for a particular society is unjustified. Costa Rica, for example, has elaborate means for making sure democracy works quite well in spite of its geographical, cultural, and economic position.

The survey's formal methodology is extremely simple. The work began with the simplest of checklists for political rights and civil liberties. Each country was evaluated against a reference book description. The original country ratings were determined on this basis. The work of the survey in subsequent years has consisted of following news about a country in a variety of sources, and occasionally changing ratings when the news did not fit the established rating level. In effect, the author developed rough models in his mind as to what to expect of a country at each rating level, reexamining his ratings only when current information no longer supported this model. Changes in ratings and adjustments in ratings were always carried out by a relativizing process, so that, for example, an apparent change might not be reflected in a changed rating because to make that change would put the country on a rating level that it did not fit. That is, because the number of ratings levels was necessarily fixed, an event or condition recorded in any one year would not lead to a change in its ratings unless it so affected the author's thinking about the country that it no longer made sense to keep the country in the group of countries with the same rating and did make sense to put it in a group of countries above or below that level. Over the years, the checklist has become a little more complex and more congruent with available information. Experience has produced some incremental growth.

The rating system of the survey consists of a seven-point scale for political rights and a seven-point scale for civil liberties.[3] The freest rating is one and the least free is seven. The survey maintained these seven-point scales primarily for consistency: once started, changing the rating system would be confusing to those who have followed the system over the years, and make comparability more difficult.

A "status of freedom" rating dividing countries into "freely," "partly free," and "not free," has also been used, primarily as a means of summarizing the data for presentation as a Map of Freedom. For some years the three-level rating lived a somewhat separate life from the seven-point scales and, to a much lesser extent, this is still the case. Understanding that in listing the seven point scales, the political rights rating is given first, it has always been true that ratings of 1-1, 1-2, 2-1, 2-2, and 2-3 led to a country being rated free, and ratings of 7-7, 7-6, 6-7, and 6-6 led to a rating of not free. Generally, those with middling ratings would then be considered partly free. However, for many years countries rated 3-2, 5-6, and 6-5 (and of course any other combinations of ratings adding up to the same thing, such as 7-4) were seen to offer an opportunity for judgment calls that allowed those countries to be placed into either the higher or lower general category. For example, one year Poland might be "6-5, Not Free," while the next it might be "6-5, Partly Free." The author had a picture in his mind as to what a five and a six were on each scale, and also a picture of what Not Free and Partly Free were. Since these were all continuous scales, the author reasoned that a "high five" and a "high six" might be considered Not Free , while a "low five" and a "low six" could be Partly Free. The logic was fine, but the result confusing. Realizing this, for the last several years all 6-5 and 5-6 countries have been rated Partly Free, as well as 3-2 countries (but not 2-3).

In any event, the seven-point scales have always been the heart of the survey, with the three-point generalized status of freedom little more than a heuristic device for printing maps or adding up doubtful totals for free or unfree peoples. For the 1988-89 surveys, the Status of Freedom was dropped from the survey. Instead, a *Freedom Rating* that simply adds together the political and civil rights ratings was employed. This rating, ranging from 2 for most free to 14 for least free, allowed for the division of countries into a variety of subgroupings, depending on the purpose. One division could be into high (1-5), medium (6-10), and low (11-14). Countries rated "high" in this accounting approximate a list of democracies as before.

Other students of the survey have remarked that the ratings on the two main scales have very high correlations, and, in fact, there might not be a sufficient reason for having two scales at all (Banks 1986). It is true that the scales and the categories they represent overlap one another to such an extent that information relevant to one scale affects the other—even the same information. This is seen particularly in information that comes in around the time of elections. The ability to discuss issues in the media, to organize demonstrations, to be free of police harassment, and so on, are indications both that the election is a fair process (political rights) and that civil liberties are being respected. For many countries information is likely to come in much more fully during election periods than for periods between elections, a circumstance that greatly lessens the difference between the indicators. Transitionally, divergence may occur. For example,when military coups occur in countries such as Ecuador, Honduras, or Nigeria with significant democratic traditions, political rights may be denied for a time while significant civil liberties are preserved. This is a typical 7-5, or 6-4 situation.

The unevenness of the sources of available information over time and its incompleteness has been a major reason why the survey never acceded to the occasional suggestion that a more objective system be devised in which many subindicators would be rated numerically, and then summed up for an overall rating. Intuitively, and after trying a few experiments, it did not seem that enough information was easily available to make such a system work. Whatever system was used there would be a temptation to fudge the figures to make them come out "reasonably." The unavoidable "apples and oranges" problem also would be compounded by such an approach. Since the critical issues in political rights and civil liberties tend to be different from country to country, the survey should not be saddled with a system that would constrain the weight that could be given particular information. For example, one might judge that the systematic execution of members of the opposition in a country was sufficient in itself for a 7 civil liberties rating, yet if only a few points were allocated to this heading in a quantitative system, this rating might be impossible.

The deeper reason for avoiding numerical grading of subfactors is that every aspect we might wish to grade has a slightly different meaning within different countries. For example, there is a checklist item for political rights that asks whether there has been a recent shift of power through elections. If, in a traditional Western parliamentary democracy, power stays in the same party for many decades, this suggests a problem in the democratic system. It suggests that somehow or other a silent conspiracy prevents the organization of an effective opposition. A high percentage of gainfully employed in government service combined with subtle political pressures on government employees might constitute such a "conspiracy." Until the mid-1970s Sweden was slightly down-rated because of such a long domination. However, there are degrees. The Christian Democrats have been the major partner in every Italian government since the forties. Yet Christian Democrats have not always held the prime ministership, and other parties from moderate Left to moderate Right have played major roles in successive governments. Japan's Liberal Democratic party has formed every government since the party was organized in the 1950s. But the "real" party system in Japan is the factional system within the Liberal Democratic party, and the public can use its votes to affect the relative power of the factions. Switzerland's longstanding rule by a four-party grand coalition operates so smoothly that it might be considered one-party government, or government by a "front" as in Malaysia. But Switzerland also has a very active initiative and referendum system that allows for direct popular input. It also distributes power to cantonal and commune levels to a degree unmatched in any other democracy. The meaning of unchanging party composition in government is much different in Switzerland than in Sweden.

As another example, let us consider public ownership of the media. It has until recently been common for newspapers to be independent and radio and/or television to be government owned in many traditional democracies. The same has become the case in many new democracies. But one would not want to consider the civil liberties' significance to be the same for a variety of reasons. In a fully literate society with very high newspaper readership, government control of a broadcasting medium is much less significant than in a country such as India, where half the population is illiterate or does not read newspapers.

Checklist for Political Rights

1. Chief authority recently elected by a meaningful process
2. Legislature recently elected by a meaningful process

   Alternatives for 1 and 2:
   a. no choice and possibility of rejection
   b. no choice but some possibility of rejection
   c. government or single-party selected candidates
   d. choice possible only among government-approved candidates
   e. relatively open choices possible only in local elections
   f. open choice possible within a restricted range
   g. relatively open choices possible in all elections
3. Fair election laws, campaigning opportunity, polling and tabulation
4. Fair reflection of voter preference in distribution of power
   —parliament, for example, has effective power
5. Multiple political parties
   —only dominant party allowed effective opportunity
   —open to rise and fall of competing parties
6. Recent shifts in power through elections
7. Significant opposition vote
8. Free of military or foreign control
9. Major group or groups denied reasonable self-determination
10. Decentralized political power
11. Informal consensus; de facto opposition power

The criteria on which the survey is based are organized into checklists. This checklist for political rights asks the investigator to determine the presence or absence of aspects of the political process common to other democratic states, and then checks for the status of other aspects of the system that may impinge on, or provide alternatives to, the normal democratic process. Although the first surveys used a simpler written checklist, this checklist, used for the last few surveys, approximates what has been done all along. The categories are developed not so much out of any theoretical understanding of democracy as from the experience that these were headings under which information relevant to the rating system has most often been available.

The "alternatives" listed after 1 and 2 reflect variations in the extent to which political systems offer citizens or subjects a chance to participate through electoral choice. These variations were found in the course of survey monitoring.

At the antidemocratic extreme are those systems with no popular process, such as inherited monarchies or purely appointive Communist systems. Little different in practice are those societies that hold elections for the legislature or president, but give the voter no alternative other than affirmation. In such elections there is neither the choice nor possibility—in practice or even sometimes in theory—of rejecting the single candidate that the government proposes for chief executive or representative. In elections at this level the candidate is usually chosen by a secretive process involving only the top elite. More democratic are those systems, such as Zambia's, that allow the voter no choice, but suggest that it is possible to reject an official candidate. In this case the results may show ten or twenty percent of the voters actually voting against an executive candidate or, rarely, rejecting an individual legislative candidate on a single list. In some societies there is a relatively more-open party process for selecting candidates. However the list of preselected candidates is prepared, there is seldom any provision for serious campaigning against the single list.

The political system is more democratic if multiple candidates are offered for each position, even when all candidates are government-or party-selected. Popular voting for alternatives may exist only at the party level—which in a few countries is a large proportion of the population—or the choice may be at the general election.Usually the country's top leader and party domination are not open to voter rejection. Many legislators, even members of the cabinet, may be rejected by the voters in such a system, although choices are restricted to what the party approves. Campaigning is restricted to questions of personality, honesty, or ability; for example, in Tanzania campaigning may not involve questions of policy. A further increment of democratic validity is effected if choice is possible among government-approved rather than government-selected candidates. In this case the government's objective is to exclude "undesirable elements" from the election. With government-selected candidates there is reliance on party faithful, but self-selection allows persons of local reputation to achieve office. Controlled electoral systems may allow open, self-selection of candidates for some local elections, but not for elections on the national scale. A system such as Iran's allows an open choice of candidates in elections, but draws narrow ideological limits around what is an acceptable candidacy.

Beyond this, there is the world of free elections as we know them, in which candidates are selected by multiple parties or self-selected. It could be argued that parliamentary systems, such as are common outside of the United States, reduce local choice by imposing party choices on voters. However, independents can and do win in most systems, and new parties, such as the "Greens" in Western Europe, test the extent to which the party system in particular countries is responsive to the desires of citizens.

Emphasis is placed on elections because elections play a critical role in democracy, and because they are events that produce easily available information on the democratic character of a state. Especially in new or partial democracies elections tend to be crises that bring out the best and the worst in political systems. But because elections are occasions for which we have a great deal of information, it does not mean that this information can be evaluated easily. For example, the fairness of elections is assumed for most traditional democracies, at least on the national level. Serious challenges to official results in such states are seldom brought, even though outside observers may note reports of inconsistencies or anomalies in their election processes. To take one example, when a losing candidate demands a recount in the United States, the count frequently turns out differently than the first time (although the discrepancy is seldom enough to change the result). Yet cheating is infrequently charged and the overall results of national elections are accepted with little complaint. But in many new or transitional countries, it is standard practice for the opposition to point out before the election how the government will "steal" the election. If the opposition loses, it will then make strenuous claims that the election was stolen. Thus the ARENA party in El Salvador has claimed fraud in each of the several elections in the 1980s; most recently it won the election and yet claimed that it was robbed of the greater win to which it was entitled. Claims and counterclaims of this nature are seldom subject to verification, even for those on the ground.

Yet one has to make a judgment. In some cases, such as elections in Liberia, Haiti, or Guyana, the traditions of the country support an assumption of unfair elections, and the assumption is generally correct. In other cases, such as the recent elections in South Korea, the apparent willingness of the people and most observers to accept the results suggests they were fair enough. It is easy to get bulldozed by the media and other observers when a result is so desirable and fervently wanted by so many of those surrounding the reporters. This was the case with the election that ousted Marcos in the Philippines. It was unfair, but the eventual "winners" were not sure enough that Marcos had literally stolen the election in the counting process to carry out an official recount.

The degree to which voter preference is expressed in actual power is a difficult call. The power given to the courts in the United States, the "unfairness" in the allocation of Senate seats, and the argument that proportional representation is fairer should all be considered. The degree of system domination by the monied few varies from society to society. In the United States money is generally used to affect narrow issues, especially defensively, but this is not by any means always the case, or universally.

Checklist item 5 on multiple parties does not mean that a state is automatically "marked down" if it does not have multiple parties. In theory it should be possible for democracy to be perfected without political parties. The founding fathers of the American Republic did not think parties were necessary. The leaders of many countries that have moved from liberal democratic models to single parties argue for the necessity to reduce the adversarial spirit of parties; they claim to be able to preserve democracy by bringing the political struggle within the confines of one party. However, practice is quite different: policy is set in single parties by a small clique at the top; those in disfavor with the government are not allowed to compete for office by legal means—indeed, they are often ejected from the single party altogether, as in Kenya.

The conclusion of the survey is that while parties may not be necessary for democracy in very small countries such as Tuvalu, for modern states they seem necessary to allow alternatives to a ruling group or policy to gain sufficient votes to make a change. Therefore, the existence or nonexistence of multiple parties is evidence for the existence of democracy, but is not absolutely conclusive. We are waiting for demonstrations of the ability of one-party or nonparty systems to achieve democracy in medium or large states. (Nepal's experiment with a nonparty system is worth watching in this connection.)

"Dominant Party" structures such as those of Malaysia or Singapore allow oppositions to mobilize to the extent that they can publicize alternative positions and effectively criticize government performance, but not so that they represent a realistic threat to the group in power. Controls over campaigning, expression of opinion, patronage, and vote manipulation, as well as "punishment" of areas that vote against the government are methods used in such systems to make sure that the governing party remains in power.

Items 6 and 7 on the checklist ask the analyst to consider whether the electoral processes result in change, or compel change. Thus, an important indicative test of democracy is the extent to which there has been a recent shift in power occasioned through the operation of the electoral process. While it is true that the people of a country may remain relatively satisfied with the performance of one party for a long period of time, it is also true that a party in power may be able over time to entrench itself in multiple ways to such a degree that it is next to impossible to dislodge it by legitimate means. The extent of democratic rights can also be empirically suggested by the size of an opposition vote. While on rare occasions a governing party or individual may receive overwhelming support at the polls, any group or leader that regularly receives seventy percent or more of the vote indicates a weak opposition, and the probable existence of undemocratic barriers in the way of its further success. When a government or leader receives over ninety percent of the vote this indicates highly restrictive freedom for those opposing the system: over ninety-eight percent indicates that elections are little more than symbolic.

The extent to which imputed foreign control over a country should lead to a reduction in its political rights rating is always contentious. All countries are to a degree controlled by other countries; it is equally obvious that some countries are controlled by others through the threat of military intervention. But in an age of dependency theories, untangling the extent to which a country's political or economic system is controlled by another is difficult. There are several tests to apply. First, one can assume that country A's politics are significantly controlled by country B, if B has troops stationed in A, and there is reason to believe that B's troops would be used against the domestic as well as foreign opponents of A's regime. Mongolia, East Germany, and Afghanistan 1980-1988 come to mind; others are Cambodia, Lebanon, and to a lesser extent former French colonies such as Gabon or the Central African Republic. In more marginal cases the threat of intervention controls a country's politics: Finland has been an obvious example; Grenada was in this category for a year or two after our intervention.

Political and military leaders in many Central American and Caribbean countries have reason to fear North American pressure, if not invasion. Our actions in Grenada seem to have brought this so strongly home to the former military leader of Suriname that he changed his politics overnight. Nevertheless, we have not used this fact to reduce the political rights ratings for these countries. The fact that the freedoms of South Africa's small neighbors are reduced by its threats and interventions is reflected in our ratings. We ask whether citizens of country A speak out openly against the interference of country B, and whether those who speak out include A's leaders. In this sense, Mexico, Cuba, and Panama (until December, 1989) have not had their freedoms taken away by the United States, while Lesotho and Swaziland have had theirs reduced by South Africa. It is less clear whether India has reduced those of Sri Lanka, or Indonesia and Australia those of Papua New Guinea.

The question of military influence is only slightly less difficult than that of foreign influence. At one extreme are countries such as Iceland or Costa Rica with no regular military. At the other extreme are those countries such as Nigeria or Niger in which military officers rule directly without other mechanisms of legitimacy beyond the exercise or threat of force. (It is a fine point whether freedom is any less because the man in charge is military rather than civilian, given that the power has been attained by the blatant use and threat of force. A revolutionary coup by civilians, say Ba'athists in Iraq, gives no more legitimacy or freedom than a military coup. Of course, if power is achieved by force on the heels of a genuine revolution involving large numbers of people, then this is a relatively "freer" path to power.)

Moving upward from Iceland are those countries such as the United States in which a military establishment regularly demands and receives a considerable budget, and is involved in intelligence and to a limited extent in policy planning. Still, in such societies the civilian leadership continues to dominate the military, for example, through a civilian secretary of defense. In addition, societies at this level have little or no tradition of military intervention, or even serious threats of intervention to support or thwart the desires of civilian leaders. Of course, the military (including the officers' corps, soldiers, civilian employees, veterans, and their families) is a legitimate pressure group in any society—as long as its supporters do not point their guns at their political opponents. At the next higher level of military influence, the first at which the political rights rating might be reduced as a result, civilian control over military leaders is continually in question. In Latin America, cabinet ministers responsible for defense, or ministers responsible for the separate services, are generally serving military officers. In these countries there has been a tradition of military interventions in the past, and fear lingers that serious instabilities will lead to new interventions. Countries such as Honduras or Guatemala, on the next level, live in continual fear that the military will again usurp civilian power. Civilian authority is circumscribed by limits on how far the government can go in exerting authority over the forces nominally under its control. Still higher in degree of military influence are those countries such as Liberia, Paraguay, or Chile in which a military leader takes power by force but then subsequently distances himself somewhat from the military by becoming ostensibly a civilian leader through a quasiconstitutional legitimizing process. Ultimately, the key issue is not "military influence", but the role of violence in attaining and keeping power.

Item 9 reminds us that a democratic polity is one in which the people as a whole feel that the process is open to them, and that on important issues all individuals can be part of a meaningful majority. If this is not true, then the democratic polity must either divide, or devise methods for those who feel they are not part of the system to have reserved areas, geographical or otherwise, in which they can expect that their interests will be uppermost. In other words there must be either external or internal self-determination. Most democracies are relatively homogeneous. But even here, without elected local or regional governments, people in some areas will feel crushed under a national majority that is unable to understand their particular problems or accept their values. Federal democracies, such as India or the United States, have devised elaborate methods for separate divisions of the country to be in important degrees self-governing. The problems of overcentralization in Europe have been addressed by countries such as France, Spain, and the United Kingdom, but in Ulster political boundaries continue to make a section of the people feel like foreigners in their own land.

The question of self-determination (10) is closely related to the extent to which political power has been decentralized. Since it would be possible for a country to have an elaborate degree of decentralization and still hand down all the important decisions from above, we must test empirically the extent to which persons or parties not under control of the center actually succeed politically. The fact, for example, that Japanese-Americans are able to play a leading role in Hawaiian politics, or that the Scots nationalists are able to achieve a significant vote in Scotland suggest an authentic devolution of political power.

Finally, the survey wants evidence for the extent to which the political decision process depends not only on the support of majorities at the polls, but also on a less adversarial process involving search for consensus among all groups on issues of major public interest. A democracy should be more than simply a society of winners and losers. The most common way to demonstrate this is to take the opposition into account in major decisions and appointments, even when it does not have to be consulted in terms of the formal requirements of the system. Sri Lanka and Lebanon are current examples of the breakdown of democratic systems when one or more groups are no longer willing to accommodate the interests of others, and accept the electoral process as an arbiter. Colombia's "la violencia" was another example, one with analogies that continue to threaten several countries in Latin America. Obviously, the distribution of informal power is particularly important in judging the degree of success of one-party "democracies" that base their claim to legitimacy on their willingness to achieve national consensuses.

The Checklist for Civil Liberties

In considering the accompanying *Checklist for Civil Liberties,* we are entering on a field made familiar by many special or annual reports on human rights violations. It is important to mention one of the chief differences between such reporting and the survey approach. The survey is looking for patterns and balances in activities, rather than numbers of failures to observe particular human rights standards. The quantitative human rights violations approach has at least four difficulties that we should strive to avoid. The first and most obvious is that countries differ dramatically in size. One case of government interference with the media in Barbados is of much greater importance to our judgment of its freedom than tens of such interferences in a country such as India. It is not just that there are infinitely more media channels in India, but also that there are so many channels that the repression of individual channels is unlikely to be effective. The second is that counting numbers of violations is often an indadequate measure of the presence or absence of the behavior at issue. Although the number of journalists imprisoned in North Korea in the 1970s might have been low, journalism was totally controlled. In South Korea journalists were much more likely to be in trouble with the law, but journalism was much freer. Finally, and most important, there is the question of the balance of positive and negative activities. For example, a very large number of civil liberties violations are reported every year in South Africa; yet every year we also find reports of a remarkable number of free and open demonstrations, new organizations, critical publications and reports, and so on. If we are to use quantitative measures, we must develop a means of measuring both demonstrations that occur and demonstrations suppressed, public criticisms not suppressed along with public criticisms suppressed.

Checklist for Civil Liberties

12. Media/literature free of political censorship
    a. Press independent of government
    b. Broadcasting independent of government

13. Open public discussion

14. Freedom of assembly and demonstration

15. Freedom of political or quasipolitical organization

16. Nondiscriminatory rule of law in politically relevant cases
    a. independent judiciary
    b. security forces respect individuals

17. Free from unjustified political terror or imprisonment
    a. free from imprisonment or exile for reasons of conscience
    b. free from torture
    c. free from terror by groups not opposed to the system
    d. free from government-organized terror

18. Free trade unions, peasant organizations, or equivalents

19. Free businesses or cooperatives

20. Free professional or other private organizations

21. Free religious institutions

22. Personal social rights: including those to property, internal and external travel, choice of residence, marriage and family

23. Socioeconomic rights: including freedom from dependency on landlords, bosses, union leaders, or bureaucrats

24. Freedom from gross socioeconomic inequality

25. Freedom from gross government indifference or corruption

The checklist begins with the communications media (12). The analyst asks whether the press and broadcasting facilities of the country are independent of government interference or direction, and serve the range of opinion that is present in the country. Clearly, if a population does not receive information about alternatives to present leaders and policies, then its ability to use any political process is impaired. In traditional democracies people are no longer imprisoned for expressing their rational views on any matter—although secrecy and libel laws do have a slight affect in some democracies. As one moves from this open situation, from ratings of (1) to ratings of (7), a steady decline in freedom to publish is noticed: the tendency increases for people to be punished for criticizing the government, or papers to be closed, or censorship to be imposed, or for the newspapers and journals to be directly owned and supervised by the government.

The methods used by governments to control the print media are highly varied. While prepublication censorship is often what Westerners think of because of their earlier history or wartime experience, direct government ownership and control of the media and postpublication censorship through warnings, confiscations, or suspensions are more common. Government licensing of publications and journalists and controls over the distribution of newsprint are other common means of keeping control over what is printed. Even in countries with a degree of democracy, such as Malaysia, press controls of these sorts may be quite extensive, often based on an ostensible legal requirement for "responsible journalism." Control of the press may be further extended by requiring papers to use a government news agency as their source of information, and by restricting the flow of foreign publications.

Broadcasting services—radio or television—are much more frequently owned by the government than the print media, and such ownership may or may not be reflected in government control over what is communicated. It is possible, as in the British case, for a government-owned broadcasting corporation to be so effectively protected from government control that its programs demonstrate genuine impartiality (generally still true in spite of some recent chinks in BBC's armor). However, in many well-known democracies, such as France or Greece, changes in the political composition of government affect the nature of what is broadcast to the advantage of incumbents. The government-owned broadcasting services of India make little effort to go beyond presenting the views of their government.

In most countries misuse of the news media to serve government interests is even more flagrant. At this level, we need to distinguish between those societies that require their media, particularly their broadcasting services, to avoid criticism of the political system or its leaders, and those that use the media to "mobilize" their peoples in direct support for government policies. In the first case the societies allow or expect their media, particularly the broadcasting services, to present a more or less favorable picture; in the second, the media are used to motivate their peoples to actively support government policies and to condemn or destroy those who oppose the governing system. In the first, the government's control is largely passive; in the second it is directly determinative of content.

The comparison of active and passive control by government raises the most difficult issue in the question of media freedom—self-censorship. It is easy to know if a government censors or suspends publications for content, or punishes journalists and reporters by discharge, imprisonment, or worse; judging the day-to-day influence of subtle pressures on the papers or broadcasting services of a country is much more difficult. Perhaps the most prevalent form of government control of the communications media is achieved through patterns of mutual assistance of government and media that ensure that, at worst, reports are presented in a bland, noncontroversial manner—a common practice in Mexico and Pakistan, at least until recently.

Open public discussion (13) is at least as important a civil liberty as free communications media. The ultimate test of a democracy is the degree to which an atmosphere for discussion in public and private exists free of fear of reprisal by either the government or opposition groups. Even in the relatively free Communist society of Yugoslavia people are still being imprisoned for the expression of critical opinions in private. Certainly Iranians have had to be careful in recent years not to express too openly opinions that go against the prevailing ideology.

Open discussion expressed through political organization, public demonstration, and assemblies is often threatening to political incumbents. There are occasions in which such assemblies may be dangerous to public order and should be closely controlled or forbidden. But in many societies this hypothetical danger is used as a pretense to deny opposition groups the ability to mobilize in support of alternative policies or leaders. In Malaysia, for example, the government's denial of public assembly to the opposition has been a principal means to restrict the ability of the opposition to effectively challenge the rule of the government. Obviously, denial of the right to organize freely for political action is the most generalized form of the attempt to prevent the effective mobilization of opposition to government policies. Control over political organization is a distinguishing characteristic of one-party states, but many multiparty states place limits on the kinds or numbers of political parties that may be organized. Controls over extremist parties that deny the legitimacy of democratic institutions, such as many Fascist or Communist parties, are understandable—still, they represent limits on freedom. Political and civil freedoms overlap closely on the right to political organization. The distinction is between denying the right to participate in elections and denying the right to organize to present alternative policies or arguments for and against change in other ways.

A democratic system is not secured unless there is a legal system that can be relied on for a fair degree of impartiality. The electoral process, for example, needs to be supervised by electoral commissions or other administrative systems that ultimately can be checked or overruled by the judicial system. People accused of actions against the state need to have some hope that their cases will be tried before the courts of the society and that the process will be fair. One of the tests that the author often applies to a country is whether it is possible to win against the government in a political case, and under what conditions. A reliable judicial system requires a guarantee of the permanence of judicial tenure, particularly at the highest levels, as well as traditions of executive noninterference developed over a period of years. Of course, in no society are all trials fair or all judges impartial; but in this respect there are vast differences between democracies and nondemocracies.

By definition, in a free society people will not fear their government (17), especially in regard to their politically related activities. To this degree, the emphasis of organizations such as Amnesty International on the extent of imprisonment, execution, or torture for reasons of conscience is closely related to any measurement of democracy. Oppressive countries imprison their opponents, or worse, both to silence the particular individuals, and to warn others of the dangers of opposing the system. Recently, exile and disappearances have been used as a further deterrent. "Disappearance" is generally a form of extrajudicial execution, often carried out in support of the ruling system. Such terrorism may or may not be directly under the orders of government leaders. These practices underscore the fact that a great deal of such internal state terrorism does not involve the normal legal process; frequently opponents are incarcerated through "detentions" that may last for years. In the Soviet Union and some other Communist countries, the practice of using psychiatric institutions to incarcerate opponents was developed on the theory that opposition to a people's state is itself a form of mental illness.

It is important in this regard to distinguish between the broader category of "political imprisonment" and the narrower "imprisonment for reasons of conscience." The former includes all cases that informed opinion would assume are related to political issues, or issues that can be defined politically in some states (such as religious belief in Communist or some Islamic societies). It includes those who have written articles that the regime finds offensive as well as those who have thrown bombs or plotted assassinations, or even caused riots, to dramatize their cause. Since clearly the latter actions cannot be accepted by any government, all states, at whatever level of freedom, may have some "political prisoners." But if we take the category of political prisoners and separate out those who appear not to have committed or planned, or been involved in supporting acts of violence, then we have the smaller category of "prisoners of conscience." Their existence must be counted against the democratic rating of any country. This is not to say that the existence of prisoners of conscience who have been involved in violence cannot also be taken in many countries as an indication that a system may not be sufficiently responsive to demands expressed nonviolently—too often there may be no effective means to express opposition without violence. The distinction between prisoners by reason of conscience and political prisoners is in practice often blurred by the outsider's difficulty in deciding whether particular incarcerated individuals have or have not committed or planned acts of violence. Nevertheless, by looking at the pattern of a regime's behavior over a period of years, it is possible to estimate the degree to which a regime does or does not have prisoners of conscience.

Democracies require freedom of organization (18-21) that goes far beyond the right to organize political parties. The rights of individuals to organize trade unions, cooperatives, business enterprises, or religious societies are certainly basic rights that may be limited only with great care in a free society. The right of union or peasant organization has been particularly significant because it allows large groups of ordinary people in many societies to balance, through numbers, the ability of the wealthy to concentrate power. However, in some societies, such as those of western Africa, the ability of medical, bar, and academic associations to mobilize or maintain alternatives to ruling groups has been of equal importance. Churches often stand between a people and complete tyranny. Democracies require freedom of organization because there must be orderly, countervailing power centers in a society—which is one definition of pluralism—if a society is going to maintain free institutions against the natural tendency of governments to aggregate power.

The role that nongovernmental restrictions on political rights and civil liberties should play in the assignment of ratings is one that has never been satisfactorily addressed. My general approach is the standard human rights position that the survey's concern is with the relationship between the government and its citizens. However, in extreme cases it has been unable to adhere to this position. For example, the ratings of Lebanon have recently been reduced to reflect the fact that the parliament and cabinet, the legal structure, have become irrelevant in most of the country. Lebanon's pluralism now looks more like a distributed totalitarianism. When added together it looks plural, but for people in particular communities or neighborhoods the relevant system must appear quite repressive. We must start to come to some firmer guidelines for a country such as Colombia where many people live outside the government's law, and where suppression of opinion may be the threat of gang execution rather than prison. In India the general freedoms accorded the people are much reduced in the Punjab under the threat of Sikh violence, or in Bihar in the face of threats from Left, Right, and the security services. Social repressions existing apart from the actions of the government or its security forces affect all countries to a greater or lesser extent, but where the analyst must start taking them into account is increasingly at issue.

Additional Thoughts Raised by the Survey

Historically, what constitutes freedom and democracy is a moving target (compare Strauss 1988). Modern democracy evolved with a more or less steady acceleration from seventeenth century origins. With few exceptions, each generation has seen an extension of democracy to more people, but also a deepening and broadening of democracy and freedom within societies calling themselves free. It is a well-known story, but one easy to forget. Democracy in the nineteenth century United States, and analogously in other democracies of the time, assumed that women, blacks, Indians, and poor people generally either would not vote or would vote as their superiors ordered. The right of such peoples to a hearing was granted grudgingly, if at all. The evolution of democracy has overcome these barriers, but we are still in the midst of defining what democracy means, and we may always be.

We should ask when and how we should judge evolving democracies in different terms, different time-senses, rather than against the particular point that we have reached in our societies at this time. It would be easy to cast doubt on this suggestion by pointing out that South Africa could by some nineteenth century standards be seen as a fully functioning democracy. On the other hand, should democracy in the United States and Great Britain be judged by the standards of countries such as Norway and Iceland in which the major parties have decided that approximately 50 percent of their cabinet ministers must be women? If this study were being done in Oslo, would it make sense to begin at that point?

Whatever we may think about South Africa and Norway, this indicates a difficulty that we must feel in finding a firm place to stand, from which to "judge." Are we not after all engaged in a form of judgment? We could assume that we are not judging, that we are simply setting up a list of criteria, devised at a particular point in history, and seeing how other societies measure up to them. But if this is so, then how are we going to mark the divisions on our ruler when it involves societies that seem to excel, or believe they do, our top marks? Should we place Iceland, etc. on a higher level than ourselves (compare Anderson 1988)? We probably will not, because we have not accepted the Icelandic definitions of democracy as indisputably adding to democracy, just as we do not include their comprehensive welfare systems (which most representatives from Scandinavian countries at international conferences often do—even after patient explanation of the difference between economic and political democracy).

We need to further explore the fact that the rating system described here must be applied to a wide variety of different cultural and situational contexts. Democratic rights have their expression in countries characterized by particular cultures and particular internal and external situations that limit, channel, or reinforce freedoms. What the survey looks for in India cannot be exactly congruent with what we look for in the United States. The Indian castes are outlawed, but a living reality; the state grants the lowest castes special favors, but the grant of these favors is widely viewed as a denial of the rights of others; the existence of castes is a denial of equality, and yet they provide the basis for a great deal of democratic political and organizational activity of a type less common in our own society. The security services in India are often repressive and brutal, and yet without striving for political power these services maintain peace in perhaps the most violent and fissiparous democracy. It is a truism that democracy in Japan exists within a cultural framework that is hard for the outsider to penetrate. What are we really to compare to the factionalized ruling party of Japan, tied closely into corporate relations with business, academia, and the media? What is the actual threat to civil liberties of a judicial-security system that makes legal challenge difficult and relies on confession as the basis of police work? Checklist items look fairly good on the surface, but one must wonder. Yet in wondering and questioning we know that we cannot allow ourselves to be seduced selectively by the critical, neo-Marxist stance toward political and civil liberties that assumes they are all merely covers for new types of repression. We are certain that countries toward the freer end of our rating continuum are very different from those at the other end, but within this certainty we often find our underpinnings shaky. It would help the common enterprise if they could be shored up.

The author has also not fully resolved another problem of democratic time (compare Strauss 1988). Countries such as Nigeria have ocscillated in recent years between democracy and nondemocracy, a few years of this, a few years of that. Others, such as West Germany and Italy, have now enjoyed forty years of democracy, but many still alive in these countries remember when freedoms were brutally denied. Others, such as the United States or the UK, have few, at least among their majority peoples, that have ever been without broad civil and political freedoms. In a year in which full democratic freedoms seem to be existing in countries with these different historical experiences, should we use history as a discriminator? If so, how, and to what degree?

Appendix A

Independent States: Comparative Freedoms in 1978 and 1988

	Political Rights[1]		Civil Liberties[1]		Freedom Rating[2]	
	1978	1988	1978	1988	1978	1988
Afghanistan	7	6	7	6	14 (NF)	12
Albania	7	7	7	7	14 (NF)	14
Algeria	6	5	6	6	12 (NF)	11
Angola	7	7	7	7	14 (NF)	14
Antigua & Barbuda	2	2	2	3	4 (F)	5
Argentina	6	2	5	1	11 (NF)	3
Australia	1	1	1	1	2 (F)	2
Austria	1	1	1	1	2 (F)	2
Bahamas	1	2	2	3	3 (F)	5
Bahrain	6	5	4	5	10 (PF)	10
Bangladesh	4	4	4	5	8 (PF)	9
Barbados	1	1	1	1	2 (F)	2
Belgium	1	1	1	1	2 (F)	2
Belize	1	1	2	2	3 (F)	3
Benin	7	7	7	7	14 (NF)	14
Bhutan	4	5	4	5	8 (PF)	10
Bolivia	5	2	3	3	8 (PF)	5
Botswana	2	2	3	3	5 (F)	5
Brazil	4	2	4	3	8 (PF)	5
Brunei	6	6	5	6	11 (NF)	12
Bulgaria	7	7	7	7	14 (NF)	14
Burkina Faso[3]	2	7	3	6	5 (F)	13
Burma	7	7	6	6	13 (NF)	13
Burundi	7	7	6	6	13 (NF)	13
Cambodia[4]	7	7	7	7	14 (NF)	14
Cameroon	6	6	5	6	11 (NF)	12
Canada	1	1	1	1	2 (F)	2

	Political Rights[1]		Civil Liberties[1]		Freedom Rating[2]	
	1978	1988	1978	1988	1978	1988
Cape Verde	6	5	6	6	12 (NF)	11
Cen. Africa Rep.	7	6	7	6	14 (NF)	12
Chad	6	6	6	7	12 (NF)	13
Chile	6	5	5	4	11 (NF)	9
China (Mainland)	6	6	6	6	12 (NF)	12
China (Taiwan)	5	5	4	3	9 (PF)	8
Colombia	2	2	3	3	5 (F)	5
Comoros	5	6	4	6	9 (PF)	12
Congo	7	7	6	6	13 (NF)	13
Costa Rica	1	1	1	1	2 (F)	2
Cote d'Ivoire [5]	6	6	5	6	11 (NF)	12
Cuba	6	7	6	6	12 (NF)	13
Cyprus (G)	3	1	4	2	7 (PF)	3
Cyprus (T)	3	2	4	3	7 (PF)	5
Czechoslovakia	7	7	6	6	13 (NF)	13
Denmark	1	1	1	1	2 (F)	2
Djibouti	2	6	3	6	5 (F)	12
Dominica	2	2	3	2	5 (F)	4
Dominican Rep.	2	1	2	3	4 (F)	4
Ecuador	5	2	3	2	8 (PF)	4
Egypt	5	5	5	4	10 (PF)	9
El Salvador	4	3	4	3	8 (PF)	6
Equatorial Guinea	7	7	7	7	14 (NF)	14
Ethiopia	7	6	7	7	14 (NF)	13
Fiji	2	5	2	4	4 (F)	9
Finland	2	1	2	2	4 (F)	3
France	1	1	2	2	3 (F)	3
Gabon	6	6	6	6	12 (NF)	12
Gambia	2	3	2	3	4 (F)	6
Germany (E)	7	7	6	6	13 (NF)	13
Germany (W)	1	1	2	2	3 (F)	3
Ghana	6	6	4	6	10 (PF)	12
Greece	2	2	2	2	4 (F)	4
Grenada	2	2	3	1	5 (F)	3
Guatemala	3	3	4	3	7 (PF)	6
Guinea	7	7	7	6	14 (NF)	13
Guinea-Bissau	6	6	6	7	12 (NF)	13
Guyana	4	5	3	5	7 (PF)	10
Haiti	7	7	6	5	13 (NF)	12

	Political Rights[1]		Civil Liberties[1]		Freedom Rating[2]	
	1978	1988	1978	1988	1978	1988
Honduras	6	2	3	3	9 (PF)	5
Hungary	6	5	5	4	11 (NF)	9
Iceland	1	1	1	1	2 (F)	2
India	2	2	2	3	4 (F)	5
Indonesia	5	5	5	5	10 (PF)	10
Iran	6	5	5	6	11 (PF)	11
Iraq	7	7	6	7	13 (NF)	14
Ireland	1	1	1	1	2 (F)	2
Israel	2	2	2	2	4 (F)	4
Italy	2	1	2	1	4 (F)	2
Jamaica	2	2	3	2	5 (F)	4
Japan	2	1	1	1	3 (F)	2
Jordan	6	6	6	5	12 (NF)	11
Kenya	5	6	5	6	10 (PF)	12
Kiribati	2	1	2	2	4 (F)	3
Korea (N)	7	7	7	7	14 (NF)	14
Korea (S)	5	2	5	3	10 (PF)	5
Kuwait	6	6	3	5	9 (PF)	11
Laos	7	6	7	6	14 (NF)	12
Lebanon	4	6	4	5	8 (PF)	11
Lesotho	5	6	4	6	9 (PF)	12
Liberia	6	5	4	5	10 (PF)	10
Libya	6	6	6	6	12 (NF)	12
Luxembourg	1	1	1	1	2 (F)	2
Madagascar	5	5	5	5	10 (PF)	10
Malawi	6	6	6	7	12 (NF)	13
Malaysia	3	4	3	5	6 (PF)	9
Maldives	5	5	5	6	10 (PF)	11
Mali	7	6	7	6	14 (NF)	12
Malta	2	1	2	2	4 (F)	3
Mauritania	6	6	6	6	12 (NF)	12
Mauritius	2	2	4	2	6 (PF)	4
Mexico	4	3	4	4	8 (PF)	7
Mongolia	7	7	7	7	14 (NF)	14
Morocco	3	4	4	5	7 (PF)	9
Mozambique	7	6	7	7	14 (NF)	13
Nauru	2	2	2	2	4 (F)	4
Nepal	6	3	5	4	11 (NF)	7

	Political Rights[1]		Civil Liberties[1]		Freedom Rating[2]	
	1978	1988	1978	1988	1978	1988
Netherlands	1	1	1	1	2 (F)	2
New Zealand	1	1	1	1	2 (F)	2
Nicaragua	5	5	5	4	10 (PF)	9
Niger	7	6	6	6	13 (NF)	12
Nigeria	5	5	3	5	8 (PF)	10
Norway	1	1	1	1	2 (F)	2
Oman	6	6	6	6	12 (NF)	12
Pakistan	6	3	5	3	11 (PF)	6
Panama	5	6	5	5	10 (PF)	11
Papua New Guinea	2	2	2	3	4 (F)	5
Paraguay	5	6	5	6	10 (PF)	12
Peru	5	2	4	3	9 (PF)	5
Philippines	5	2	5	3	10 (PF)	5
Poland	6	5	5	5	11 (PF)	10
Portugal	2	1	2	2	4 (F)	3
Qatar	5	5	5	5	10 (PF)	10
Romania	7	7	6	7	13 (NF)	14
Rwanda	6	6	5	6	11 (NF)	12
St. Kitts-Nevis	2	1	3	2	5 (F)	3
St. Lucia	2	1	3	2	5 (F)	3
St. Vincent	2	1	2	2	4 (F)	3
Sao Tome & Prin.	6	6	5	7	11 (NF)	13
Saudi Arabia	6	6	6	7	12 (NF)	13
Senegal	4	3	3	4	7 (PF)	7
Seychelles	6	6	4	6	10 (PF)	12
Sierra Leone	6	5	5	5	11 (PF)	10
Singapore	5	4	5	5	10 (PF)	9
Solomon Islands	2	2	2	2	4 (F)	4
Somalia	7	7	7	7	14 (NF)	14
South Africa	5	5	6	6	11 (PF)	11
Spain	2	1	3	2	5 (F)	3
Sri Lanka	2	3	3	4	5 (F)	7
Sudan	5	4	5	5	10 (PF)	9
Suriname	2	3	2	2	4 (F)	5
Swaziland	6	5	5	6	11 (PF)	11
Sweden	1	1	1	1	2 (F)	2
Switzerland	1	1	1	1	2 (F)	2
Syria	5	6	6	7	11 (PF)	13
Tanzania	6	6	6	6	12 (NF)	12
Thailand	6	3	4	3	10 (PF)	6

	Political Rights[1]		Civil Liberties[1]		Freedom Rating[2]	
	1978	1988	1978	1988	1978	1988
Togo	7	6	6	6	13 (NF)	12
Tonga	5	5	3	3	8 (PF)	8
Transkei	5	7	5	6	10 (PF)	13
Trinidad & Tobago	2	1	2	1	4 (F)	2
Tunisia	6	6	5	4	11 (NF)	10
Turkey	2	2	3	4	5 (F)	6
Tuvalu	2	1	2	1	4 (F)	2
Uganda	7	5	7	5	14 (NF)	10
USSR	7	6	6	5	13 (NF)	11
Un. Arab Emirates	5	5	5	5	10 (PF)	10
United Kingdom	1	1	1	1	2 (F)	2
United States	1	1	1	1	2 (F)	2
Uruguay	6	2	6	2	12 (NF)	4
Vanuatu	3	2	3	4	6 (PF)	6
Venezuela	1	1	2	2	3 (F)	3
Vietnam	7	6	7	7	14 (NF)	13
Western Samoa	4	4	2	3	6 (PF)	7
Yemen (N)	6	5	5	5	11 (NF)	10
Yemen (S)	7	7	7	7	14 (NF)	14
Yugoslavia	6	5	5	5	11 (NF)	10
Zaire	7	6	6	7	13 (NF)	13
Zambia	5	6	5	5	10 (PF)	11
Zimbabwe	5	6	5	5	10 (PF)	11

Notes to Table

1.   The scales use the numbers 1–7, with 1 comparatively offering the highest level of political or civil rights and 7 the lowest. The Freedom Rating simply sums the figures for political rights and civil liberties. The F, PF and NF in parenthesis under the 1978 Freedom Rating refers to the method of grouping freedom ratings used until 1988, a method that was slightly more complicated than simply adding the figures for the two rights. (See the foregoing text.) In retrospect, certain 1978 ratings appear incorrect, for example China (Taiwan), Morocco, or Western Samoa.

2.   The Freedom Rating sums the first two scales.

3.   Formerly Upper Volta.

4.   Often written Kampuchea.

5.   Formerly Ivory Coast.

Appendix B

Sample Checklist Analysis for Two Countries

Political Rights

		INDIA	CHINA
1.	Election of chief authority	—parliamentary system	—behind-the scenes maneuvering by small elite
2.	Effective choice allowed in legislative elections	—regular free elections	—mostly single-party; very little choice
3.	Fairness of election procedures, campaign opportunities, etc.	—adequate laws, intensive campaigning at all levels, violence interrupts process locally on occasion	—little campaigning; media monopolized; manipulation of results
4.	Effect of elections on distribution of power	—parliament rules	—legislative bodies are not the locus of power
5.	Multiplicity of political parties	—many parties, opposition attains power in many states, but ruling party's power entrenched nationally	—effectively single party; marginal minor parties occasionally take independent positions
6.	Do elections shift power?	—since the 1970s only regional shifts	—elections have not shifted power
7.	Significant opposition vote?	—cumulatively, opposition generally outpolls government	—isolated examples of protest votes
8.	Military or foreign control?	—military has no record of interference in politics	—in crises military becomes very influential; otherwise stays out of politics
9.	Denial of self-determination to ethnic or other subgroups	—extensive efforts to balance religious, ethnic, and caste rights through special local and regional divisions and quotas	—although most ethnic cultures are given some respect, the political rights of minorities are denied
10.	Decentralization of political power	—regional and local government with relatively extensive powers; highly responsive to ethnic demands	—in theory, and largely in practice, highly centralized

Political Rights

	INDIA	CHINA
11. Informal consensus; de facto opposition power	—consensus and opposition power plays a major role at local and regional levels, less so nationally	—response to popular demands has been episodic at best; generally little attempt to respond to the political demands of those outside a narrow circle
12. Media/literature free of political censorship	—newspapers and journals free and varied, although some pressures on major publications; radio and TV are government controlled	—all mass media under direct government control and generally compelled to follow government line; less compulsion in new independent publications
13. Open public discussion	—discussion is open, vehement and largely free of fear	—conversation and discussion often open; still, informal pressures and informers
14. Freedom of assembly and demonstration	—demonstrations of all kinds are frequent, although often end in violence and arrests	—most assembly and demonstration orchestrated or controlled, but some free
15. Freedom of political organization	—traditionally highly organized politically and socially; many modern cause groups	—Effectively, only one political party allowed; but its factions represent a variety of positions
16. Nondiscriminatory rule of law in politically relevant cases	—independent judiciary, but very slow and occasionally pressured; security forces occasionally react brutally	—No judicial independence in political cases; police brutality occasional
17. Free from unjustified political terror or imprisonment	—exceptional cases of political imprisonment; generally free of fear of government	—general use of imprisonment against nonviolent opponents; frequent torture
18. Free trade unions, peasant organizations, or equivalents	—independent unions, and farmers organization are unconstrained	—essentially all economic organizations of this type government controlled
19. Free businesses or cooperatives	—independent businesses and cooperatives	—many small ones are independent; larger are government or foreign owned

Political Rights

	INDIA	CHINA
20. Free professional or other private organizations	—extensive network of independent professional and other organizations	—professional groups are government controlled or supervised
21. Free religious institutions	—religious freedom, but some gov. interference in activities	—only if strictly religious and free of foreign control
22. Personal social rights	—private rights accepted; extensive social restrictions on women	—substantial control over number of children, occupation, overseas travel, and residence
23. Socioeconomic rights	—large parts of the population in feudal or semi-bondage relationships	—no feudal dependencies; many bureaucratic ones
24. Freedom from gross socioeconomic inequality	—gross inequality	—inequalities comparatively minor
25. Freedom from government indifference or corruption	—government indifference and corruption common	—widespread corruption

Notes

1. Criticisms of the survey have been discussed in earlier editions of the survey (especially Gastil 1987: 79–87). Many criticisms discussed here were presented in the *Human Rights Quarterly* (1986), which is largely devoted to statistical measures of human rights. Surveys covering ground similar to the Comparative Survey are presented in Gastil (1988); others are discussed in Gastil (1987: 79–97). The claim for lack of institutional bias may not be valid for surveys produced after July 1989.
2. The author was always impressed with the way in which Ralph White (1968) was able to use the standard run of journalistic reporting on the Vietnam war, often written by reporters very critical of the American effort, as a basis for a quite fair-minded analysis of the situation.
3. Much of the following discussion, as well as the accompanying charts, are edited from Gastil (1988, 1989), especially the section "Freedom in the Comparative Survey: Definitions and Criteria", beginning on page 3.

References

ANDERSON, THOMAS D.
    1988   Civil and political liberties in the world: A geographical analysis. In Gastil (1988: 89–100).
BANKS, DAVID L.
    1986   The analysis of human rights data over time. *Human Rights Quarterly* 8, 4 (November): 654–680.
ELAZAR, DANIEL
    1970   *Cities of the prairie*. New York: Basic Books.
    1972   *American federalism, 2d ed*. New York: Crowell Publishers.
GASTIL, RAYMOND D.
    1973   The new criteria of freedom. *Freedom at Issue*. 17 (January-February): 2–5, 20–23.
    1974   Comparative survey of freedom III. *Freedom at Issue* 23 (January-February): 8–10. (1973 and 1974 also had mid-year surveys.)
    1975–   (The Survey was published as *The comparative survey of freedom*, usually with a roman numeral
    1989   attached, in every J-F issue of FAI.)
    1978   *Freedom in the world: 1978*. Boston: G. K. Hall.
    1979   *Freedom in the world: 1979*. Boston: G. K. Hall.

1980   *Freedom in the world: 1980.* New York: Freedom House.
1981   *Freedom in the world: 1981.* Westport: Greenwood Press.
1982   *Freedom in the world: 1982.* Westport: Greenwood Press.
1984   *Freedom in the world: 1983–1984.* Westport: Greenwood Press.
1985   *Freedom in the world: 1984–1985.* Westport: Greenwood Press.
1986   *Freedom in the world: 1985–1986.* Westport: Greenwood Press.
1987   *Freedom in the world: 1986–1987.* Westport: Greenwood Press.
1988   *Freedom in the world: 1987–1988.* New York: Freedom House.
1989   *Freedom in the world: 1988–1989.* New York: Freedom House. (Published after the article was essentially complete.)
HUMAN RIGHTS QUARTERLY
1986   8, 4 (November). (Special edition on measures.)
STRAUSS, IRA
1988   Defining democracy: The three approaches. *AUD Occasional Paper.* No. 1 (April).
WHITE, RALPH K.
1968   *Nobody wanted war.* New York: Doubleday and Company.

3

Measuring Polyarchy

Michael Coppedge and Wolfgang H. Reinicke

The authors have developed a scale based on Robert Dahl's concept of polyarchy. The scale measures the degree to which national political systems meet the minimum requirements for political democracy, where real-world "democracies" rather than abstract ideals are the standard. The Polyarchy Scale is constructed from indicators of freedom of expression, freedom of organization, media pluralism, and the holding of fair elections. The scale is (1) well grounded in democratic theory, (2) world-wide in scope, (3) demonstrably valid, (4) solves problems of weighting indicators, and (5) is easy to interpret and replicate. Some limitations in the scale's applicability are discussed and suggestions are made for improvements and future research.

The Concept of Polyarchy

The term "polyarchy" was originally coined in Dahl and Lindblom (1953), but was developed most fully in Dahl (1971). Polyarchy is defined as the set of institutional arrangements that permits public opposition and establishes the right to participate in politics. In these two respects—public contestation and inclusiveness—polyarchy is similar to the concept of democracy. However, polyarchy is not, and was not intended to be, exactly equivalent to democracy, so it is important to clarify at the outset the various ways in which polyarchy differs from some other conceptions of democracy.

First, the term "democracy" inevitably calls to mind a host of ideals that no actual political system has ever approached. But we also refer to certain actual systems as "democracies," which is often confusing. In order to "maintain the distinction between democracy as an ideal system and the institutional arrangements that have come to be regarded as a kind of imperfect approximation of an ideal," Dahl and Lindblom introduced the term "polyarchy" to denote the latter (Dahl 1971, 9n).

Michael Coppedge is assistant professor in the Latin American Studies Program at the Paul H. Nitze School of Advanced International Studies (SAIS). He is completing a book on party factions and presidential democracy in Venezuela.

Wolfgang H. Reinicke is a Ph.D. candidate at Yale University and a research fellow at the Brookings Institution. He is currently completing a dissertation on the politics of global integration in banking and finance.

Second, like democracy, polyarchy is a quality of a political system; but unlike democracy (at least as it is usually conceived), polyarchy is also a dimension. There are degrees of polyarchy, ranging from full polyarchy to the absence of polyarchy, or hegemony. Those who are looking for a measure that will permit them to make comparisons among democratic states may therefore find a measure of polyarchy odd, in that it says more about the many gradations of failure to achieve full polyarchy than it says about the most democratic extreme.

Third, because polyarchy is concerned with imperfect approximations rather than ideals, the standard for the most democratic regimes is rather low. The concept of polyarchy is limited to the most basic institutional requirements for democracy, specifically those that had been met in most Western European countries by the end of the First World War. A country can qualify as a full polyarchy even if it does not allow workplace or communitarian democracy, proportional representation, referenda, or party primaries.

Fourth, polyarchy does not take into account varying degrees of democracy at different levels of the polity; it is concerned with the national regime only (Dahl 1971: 10–14). And fifth, no particular level of socioeconomic equality is required for a country to be fully polyarchic. Political and social scientists working in some traditions of scholarship would include social and economic equality in the definition of democracy, but in *Polyarchy*, Dahl discussed socioeconomic equality only as a condition that favors the development of polyarchy. So it should be clear that polyarchy reflects political, not social or economic, democracy. Our scale of polyarchy, then, measures the degree to which national political systems meet the minimum requirements for political democracy, where real-world "democracies" rather than abstract ideals are the standard.

As formulated in *Polyarchy* (Dahl 1971: 3), these minimum requirements for political democracy were:

1. Freedom to form and join organizations
2. Freedom of expression
3. The right to vote
4. Eligibility for public office
5. The right of political leaders to compete for support
6. Alternative sources of information
7. Free and fair elections
8. Institutions for making government policies depend on votes and other expressions of preference.

These requirements serve as both a conceptual and an operational definition of polyarchy, which greatly simplifies the problem of constructing a valid measure.

Polyarchy has by no means replaced democracy as an analytical concept in political science, but it is one of "democracy's" closest competitors. Polyarchy is a concept familiar to most American political scientists. A sizable body of theoretical speculation and empirical research concerning polyarchy has been built up, not only in *Polyarchy*, but in Dahl's more recent works and in publications by other political scientists.[1] The Polyarchy Scale developed in this article will provide a useful tool for evaluating many of the previously-untested hypotheses about polyarchy.

A Comprehensive Data Base

An ideal measure of polyarchy would be based on all existing nations. Until recently, comprehensive studies were not possible due to the lack of adequate political data on the smaller, newer, and least-developed nations. For example, in an earlier attempt to construct a Guttman scale of polyarchy, Norling and Williams (Dahl 1971: App. A) were handicapped by inadequate data. As a consequence, they had to exclude from their analysis twenty-one countries that were independent by 1968. Another consequence was that data were missing for a large number of the countries that *were* included in the analysis, which biased the ranking in favor of the countries about which less was known.[2]

Today the data are much more detailed and complete. Thanks to systematic data collection efforts by the Department of State, Raymond Gastil of Freedom House, Charles Humana, and others, there have been multiple sources of information on the political systems of every country in the world since the early 1980s. Using the information they had gathered, we were able to base our scale on the universe of the 170 independent nations that existed in 1985.[3] Only dependent territories were excluded. Usually these sources provide detail sufficient to rate each country on each of the relevant criteria. The information is surprisingly current: even though our research was done in the summer of 1986, there was enough recent information to make our analysis a snapshot of the situation as of mid-1985.

Defining the Variables

With a few substantively minor adjustments, the component variables in the Polyarchy Scale correspond directly to Dahl's eight institutional requirements. Thus, we coded one variable for the extent of the suffrage, one for freedom of expression, one for freedom of organization, and one for the existence of alternative sources of information. Three of the remaining four institutional requirements were easily combined into a single variable measuring free and fair elections. It proved impossible to create a separate variable for the remaining institutional requirement, "Eligibility for public office," because information on this requirement is still incomplete. However, the information available suggests that eligibility for office differs very little from eligibility to vote, so little is lost by omitting this guarantee. The suffrage variable was eventually dropped from the final scale because it contributed very little empirically to the measurement of polyarchy. This amendment is discussed in greater detail below.

Following are descriptions of the variables and their categories.

The variable measuring free and fair elections is FAIRELT, which contains three categories:

1. Elections without significant or routine fraud or coercion.
2. Elections with some fraud or coercion.
3. No meaningful elections: elections without choice of candidates or parties, or no elections at all.

The freedom of organization variable, FREORG, has four categories:

1. Some trade unions or interest groups may be harassed or banned but there are no restrictions on purely political organization.
2. Some political parties are banned and trade unions or interest groups are harassed or banned, but membership in some alternatives to official organizations is permitted.
3. The only relatively independent organizations that are allowed to exist are nonpolitical.
4. No independent organizations are allowed. All organizations are banned or controlled by the government or the party.

The variable measuring freedom of expression, FREXT, contains three categories:

1. Citizens express their views on all topics without fear of punishment.
2. Dissent is discouraged, whether by informal pressure or by systematic censorship, but control is incomplete. The extent of control may range from selective punishment of dissidents on a limited number of issues to a situation in which only determined critics manage to make themselves heard. There is some freedom of private discussion.
3. All dissent is forbidden and effectively suppressed. Citizens are wary of criticizing the government even privately.

The fourth variable, ALTINF, is a measure of availability of alternative sources of information. It contains four categories:

1. Alternative sources of information exist and are protected by law. If there is significant government ownership of the media, they are effectively controlled by truly independent or multi-party bodies.
2. Alternative sources of information are widely available but government versions are presented in preferential fashion. This may be the result of partiality in and greater availability of government-controlled media; selective closure, punishment, harassment, or censorship of dissident reporters, publishers, or broadcasters; or mild self-censorship resulting from any of these.
3. The government or ruling party dominates the diffusion of information to such a degree that alternative sources exist only for nonpolitical issues, for short periods of time, or for small segments of the population. The media are either mostly controlled directly by the government or party or restricted by routine prior censorship, near-certain punishment of dissident reporters, publishers, and broadcasters, or pervasive self-censorship. Foreign media may be available to a small segment of the population.
4. There is no public alternative to official information. All sources of information are official organs or completely subservient private sources. The media are considered instruments of indoctrination. Foreign publications are usually unavailable or censored, and foreign broadcasts may be jammed.

The indicator of the right to vote is SUFF, which has the following categories:

1. Universal adult suffrage.
2. Suffrage with partial restrictions.
3. Suffrage denied to large segments of the population.
4. No suffrage.

It should be noted that quite a few countries that do not hold elections nevertheless provide for universal adult suffrage. We coded the suffrage variable according to the legal provisions of each country, leaving their interpretation to a later stage of analysis.

TABLE 1
1985 Distribution of Countries on Two-Dimensional Scale of Polyarchy

Degree of Public Contestation Scale Types	Extent of Suffrage			
	Full	**Partial**	**Very Restricted**	**None**
Full 0	41	0	1	0
1	10	0	0	0
2	11	0	0	1
3	1	0	1	0
4	14	1	0	0
5	8	0	0	0
6	6	0	1	2
7	15	0	0	4
8	13	0	0	6
9	5	0	0	2
None 10	20	0	1	6
Totals	144	1	4	21

Coding the Variables

For the coding, we relied on sources that differ widely in the quality, format, and completeness of the information they provide. Some cover all countries, others omit the smaller ones. A few sources present information in precoded variables, others in a descriptive format. Some sources are useful for measuring all of the requirements for polyarchy, while others are useful for only one or a few. Rather than attempting to combine this disparate information into some untested index or weighing scheme, we decided to utilize it to code our own new variables. Fresh coding allowed us to draw on different sources and differently formatted data for each variable. All ratings were assigned initially by one coder consulting multiple sources. The sources consulted for each variable are listed in appendix A.

Unidimensionality

Since Dahl intended polyarchy to be a two-dimensional concept, we constructed two separate measures. The measure of the dimension of inclusiveness was SUFF, the "right to vote" variable. Public contestation was measured by constructing an ordered typology in the form of a Guttman scale.[4] This scale ranged from systems with full public contestation (Type 0) to those that allow no contestation (Type 10).

A frequency cross tabulation of the measurements on the two dimensions (Table 1) led us to question the usefulness of inclusiveness as a criterion for polyarchy. Eighty-five percent of all countries in 1985 provided for universal suffrage, whether they held meaningful elections, approval elections, or no elections at all. Furthermore, all but two of the countries which had less than full suffrage in 1985 did not have meaningful elections in the first place. These two countries—South Africa and Western Samoa—should not be ranked as high as countries with the same polyarchy scores, but it is much simpler to treat these two cases as anomalies than to create a separate conceptual dimension to take them into account.

Some readers might feel that it would be worthwhile to keep the inclusiveness dimension in order to distinguish between nondemocratic regimes with limited hypothetical suffrage and nondemocratic regimes with no hypothetical suffrage at all. We disagree, but the ratings on the suffrage variable are included in the Appendix for the benefit of these readers. Dropping the suffrage dimension leaves us with a unidimensional scale of polyarchy that is identical to the scale of public contestation. Its coefficients of reproducibility and scalability are .900 and .829, respectively.[5]

Two other measures of democracy do not deal adequately with the question of unidimensionality. Gastil (1986) compiles separate indexes for political rights and civil liberties even though they are very highly correlated. Bollen (1988) insists on dividing Dahl's institutional requirements for polyarchy into separate conceptual dimensions (''political rights'' and ''political liberties'') even though in building his earlier Index of Political Democracy (Bollen 1980), he demonstrated that the components of political democracy were unidimensional.[6] Common sense dictates that a one-dimensional phenomenon be measured with a one-dimensional indicator. Once the unidimensionality of the phenomenon has been established, insisting on two-dimensional indicators is like trying to measure length in acres.

A Solution to the Problem of Weights

One problem that frequently arises in scale and index construction is assigning weights to the variables. How important is having a free press compared to having freedom of organization? Do you penalize a country more for having fraudulent elections than you do for sporadic press censorship? Most scaling techniques offer no definitive solutions to these problems. One great advantage of Guttman scaling is that it makes it possible to rank countries without having to decide on the relative weights of the component variables, as long as the countries' ratings match the perfect scale types. In effect, the variables are weighted equally. However, the weights are irrelevant to the scale; they could just as easily be grossly unequal, and the ranking of the scale types would remain completely unchanged. For example, any country that fits type 0 perfectly will always rank higher than any country that fits type 1 perfectly, no matter how the component variables are weighted

Owing to this special property of Guttman scaling, the Polyarchy Scale produces an unequivocal ranking of 137 of the world's 170 independent nations for the year 1985. For the remaining thirty-three countries that do not fit the scale types perfectly, ranking is more problematic. There is no *a priori* way to weight the variables in order to decide whether these countries rank above, below, or on par with the countries that have the same scale score and match the perfect scale types.

Nevertheless, we can make a convenient distinction between two types of deviating cases. One group consists of twenty-six countries whose ratings differ only slightly from the corresponding perfect scale type: no rating is more than one category removed from the expected level, and no more than two rating are off. We call these cases ''approximately equivalent variants.'' Doubling the weight of one of the variables would move these countries only one rank up or down, so their ranks can safely be considered approximately correct.

The other group consists of anomalies: countries with one or more ratings that are two or more levels removed from the norm, or have three or more odd ratings altogether. The ranks of these countries change more drastically as the variable weights are modified, so that the ranks of anomalies cannot safely be considered approximately correct. Take, for example, the small European principalities of Andorra, Liechtenstein, and Monaco. In media pluralism, freedom of expression, and freedom of organization, they are like Type 0 polyarchies. But the effective leaders of their governments are not elected; they are either born to the office or appointed by other unelected officials. We prefer not to guess where these odd cases should be ranked. Fortunately, there are only a few—Andorra, Liechtenstein, Monaco, Vatican City, and Syria. South Africa and Western Samoa are also considered anomalies because of their restricted suffrage. Appendix B shows the Polyarchy Scale scores and their interpretations, along with a listing of the perfect scale types, approximately equivalent variants, and the anomalies.

Implications for the Measurement of Polyarchy

The most obvious implication of this scale is that polyarchy can be measured, albeit roughly. It is impossible to rank each country one by one on a unidimensional scale that spans the whole range from polyarchy to nonpolyarchy, because as soon as we try to rank countries within types, we encounter a multidimensional reality that does not allow simple comparisons such as rankings.[7] This is analogous to measuring a thread with a ruler. On a human scale, a thread is effectively one-dimensional and can be measured with a one-dimensional instrument. On a microscopic scale, with microscopic instruments, the three-dimensional structure of the thread is harder to ignore.

We have not developed a finely calibrated instrument suitable for measuring the complex differences among countries at the same level of polyarchy. What we have produced is a coarsely calibrated instrument: an ordered typology with ten to twelve types that apply to many countries at once. This Polyarchy Scale should be very useful for identifying countries that are similar in the degree of polyarchy they possess, and for making broad comparisons of dissimilar types.

The scale is also useful as a checklist: it tells the researcher who is making comparisons involving polyarchy, which characteristics of political systems to pay attention to, and which to ignore. Broadly speaking, someone who is interested in how polyarchic a country is compared to other countries in the world should examine four factors: elections, freedom of organization, freedom of expression, and alternatives to official sources of information.

The Polyarchy Scale also provides more specific items for a checklist. Success in constructing a scale depends as much on how each variable is divided into categories as it does on selecting the correct variables. Based on the category descriptions for each variable, then, the important things to know in measuring polyarchy are:

1. whether or not elections are held that offer voters a meaningful choice of parties or candidates;
2. whether or not election outcomes are affected by significant fraud or coercion;

3. whether all, some, or no political organizations are banned;
4. if all political organizations are banned, whether some or no nonpolitical organizations are allowed to function independently;
5. whether freedom of expression is complete, nonexistent, or somewhere in between;
6. whether the media are pluralistic or government-dominated;
7. if the media are pluralistic, whether official views receive preferential or balanced treatment; and
8. if the media are government-dominated, whether control is complete or incomplete

The process of scale construction also revealed that several distinctions we assume to be relevant to polyarchy are not, in fact, useful for measuring polyarchy. There were five distinctions that we included in original working definitions of our variables, but eliminated because they frustrated our preliminary attempts to construct a scale. Their incompatibility with the other criteria under the constraints of unidimensionality does not mean they are unimportant distinctions for other concepts or issues; it simply means that they vary independently of the more basic components of polyarchy.

The original version of FAIRELT (fair elections) included categories that distinguished between countries that held approval elections (without a choice of candidates) and countries that held no elections at all for the effective leaders of the government. It also distinguished between degrees of fraud or coercion that probably determined the winner of the election, and those that only changed the margin of victory. FREORG (freedom of organization) began with seven categories, but had to be collapsed into four to produce a scale. This adjustment eliminated two distinctions: that between one-party and no-party states, and that between states that allow freedom of purely political organization but harass or ban trade unions or other interest groups, and those that guarantee freedom of both political and nonpolitical organization. The original version of FREXT (freedom of expression) contained two middle categories instead of one, in order to distinguish between exceptional and routine suppression of dissent, where control was nevertheless incomplete.

After collapsing a few categories in the original variables, we found that it was possible to generate more than one scale that met the minimum criterion of a coefficient of reproducibility of at least .900. The final scale was chosen because it does the best job of discriminating between countries that are subjectively dissimilar while still meeting the reproducibility requirement (at exactly .900). The substantive implication of the collapsed categories is that the following distinctions are not useful for measuring polyarchy:

1. elections without choice vs. no elections;
2. one-party states vs. no-party states;
3. exceptional vs. routine suppression of dissent;
4. electoral fraud or coercion that changes the winner of an election vs. fraud or
   coercion that changes only the margin of victory;
5. in states with full freedom of political organization, full vs. partial freedom of
   nonpolitical organization;

For example, the first two distinctions listed above were designed to distinguish between authoritarian and totalitarian regimes. Their irrelevance means that some authoritarian and totalitarian regimes can be roughly equally "unpolyarchic."

Reliability

In this kind of research the two principal causes of error, and therefore the greatest threats to reliability, are the biases of the sources consulted and subjectivity in the coders' scoring.[8] We minimized contamination by the sources' biases by using multiple sources of information whenever possible. For some of the ratings, it was necessary to rely on a single source, but the number of countries affected is small: over ninety-one percent of the ratings are based on more than one source. The average number of sources consulted for all the ratings was 2.3.

Our original procedure was for each coder to pool the information obtained from all of the sources before assigning a rating. Where there were superficial disagreements among the sources, the coder tried to read between the lines to see a reality that was compatible with all of the descriptions. Where these differences were irreconcilable, two coders reviewed the sources and jointly agreed on the correct rating, sometimes after consulting additional sources.[9]

In our original procedure, there was no way to test the assumption that the use of multiple sources would improve the scale's reliability. In order to check the reliability of our ratings, we asked a research assistant to repeat the coding procedure, this time keeping records on consensus or disagreement among sources.[10] Sixty-two percent of her ratings were based on complete consensus among all sources consulted. Another 23 percent were based on at least two-thirds consensus, and for the remaining fifteen percent, it was impossible to assign a rating without pooling information from the sources or consulting additional sources. To the extent that consensus among sources is an indicator of reliability, then, approximately three-fifths of our ratings can be considered very reliable, 85 percent can be considered at least fairly reliable, and about fifteen percent are of uncertain reliability.

Reliability is also affected by coding errors. Our original check on coding errors was to discuss together all ratings on which there seemed to be irreconcilable disagreement among the sources. As it turned out, we discussed fewer than fifty ratings, either because of consensus among sources or, perhaps in part, our own willingness to resolve apparently superficial disagreements by reading between the lines.

We also checked on coding errors by comparing our ratings with the ratings assigned by the research assistant. As mentioned earlier, she was unable to assign a rating to fifteen percent of the cases because of disagreement among sources. But 86.5 percent of the remaining ratings from the attempted replication agreed perfectly with ours. If the comparison is limited to just the ratings for which there was full consensus among sources, the rate of agreement between the original and replicated ratings rises to 93 percent.

Obviously, for a measure that passes judgment on entire nations, perfect reliability is desirable. While perfection is not attainable, there are simple ways to improve the reliability of the Polyarchy Scale that could easily be tried in the future. The most pressing need is for more explicit coding criteria. The authors of this article shared many assumptions regarding coding decisions that did not find their way into the written category descriptions. As a result, the replicated ratings were based on somewhat different assumptions. We believe that most of the differences between the original and the replicated ratings would disappear if the coding criteria were more detailed. Coders should be thoroughly trained, and at least two coders should be used. In addition, where disagreements among sources or between coders prevent the assignment of a rating, coders should discuss the discrepancies and consult experts or additional sources.

All of these improvements must be made before every single rating can be regarded as highly reliable. However, that degree of reliability is not necessary for research involving comparisons of large numbers of countries, since most statistical analyses incorporate techniques for dealing with measurement error. We therefore feel safe in claiming that the Polyarchy Scale is already reliable enough for research on the relationship between polyarchy and other characteristics of whole political systems.

Validity

Validity is always difficult to establish, which explains why most attempts to measure democracy have claimed only face validity, which is entirely subjective. The validity of our scale is, however, one of its strongest points, with the understanding that it is a measure of polyarchy rather than democracy. Creating a measure with high construct validity is a question of (1) choosing the correct indicators, and (2) combining them correctly.[11] The fact that polyarchy is an operationally defined construct enabled us to satisfy the first requirement: with minor exceptions, there is a one-to-one correspondence between the guarantees that Dahl used to define polyarchy and the component variables that we used to measure his concept.

We did not code a separate variable for guarantee number 8, "Institutions for making government policies depend on votes and other expressions of preference," because in a more recent reformulation of these criteria, Dahl stipulated that officials who have "control over government decisions about policy," rather than the policies themselves, should depend on votes (Dahl 1982, 10–11). This amendment made the eighth guarantee essentially equivalent to number 7, "free and fair elections." It was not necessary to construct a variable for number 5, "Right of political leaders to compete for support," because this requirement is implicit in three others—"free and fair elections," "freedom to form and join organizations," and "freedom of expression." Aside from these adjustments, the component variables are by definition valid indicators of polyarchy.

But there are two sides to choosing the correct indicators. So far we have shown that we included indicators of all of the aspects of polyarchy; we must also be careful to include indicators of just those aspects and no others. This second requirement was satisfied by the process of constructing the Guttman scale, for we began our scale construction with variables that were more finely calibrated than the ones that appear in the final scale.[12] That is, our original variables included "extra" information that we presumed to be useful for measuring polyarchy as a unidimensional concept, but which scalogram analysis showed to be unrelated to polyarchy. By eliminating this extra information, we pared down our variables to the most valid possible set of indicators.

Additional support for the validity of the scale comes from its association with other constructs thought to be correlated with democracy. The Pearson product-moment correlations between our scale (with the seven anomalies excluded) and Gastil's indexes of political rights and civil liberties are .938 and .934, respectively.[13]

The Polyarchy Scale should be used with caution in multiple regression since it is ordered categorical data rather than ratio data. The fact that it lacks an absolute zero point and there is no guarantee that the categories are evenly spaced violates one of the assumptions of regression. Log-linear and logit models are more appropriate, as they are for most other measures of democracy. Given the finite universe of 170 countries, the other variables in such models should not have a total of more than three or four categories, unless the Polyarchy Scale is collapsed into a smaller number of categories for the purposes of analysis.

Straightforward Interpretation

The reproducibility of a Guttman scale means that if one knows the score of a country on the scale, one can reproduce, or reconstruct, the country's ratings on each of the component variables. (Actually, with the minimum coefficient of reproducibility of .900, one can reproduce ninety percent of the ratings.) This one-to-one correspondence between scores and combinations of characteristics, or "perfect scale types," makes Guttman scale scores very easy to interpret.

For example, Chile's scale score of 5 tells one much more than the fact that Chile ranks higher than Jordan, lower than Mexico, and about on par with Liberia; it also tells one that in Chile, no meaningful elections are held, some independent political organizations are banned, some public dissent is suppressed, and there is preferential presentation of official views in the media. And by comparing these conditions with the standard conditions in the adjacent scale types, one can determine what the substantive difference is between Chile and the countries that are ranked higher or lower. For example, the relevant difference between Chile and Mexico is that there are meaningful elections in Mexico, even though they are marred by fraud or coercion; and the difference between Chile and Jordan is that some independent political organizations exist in Chile, while in Jordan they are all banned.

Easy Replication

The final attractive charcteristic of the Polyarchy Scale is that it is relatively easy to replicate. Fresh coding of the variables means that it is not necessary to wait for an updated edition of the *Political Handbook* in order to decide how polyarchic a country is. Anyone having access to the sources and to the category definitions could rate countries individually or in groups. With a more detailed coding guide, relatively little training would be required to do an adequate job of this, thanks to the

information collected by other scholars. Our principal sources update their information annually, so as long as they continue to do so, the Polyarchy Scale could also
be updated annually. Since it relies on multiple sources, it could continue to be
updated even if some of the sources are discontinued or replaced by others. Replication by other researchers, preferably with teams of coders, is the best check on
reliability.

Conclusions

The Polyarchy Scale that we have constructed is theoretically well-grounded, empirically comprehensive, demonstrably valid, and easy to interpret and replicate.
While its reliability needs to be improved, it is already useful for large-scale comparative research on polyarchy. The scale is somewhat disappointing in that it
locates such a disproportionate number of countries in the top category. This result
is inevitable, given the fact that polyarchy is concerned with the *minimum* requirements for political democracy.

Still, one would like to be able to compare the quality of democracy among the
full polyarchies. A ''Polyarchy Plus''scale would be constructed by adding a new
variable or variables, or subdividing the top category of one of the existing variables,
in order to incorporate an additional criterion that is useful for making distinctions
among the full polyarchies. Unfortunately, there are many such criteria that could be
incorporated into the scale. Incorporating all of these would almost certainly violate
unidimensionality; incorporating just one or some of them would require making
difficult and controversial judgments. Until a scholarly consensus develops on the
essential characteristics of higher levels of democracy, the Polyarchy Scale is probably as precise as we can make it.

To conclude on a cautionary note, we believe it is unwise to discuss measurement
of democracy or polyarchy without paying attention to regime stability. While
stability and polyarchy are very distinct aspects of a political system, instability has
an undeniable impact on the quality of political life. A precarious or unconsolidated
polyarchy is very different from a fully consolidated one. We therefore urge those
who may contemplate using our scale to remember that there are important characteristics of democracy that it does not reflect.

Appendix A

Sources Consulted for Coding Variables

Fair Elections (FAIRELT): Gastil 1986, Statesman's Yearbook 1986, Banks and Textor
    1985, Europa 1986a-d; and in some cases, Phillips 1984, Delury 1983, DOS 1986, Watch
    Committees 1986, Humana 1986, and McHale 1983.
Freedom of Expression (FREXT): Humana 1986, Gastil 1986, DOS 1986, and Watch
    Committees 1986.
Media Pluralism (ALTINF): Humana 1986, Gastil 1986, DOS 1986, and Watch Committees
    1986.
Freedom of Organization (FREORG): Humana 1986, Gastil 1986, DOS 1986; and in some
    cases Europa 1986a-d, Phillips 1984, Statesman's Yearbook 1986, Banks and Textor
    1985, McHale 1983, Delury 1983, and Alexander 1982.
Extension of Suffrage (SUFF): Banks and Textor 1985, Delury 1983, Alexander 1982,
    McHale 1983, Fukui 1985, and Europa 1986a-d.

Appendix B

The Polyarchy Scale 1985

The series of numbers in parentheses are the combinations of ratings received by the
countries in that column. The first digit is the rating on FAIRELT, the second is for
FREORG, and the third is for FREXT, and the fourth is for ALTINF.

Scale
Score   N
0   41   Perfect Scale Type (1 1 1 1):
            Meaningful fair elections are held, there is full freedom for political organization
            and expression, and there is no preferential presentation of official views in the
            media.

Argentina	Finland	Luxembourg	San Marino
Australia	France	Nauru	Spain
Austria	Germany, West	Netherlands	Sweden
Barbados	Grenada	New Zealand	Switzerland
Belgium	Honduras	Norway	Trinidad & Tobago
Belize	Iceland	Papua New Guinea	Tuvalu
Brazil	Ireland	Portugal	United Kingdom
Canada	Italy	St. Christopher & Nevis	United States
Colombia	Japan	St. Lucia	Uruguay
Costa Rica	Kiribati	St. Vincent & The Grens.	Venezuela
Denmark			

Scale
Score N
  1   10 Perfect Scale Type (1 1 1 2):
           Meaningful fair elections are held, and there is full freedom for political orga-
           nization and expression, but there is preferential presentation of official views in
           the media.

           Botswana   Ecuador
           Cyprus   Mauritius
           Dominica   Solomon Islands
           Dominican Republic
           Approximately Equivalent:
           Israel, Peru (1 1 2 1)
           Fiji (2 1 1 1)

  2   9 Perfect Scale Type (1 1 2 2):
           Meaningful fair elections are held and there is full freedom for political organi-
           zation, but some public dissent is suppressed and there is preferential presenta-
           tion of official views in the media.

           Antigua & Barbuda
           Bahamas
           Bolivia
           India
           Thailand
           Approximately Equivalent:
           Vanuatu (1 1 2 3)
           Greece, Jamaica (2 1 1 2)
           Panama (2 2 1 1)

  3   0 (1222/2122): Undefined due to lack of cases.

  4   16 Perfect Scale Type (2 2 2 2):
           Elections are marred by fraud or coercion, some independent political organi-
           zations are banned, some public dissent is suppressed, and there is preferential
           presentation of official views in the media.

           Egypt   Philippines
           El Salvador   Singapore
           South Korea   Sri Lanka
           Malta   Turkey
           Mexico
           Approximately Equivalent:
           Senegal (2 2 1 2)
           Malaysia, Nicaragua, Zimbabwe (1 2 2 3)
           Maldives, Morocco (3 1 2 2), Lebanon (3 2 2 1)

Scale
Score N

5 7 Perfect Scale Type (3 2 2 2):
No meaningful elections are held, some independent political organizations are banned, some public dissent is suppressed, and there is preferential presentation of official views in the media.

Bangladesh   Guatemala
Chile   Liberia
Approximately Equivalent:
Gambia, Indonesia, Guyana (2 2 2 3)

6 9 Perfect Scale Type (3 3 2 2):
No meaningful elections are held, only nonpolitical organizations are allowed to be independent, some public dissent is suppressed, and there is preferential presentation of official views in the media.

Jordan   Sudan
Kuwait   Tunisia
Approximately Equivalent:
Lesotho, Madagascar, Pakistan, Paraguay (3 2 2 3)
Bhutan (3 4 1 2)

7 19 Perfect Scale Type (3 3 2 3):
No meaningful elections are held, only non-political organizations are allowed to be independent, some public dissent is suppressed, and alternatives to the official media are very limited.

Brunei   Ghana   Suriname
Burkina Faso   Guinea   Swaziland
C. A. R.   Haiti   Taiwan
Chad   Poland   Tonga
Djibouti   Rwanda   Yugoslavia
Gabon   Sierra Leone   Zambia
Approximately Equivalent:
Iran (3 2 3 3)

8 18 Perfect Scale Type (3 4 2 3):
No meaningful elections are held, all organizations are banned or controlled by the government or official party, some public dissent is suppressed, and alternatives to the official media are very limited.

Bahrain   Congo   Nigeria
Benin   Hungary   Seychelles
Burundi   Ivory Coast   Uganda
Cameroon   Kenya   United Arab
Cape Verde   Mauritania   Emirates
Comoros   Nepal   North Yemen
Approximately Equivalent:
Qatar (3 3 2 4)

Scale
Score   N
 9   7   Perfect Scale Type (3 4 2 4):
             No meaningful elections are held, all organizations are banned or controlled by
             the government or official party, some public dissent is suppressed, and there is
             no public alternative to official information.

             Algeria   Tanzania
             Equatorial Guinea   Zaire
             Oman
             Approximately Equivalent:
             Malawi (3 3 3 4)
             Niger (3 3 3 4)

Scale
Score   N
 10   27   Perfect Scale Type (3 4 3 4):
             No meaningful elections are held, all organizations are banned or controlled by
             the government or official party, all public dissent is suppressed, and there is no
             public alternative to official information.

             Afghanistan   Germany, East   Mozambique
             Albania   Guinea-Bissau   Romania
             Angola   Iraq   Sao Tome &
             Bulgaria   Kampuchea   Principe
             Burma   Korea, North   Saudi Arabia
             China   Laos   Somalia
             Cuba   Libya   Togo
             Czechoslovakia   Mali   USSR
             Ethiopia   Mongolia   Viet Nam
                                                        South Yemen

Anomalies excluded from the ranking are:
Andorra, Liechtenstein, Monaco, Vatican City (3 1 1 1); Syria (3 2 3 4); and South Africa and Western Samoa
(1 2 2 2 and 1 1 1 1 with limited suffrage).

Appendix C

1985 Country Ratings on Criteria for Polyarchy
(Numbers correspond to category numbers in text.)

NATION	FAIRELT	FREORG	FREXT	ALTINF	SUFF
AFGHANISTAN	3	4	3	4	4
ALBANIA	3	4	3	4	1
ALGERIA	3	4	2	4	1
ANDORRA	3	1	1	1	1
ANGOLA	3	4	3	4	3
ANTIGUA & BARBUDA	1	1	2	2	1
ARGENTINA	1	1	1	1	1
AUSTRALIA	1	1	1	1	1
AUSTRIA	1	1	1	1	1
BAHAMAS	1	1	2	2	1
BAHRAIN	3	4	2	3	4
BANGLADESH	3	2	2	2	1
BARBADOS	1	1	1	1	1
BELGIUM	1	1	1	1	1
BELIZE	1	1	1	1	1
BENIN	3	4	2	3	1
BHUTAN	3	4	1	2	1
BOLIVIA	1	1	2	2	1
BOTSWANA	1	1	1	2	1
BRAZIL	1	1	1	1	1
BRUNEI	3	3	2	3	4
BULGARIA	3	4	3	4	1
BURKINA FASO	3	3	2	3	1
BURMA	3	4	3	4	1
BURUNDI	3	4	2	3	1
CAMEROON	3	4	2	3	1
CANADA	1	1	1	1	1
CAPE VERDE	3	4	2	3	1
CENTRAL AFRICAN REP.	3	3	2	3	1
CHAD	3	3	2	3	1
CHILE	3	2	2	2	1
CHINA	3	4	3	4	1
COLOMBIA	1	1	1	1	1
COMOROS	3	4	2	3	1
CONGO	3	4	2	3	1
COSTA RICA	1	1	1	1	1
CUBA	3	4	3	4	1
CYPRUS	1	1	1	2	1
CZECHOSLOVAKIA	3	4	3	4	1
DENMARK	1	1	1	1	1
DJIBOUTI	3	3	2	3	1

NATION	FAIRELT	FREORG	FREXT	ALTINF	SUFF
DOMINICA	1	1	1	2	1
DOMINICAN REPUBLIC	1	1	1	2	1
ECUADOR	1	1	1	2	1
EGYPT	2	2	2	2	1
EL SALVADOR	2	2	2	2	1
EQUATORIAL GUINEA	3	4	2	4	1
ETHIOPIA	3	4	3	4	4
FIJI	2	1	1	1	1
FINLAND	1	1	1	1	1
FRANCE	1	1	1	1	1
GABON	3	3	2	3	1
GAMBIA	2	2	2	3	1
GERMANY, EAST	3	4	3	4	1
GERMANY, WEST	1	1	1	1	1
GHANA	3	3	2	3	4
GREECE	2	1	1	2	1
GRENADA	1	1	1	1	1
GUATEMALA	3	2	2	2	1
GUINEA	3	3	2	3	4
GUINEA-BISSAU	3	4	3	4	4
GUYANA	2	2	2	3	1
HAITI	3	3	2	3	1
HONDURAS	1	1	1	1	1
HUNGARY	3	4	2	3	1
ICELAND	1	1	1	1	1
INDIA	1	1	2	2	1
INDONESIA	2	2	2	3	1
IRAN	3	2	3	3	1
IRAQ	3	4	3	4	1
IRELAND	1	1	1	1	1
ISRAEL	1	1	2	1	1
ITALY	1	1	1	1	1
IVORY COAST	3	4	2	3	1
JAMAICA	2	1	1	2	1
JAPAN	1	1	1	1	1
JORDAN	3	3	2	2	1
KAMPUCHEA	3	4	3	4	1
KENYA	3	4	2	3	1
KIRIBATI	1	1	1	1	1
KOREA, NORTH	3	4	3	4	1
KOREA, SOUTH	2	2	2	2	1
KUWAIT	3	3	2	2	3
LAOS	3	4	3	4	4
LEBANON	3	2	2	1	2
LESOTHO	3	2	2	3	4

NATION	FAIRELT	FREORG	FREXT	ALTINF	SUFF
LIBERIA	3	2	2	2	1
LIBYA	3	4	3	4	1
LIECHTENSTEIN	3	1	1	1	1
LUXEMBOURG	1	1	1	1	1
MADAGASCAR	3	2	2	3	1
MALAWI	3	3	3	4	1
MALAYSIA	1	2	2	3	1
MALDIVES	3	1	2	3	1
MALI	3	4	3	4	1
MALTA	2	2	2	2	1
MAURITANIA	3	4	2	3	4
MAURITIUS	1	1	1	2	1
MEXICO	2	2	2	2	1
MONACO	3	1	1	1	1
MONGOLIA	3	4	3	4	1
MOROCCO	3	1	2	2	1
MOZAMBIQUE	3	4	3	4	4
NAURU	1	1	1	1	1
NEPAL	3	4	2	3	1
NETHERLANDS	1	1	1	1	1
NEW ZEALAND	1	1	1	1	1
NICARAGUA	1	2	2	3	1
NIGER	3	3	3	4	4
NIGERIA	3	4	2	3	4
NORWAY	1	1	1	1	1
OMAN	3	4	2	4	4
PAKISTAN	3	2	2	3	1
PANAMA	2	2	1	1	1
PAPUA NEW GUINEA	1	1	1	1	1
PARAGUAY	3	2	2	3	1
PERU	1	1	2	1	1
PHILIPPINES	2	2	2	2	1
POLAND	3	3	2	3	1
PORTUGAL	1	1	1	1	1
QATAR	3	3	2	4	4
ROMANIA	3	4	3	4	1
RWANDA	3	3	2	3	1
ST. CHRISTOPHER & NEVIS	1	1	1	1	1
ST. LUCIA	1	1	1	1	1
ST. VINCENT & GREN.	1	1	1	1	1
SAN MARINO	1	1	1	1	1
SAO TOME & PRINCIPE	3	4	3	4	1
SAUDI ARABIA	3	4	3	4	4
SENEGAL	3	2	1	2	1

NATION	FAIRELT	FREORG	FREXT	ALTINF	SUFF
SEYCHELLES	3	4	2	3	1
SIERRA LEONE	3	3	2	3	1
SINGAPORE	2	2	2	2	1
SOLOMON ISLANDS	1	1	1	2	1
SOMALIA	3	4	3	4	1
SOUTH AFRICA	1	2	2	2	3
SPAIN	1	1	1	1	1
SRI LANKA	2	2	2	2	1
SUDAN	3	3	2	2	4
SURINAME	3	3	2	3	4
SWAZILAND	3	3	2	3	1
SWEDEN	1	1	1	1	1
SWITZERLAND	1	1	1	1	1
SYRIA	3	2	3	4	1
TAIWAN	3	3	2	3	1
TANZANIA	3	4	2	4	1
THAILAND	1	1	2	2	1
TOGO	3	4	3	4	1
TONGA	3	3	2	3	1
TRINIDAD & TOBAGO	1	1	1	1	1
TUNISIA	3	3	2	2	1
TURKEY	2	2	2	2	1
TUVALU	1	1	1	1	1
UGANDA	3	4	2	3	4
UNITED ARAB EMIRATES	3	4	2	3	1
UNITED KINGDOM	1	1	1	1	1
UNITED STATES	1	1	1	1	1
URUGUAY	1	1	1	1	1
USSR	3	4	3	4	1
VANUATU	1	1	2	3	1
VATICAN CITY	3	1	1	1	4
VENEZUELA	1	1	1	1	1
VIET-NAM	3	4	3	4	1
WESTERN SOMOA	1	1	1	1	3
YEMEN, NORTH	3	4	2	3	1
YEMEN, SOUTH	3	4	3	4	1
YUGOSLAVIA	3	3	2	3	1
ZAIRE	3	4	2	4	1
ZAMBIA	3	3	2	3	1
ZIMBABWE	1	2	2	3	1

Notes

We are deeply indebted to Robert Dahl for conceiving this project, entrusting it to us, and giving us encouragement and intellectual guidance along the way. We have also benefited from comments by Kenneth Bollen, Martin Lipset, and Larry Diamond, and from the research assistance of Anna Pappavlachopoulou. Responsibility for errors, however, is ours alone.

1. The *Social Sciences Citation Index* lists 182 references to *Polyarchy* since its publication.

2. Another problem with the scaling attempt by Norling and Williams was that the data did not match Dahl's

criteria for polyarchy very closely. Norling and Williams relied on updated versions of ten variables from Banks and Textor's 1963 *Cross-Polity Survey* that seemed to be related to the requirements for polyarchy. But they never tested the Banks and Textor variables to see whether they were conceptually valid substitutes for Dahl's eight criteria. Instead, they simply tried to scale the ten variables directly, with results that were optimistically judged "moderately satisfactory." Their coefficient of reproducibility was only .829, even though it was calculated by a controversial method of counting errors that tends to raise the coefficient artificially (McIver and Carmines 1981, 42-45).

3. We did not use Gastil's Indexes of Civil Rights and Political Liberties directly, since they are summary measures; instead, we used the descriptive information that he provides as justification for the ratings.

4. For an introduction to Guttman scaling, see Gorden, 1977.

5. Those who are accustomed to Guttman scales based on dichotomous variables may find our polychotomous variables unorthodox, but there is no cause for concern; the coefficients reported in the text *underestimate* the unidimensionality of the scale, if they are inaccurate at all. Each n-chotomous variable can be disaggregated into n-1 dichotomous variables, generating an equivalent scale of ten dichotomous variables. The coefficients of reproducibility and scalability of this new scale are ever more impressive, at .957 and .869, respectively. Conventionally, the coefficient of reproducibility should be at least .900 and the coefficient of scalability should be at least .600 (Dunn-Rankin 1983, 106-107).

6. Bollen's Index, like ours, did not incorporate a component of inclusiveness.

7. In technical terms, if we try to construct a more precise scale by increasing the number of categories in each variable so that each institutional guarantee is measured more accurately, the coefficient of reproducibility falls below .900.

8. Some commonly used indicators of reliability, such as coefficient alpha, are not appropriate for the Polyarchy Scale. These measures were developed for psychological testing, in which reliability depends much more on the internal consistency of the instruments than it does on measurement error. For a task such as measuring polyarchy, measurement error due to the subjectivity of the sources and the coding is much more important. The coefficient of reliability is best regarded in this situation as an upper limit on the reliability of the scale based on its internal consistency—i.e., the number of variables and the degree to which they all measure the same thing. (In this sense, reliability is also measured by the coefficient of scalability, reported in the discussion of validity.) However, reliability coefficients can be calculated. For the Polyarchy Scale, the value of KR-20, the Kuder-Richardson version of coefficient alpha for dichotomous items, is .946. To calculate it, we decomposed our four multiple-choice variables into ten dichotomous variables. A coefficient of .946 indicates the extremely high degree of reliability that one would like to have for a measure that woud be used to make important decisions, such as an IQ score that would be used to assign children to special education classes (Nunnally 1967, 226).

9. Actual procedures varied slightly from variable to variable, depending on the quality of the source information. For example, one of the authors made use of an extraneous variable previously coded by the other author, on "Bans on Political Parties," because two of the categories exactly matched categories in the "freedom of organization" variable. An unusually high proportion (22 percent) of the freedom of expression ratings were based on only one source because Charles Humana's *World Human Rights Guide* (Humana 1986) contained especially complete, hard information. These variations occurred only because it was a new research project, and procedures evolved as they were being carried out. In future measurements, standardized, consistent procedures can be followed.

10. The research assistant was a foreign-born, U.S.-educated master's student in international relations. Her minimal training consisted of reading portions of Dahl's *Polyarchy* and a preliminary version of this paper (with the ratings removed). She consulted the same sources that we used originally.

11. For a lucid discussion of construct validity, see Nunally (1967, 83-102).

12. See the discussion under "Implications for the Measurements of Polyarchy."

13. The ratings can be found in Raymond Gastil, ed., *Freedom in the World: Political Rights and Civil Liberties, 1987-1988* (Lanham, Md.: University Press of America, 1988), Table 6.

References

ALEXANDER, ROBERT J., ed.
  1982   *Political parties of the Americas: Canada, Latin America, and the West Indies.* Westport, CT: Greenwood Press.
BANKS, ARTHUR S., ed.
  1985   *Political handbook of the world.* New York: McGraw-Hill.
BANKS, ARTHUR S. and ROBERT B. TEXTOR
  1963   *A cross-polity survey.* Cambridge: M.I.T. Press.
BOLLEN, KENNETH A.
  1988   Political democracy: Conceptual and measurement traps, paper prepared for conference on "The Measurement of Democracy" held at the Hoover Institution, Stanford University, May 27-28, 1988.
  1980   Issues in the comparative measurement of political democracy, *American Sociological Review* 45 (June): 370-390.

DAHL, ROBERT A.
    1971   *Polyarchy: Participation and opposition.* New Haven: Yale University Press.
    1982   *Dilemmas of pluralist democracy.* New Haven: Yale University Press.
DAHL, ROBERT A. and CHARLES LINDBLOM
    1953   *Politics, economics, and welfare.* New York: Harper and Brothers.
DELURY, GEORGE E., ed.
    1983   *World encyclopedia of political systems and parties.* Harlow, Essex, UK: Longman.
DEPARTMENT OF STATE
          See United States Government
DUNN-RANKIN, PETER
    1983   *Scaling methods.* Hillsdale, N.J.: L. Erlbaum.
EUROPA
    1986   *The Europa yearbook.* London: Europa Publications.
    1986a   *South America, Central America and the Caribbean.* London: Europa Publications.
    1986b   *The Far East and Australasia.* London: Europa Publications.
    1986c   *Africa south of the Sahara.* London: Europa Publications.
    1986d   *The Middle East and North Africa: A survey and directory of the countries of the Middle East.* London: Europa Publications.
FUKUI, HARUHIRO, ed.
    1985   *Political parties of Asia and the Pacific.* Westport, CT: Greenwood Press
GASTIL, RAYMOND L
    1986   *Freedom in the world: Political rights and civil liberties, 1985-1986.* Westport, CT: Greenwood Press.
GORDEN, RAYMOND L.
    1977   *Unidimensional scaling of social variables: Concepts and procedures.* New York: Free Press.
HUMANA, CHARLES
    1986   *World human rights guide.* New York: Facts on File.
McHALE, VINCENT E., ed.
    1983   *Political parties of Europe.* Westport, CT: Greenwood Press.
McIVER, JOHN P. and EDWARD G. CARMINES
    1981   *Unidimensional scaling.* Beverly Hills: Sage Publications.
NUNNALLY, JUM C.
    1967   *Psychometric theory.* New York: McGraw-Hill.
PHILLIPS, CLAUDE S.
    1984   *The African political dictionary.* Santa Barbara, Calif.: ABC-Clio.
The statesman's year-book
    1986   *Statistical and historical annual of the states of the world.* London and New York: Macmillan, St. Martin's Press.
United States Government, Department of State
    1986   *Country reports on human rights practices for 1985.* Washington: United States Government Printing Office.
Watch Committees, The Lawyers Committee for Human Rights
    1986   *Critique: Review of the Department of State's country reports on human rights.* New York: Fund for Free Expression for the Watch Committees and the Watch Committees and the Lawyers Committee for Human Rights.

4

The Transformation of the Western State: The Growth of Democracy, Autocracy, and State Power since 1800

Ted Robert Gurr, Keith Jaggers, and Will H. Moore

This article uses POLITY II, a new dataset on the authority traits of 155 countries, to assess some general historical arguments about the dynamics of political change in Europe and Latin America from 1800 to 1986. The analysis, relying mainly on graphs, focuses first on the shifting balance between democratic and autocratic patterns in each world region and identifies some of the internal and international circumstances underlying the trends, and deviations from them. Trends in three indicators of state power also are examined in the two regions: the state's capacity to direct social and economic life, the coherence of political institutions, and military manpower. The state's capacity has increased steadily in both regions; coherence has increased in the European countries but not Latin America; while military power has fluctuated widely in both regions. The article is foundational to a series of more detailed longitudinal studies of the processes of state growth.

Ted Robert Gurr is a professor of government and politics at the University of Maryland and Distinguished Scholar at the University's Center for International Development and Conflict Management. Among his 14 books and monographs are *Why Men Rebel* (awarded the Woodrow Wilson Prize as best book in political science of 1970). *Patterns of Authority: A Comparative Basis for Political Inquiry* (with Harry Eckstein, 1975), and *Violence in America* (3d edition. 1989). He is engaged in a long-term global study of minorities' involvement in conflict and its consequences and resolution.

Keith Jaggers is a Ph.D. candidate in the Department of Political Science at the University of Colorado and research assistant in the Department's Center for Comparative Politics. He is co-author with Will H. Moore of "Deprivation, Mobilization, and the State," recently published in the *Journal of Developing Societies*, and is currently working on an empirical study of the impact of war on the growth of the state.

Will H. Moore is a Ph.D. candidate in the Department of Political Science at the University of Colorado and research assistant in the Department's Center for Comparative Politics. He is also a co-author with Maro Ellena of a forthcoming article in *Western Political Quarterly* on the cross-national determinants of political violence. His current research interests include the resolution of internal wars and the formation of coercive states.

Three broad processes have reshaped the global landscape of state structures during the last two centuries. One is an extraordinary expansion in the absolute and relative power of the state, a process that began in Europe. The new states created by the American and French revolutions marked the threshold between a political world dominated by monarchies, whose claims to absolutism were belied by the fact that most social and economic life was autonomous from state control or extraction, and the modern political world in which state power is based on ever-widening control and mobilization of human and material resources in exchange for broadened rights of popular participation. An integral part of this process has been the development of bureaucracies with high capacities to regulate, tax, and mobilize people in the service of state policy.[1] The industrial revolution provided the material means for this expansion, but the state share grew faster than did productivity in the private sector. In four West European countries for which time-series data are available, the budgeted expenditures of the central government increased from an average of 6.4 percent of GNP in 1875 to 11.2 percent in 1925 and 44.1 percent in 1982.[2] War was the principal engine of state growth in past centuries: there was a ten-fold increase in the size of the armies fielded in war relative to total population in France and England from 1066 to World War II.[3] In the present century, especially since 1918, politicized demands for state intervention and subsidy have been the major driving force in state expansion.

The second process has been the transformation of the structures of political participation and legitimation. This transformation followed one of two paths, toward plural democracy or mass-party autocracy. The popular side of the bargain by which most West European rulers built state power in the nineteenth century was to acknowledge the right of widespread participation in policy making. This right was given institutional expression in elected assemblies that could review, and sometimes initiate, public policy; in contested elections, direct or indirect, of chief ministers; and in recognition of citizens' rights to voice and act on political opinions. The concept of bargain is a metaphor for sequences of political crises and reforms in which these rulers granted rights of participation, however limited, to all significant social classes and groups, while simultaneously extending the state's right and capacity to regulate, tax, and mobilize the human and material bases of state power.

The process of political democratization had its own logic and dynamic which, in most of Western Europe, eroded all but a few symbolic vestiges of traditional autocracy (see for example Bendix 1978). Nonetheless, pressures to extend democratization have always contended with the self-interested desire of rulers to preserve and enhance their autonomy from political constraints. The empires of Central and Eastern Europe—Germany, Russia, Austro-Hungary—implemented some of the trappings but not the substance of effective democratic participation in the late nineteenth and early twentieth centuries. And all of them collapsed under the combined pressure of unsuccessful war and internal dissension. The revolutionary Soviet state in Russia provided a new model of autocracy, one which combined democratic forms—a mass party and nominally representative institutions—with near-absolute state control of social, economic, and political life. In the middle run the new model has proven, in Europe and China, to be almost as resilient as the Western democratic forms, although less efficient for some social and economic purposes, and susceptible to collapse in the face of internal pressures for greater participation.

The third general process has been the "Westernization" of state structures elsewhere in the world. The European-derived models have been widely imitated, beginning with the establishment of derivative democracies in the newly independent states of nineteenth century Latin America and concluding with the Socialist autocracies of most of the post-revolutionary states of contemporary Afro-Asia.

In bold outline, then, the last two centuries of Western political development have been characterized by an enormous increase in the power of those states that have survived war and revolution. In the nineteenth century democratizing states were in the ascendent, and by 1918 the most successful of them had, in coalition, largely displaced and defeated the less adaptable imperial autocracies of Central and Eastern Europe. But a new, more effective and powerful form of autocracy emerged out of the Russian Revolution, one which has provided an attractive model for many other rulers, especially those of new African and Asian states, who want to build national power without sacrificing their autonomy to the demands of fractious citizens. The late twentieth century consequence of this process, which was far more complex than this brief sketch suggests, is the political domination of the northern part of the globe by the most powerful human agencies ever devised. The states typified by the regimes of the United States, France, the USSR and China command more resources, absolutely and in proportion to the resources of their societies, and have greater capacities to organize and deploy human and material resources in the service of state policies, that any historical political systems.

The successful political systems of the northern hemisphere have matured into two increasingly distinct and internally consistent types: coherent multiparty democracies and one-party autocracies. The political patterns of Latin America and the postcolonial Third and Fourth worlds are far more heterogeneous. Their histories of experimentation with democracy, autocracy, and mixed regimes are fraught with instability and few show evidence of sustained linear progression toward one or another of the increasingly pure types that prevail in the northern hemisphere.

Background to the Present Study

There is suggestive evidence for most of the assertions in the preceding paragraphs but few studies have used data to trace out the postulated sequences and relationships.[4] This foundational article describes the basic assumptions, procedures, and some initial results of a longitudinal study of the authority characteristics of all the world's larger countries from 1800, or independence, through 1986. Later papers will examine in more detail the sequences and dynamics of political change over this span.

The present study builds on the first author's earlier study of "Persistence and Change in Political Systems, 1800–1971," which used a more restricted dataset of the same kind to determine which authority traits characterized the more durable political systems, in different regions and in different historical periods (Gurr 1974). In the POLITY I study, the unit of analysis was the "polity" or political system, each of which was described in terms of six dimensions of authority patterns. When a polity was altered by an abrupt, major change in one or more of these authority characteristics, the change was treated as the termination of the old polity and the establishment of a new one. A total of 336 polities were identified in the 91 countries that were sovereign members of the international system before 1940.[5] The dependent variables in the analysis were the persistence and adaptability of each historical and contemporary polity. The measure of persistence was the number of years a polity endured without abrupt, major change; adaptability was the number of minor and gradual changes in a polity's authority traits during its lifespan.

The median lifespan of the 267 historical polities (those which ended before 1971) was 32 years; the mean age of the 67 continuing polities in 1971 was 42 years. Not surprisingly, the more persistent polities proved to have undergone a number of minor or gradual changes in authority characteristics: their persistence was inferred to be a consequence of their adaptability. A more significant finding was that polities which had internally consistent ("coherent") democratic or autocratic traits tended to be more durable than polities characterized by mixed (incoherent) or weakly institutionalized (anocratic) authority patterns. Overall, coherent polities had average lifespans of 56 years compared with 24 and 21 years for the other two groups. The coherent polities were more durable in every subset of polities: in historical as well as continuing polities; in Europe; and (by lesser margins) in Latin America and Afro-Asia.

The effects of democracy and autocracy on the lifespan of polities also were closely examined, but with less consistent results.[6] Only in Europe were democratic regimes significantly more durable than autocracies, 60 years on the average compared with 35 years. In the other three world regions the autocratic regimes were more durable. The evidence also showed that the connection between democracy and durability is specific to contemporary polities, not historical ones. Among the polities that ended before 1971, autocracies had lifespans three times longer than those of democracies. The processes responsible for the greater longevity of historical autocracies versus democracies include the demise of many long-lived Eurasian autocracies in the nineteenth and early twentieth centuries and a great many attempts to establish democratic polities in Europe and Latin America, most of which failed. The greater durability of contemporary democracies reflects the exceptional longevity of a handful of democratic experiments, mainly in the English-speaking societies and Scandinavia.

Some of these findings were confirmed, others qualified in subsequent reanalyses of the POLITY I data by Ward (1974), Harmel (1980), Lichbach (1984), and Thiessen and Bays (1986). Harmel employed more restrictive definitions of abrupt polity change which reduced the number of polities to 238/260 (in two different analyses) and replicated the comparisons. The relative longevity of democracies versus autocracies versus the incoherent and uninstitutionalized types of polities in Europe and among continuing polities was confirmed. But his results contradicted the first author's conclusion (Gurr 1974: 1499-1500) that there was a consistent connection between coherence and persistence. Rather, Harmel found that, outside Europe, the most persistent and adaptable polities tended to be the incoherent ones. Moreover, his analysis of the directions in which they changed showed that those which shifted toward democracy or anocracy were more persistent than those which remained unchanged or that shifted toward autocracy.

Whereas the reanalyses by Harmel, Ward (1974), and Thiessen and Bays (1986) were cross-sectional and cross-regional, Lichbach (1984) was concerned with sequences of political development in 49 historical and contemporary European states. He found no evidence that European states as a group followed similar patterns of change over time with respect to any one authority trait or with regard to summary indicators of democracy or autocracy. Consistent with Harmel's findings, though, Lichbach did find that "Incoherent polities tended, eventually, to become coherent. Coherent polities tended to remain that way. That is, incoherent polities were short-lived experiments while coherent polities were longer-lived systems" (Lichbach 1984: 137). In other words there was no common, unidirectional movement in European societies toward coherent democracies. Rather, there was a century-long process of political experimentation in which the surviving polities gradually bifurcated into two sharply distinct groups: coherent democracies and coherent autocracies. And Harmel's analysis suggests that the former have been more persistent than the latter.

It was difficult to use the original polity dataset for longitudinal analyses because of its structure: each polity's authority pattern was profiled only twice, once at its inception and once at its termination. Beginning in 1986, the authors of this article began work on a new dataset, POLITY II, in which the authority traits are coded annually.[7] This has required more thorough screening of historical sources to identify and code minor changes in authority traits. At the same time, the dataset has been updated to 1986, and a number of additional countries added. As presently constituted, the dataset encompasses 134 contemporary countries, including all whose population in the mid-1980s approached or exceeded one million. The long-established members of the international system are coded beginning in 1800. More recently established countries are coded from the year in which their first independent government was formed—usually the year of independence, sometimes a few years earlier or later. The polities of 21 historical countries also are included, that is, the polities of states like Bavaria and Latvia before their absorption by others, and the United Provinces of Central America and the Ottoman Empire, before their dissolution.

The POLITY II dataset also incorporates some conceptual changes. Nine authority traits, identified below, are coded for each polity in contrast with the six traits coded in POLITY I. And more precise operational guidelines have been devised for coding institutional developments during periods of transition from one authority pattern to another.

Authority Traits: Concepts and Indicators

The conceptual framework for the polity studies was derived from Harry Eckstein's analytic scheme for describing patterns of authority. The scheme was designed "to apply to authority patterns in any and all social units, regardless of variations . . . and regardless of whether the units exhibit great or little overall asymmetry between superordinates and subordinates," (Eckstein and Gurr 1975:41). It identifies six different clusters of dimensions on which authority patterns vary, including four dimensions of influence relations between superordinate and subordinate strata (Directiveness, Participation, Responsiveness, and Compliance); two dimensions of inequality between these strata (Distance and Deportment); three dimensions characterizing relations among superordinates (Conformation, Decision-Rules, and Decision-Behavior); the competitiveness of recruitment to superordinate positions; and the bases of legitimacy, whether personal, substantive, or procedural. A number of these dimensions consist of several subdimensions. The polarities of each dimension are identified, along with intervening categories on them.

This complex schema permits far more detailed analysis and more subtle distinctions among authority patterns than does a simple democratic-autocratic continuum. On the other hand, only some of its distinctions are relevant to our understanding of differences among political systems, and not all of these can be assessed operationally over the long historical run. Consequently the POLITY II project focuses on nine operational indicators of political authority patterns, with special attention to the influence dimensions, the recruitment of chief executives, and aspects of conformation, that is, governmental structure. We also give particular attention to the institutionalization of a polity's patterns of authority. The extent to which authority relations are codified and embodied in institutions that enable them to persist over time is, in our view, an essential element of their description.

The coding scheme is applied to national patterns and practices of authority relations, not to local ones. National patterns usually are replicated in local and regional governments, but there are some exceptions, for example, in Taiwan, where local government is more democratic than national government has been (Alex Inkeles, personal communication, 1988).

Influence Relations: The Regulation of Participation

The extent to which all members of a polity have regular means of expressing political preferences is a critical variable in Eckstein's scheme and in virtually all Western conceptions of democracy. We differentiate between two aspects of political participation, regulation and competitiveness.

Participation is regulated to the extent that there are binding rules on when, whether, and how political preferences are expressed. One-party states and Western democracies both regulate participation but they do so in different ways, the former by channeling participation through a single party structure, with sharp limits on diversity of opinion; the latter by allowing relatively stable and enduring groups to compete nonviolently for political influence. The polar opposite is unregulated participation, in which there are no enduring national political organizations and no effective regime controls on political activity. In such situations, political competition is fluid and usually characterized by recurring violent conflict among shifting coalitions of partisan groups. A five-category scale is used to code this dimension of participation:[8]

Regulation of Participation

Code	Label	Characterization
1	Unregulated	Political participation is fluid; there are no enduring national political organizations and no systematic regime controls on political activity
2	Factional/ transitional	Relatively stable and enduring political groups compete for political influence but competition among them is intense, hostile, and frequently violent. Also used to characterize transitions between Unregulated and Factional/Restricted.
3	Factional/ restricted	Polities which oscillate more or less regularly between intense factionalism and restriction: when one group secures power it restricts its opponents' political activities until it is displaced in turn.
4	Restricted	Some organized political participation is permitted without intense factionalism, but significant groups, issues, and/or types of conventional participation are regularly excluded from the political process.
5	Institution- alized	Relatively stable and enduring political groups regularly compete for political influence and position with little use of coercion. No significant groups, issues, or types of conventional political action are regularly excluded from political process.

Influence Relations: The Competitiveness of Participation

The competitiveness of participation refers to the extent to which alternative preferences for policy and leadership can be pursued in the political arena. Political competition implies a significant degree of civil interaction, so polities which are coded "unregulated" on the preceding variable are not coded for competitiveness. This dimension is coded on a five-category scale:

Competitiveness of Participation

Code	Label	Characterization
1	Suppressed	No significant oppositional activity is permitted outside the ranks of the regime and ruling party.
2	Restricted/ transitional	Some organized political competition occurs outside government, without serious factionalism, but significant groups or types of peaceful political competition are regularly excluded from the political process. Also used to characterize transitions between Factional and Suppressed.
3	Factional	Polities with factional or factional/restricted patterns of competition, as defined above under Regulation of Participation.
4	Transitional	Any transitional arrangements from Restricted, Factional, or Uninstitutionalized patterns to fully Competitive patterns. Transitions to Competitive are not complete until a national election is held on a fully competitive basis.

Competitiveness of Participation

5   Competitive   Relatively stable and enduring political groups regularly compete for political influence and position with little use of violence or disruption. No significant groups are regularly excluded.

Influence Relations: Constraints on the Executive

The fact of political participation per se does not assure that political leaders have any obligation to respond to expressions of political preference. This variable refers to the extent of institutionalized constraints on the decision-making powers of chief executives. Such constraints may derive from a legislature, a mass party—not all such parties are wholly under the control of the national leader—or some other accountability group, including the military. A seven-category scale is used:

Constraints on the Chief Executive

Code	Characterization
1	Unlimited authority: There are no regular limitations on executive authority (other than irregular limitations such as the threat or actuality of coups and assassinations).
2	(Intermediate category)
3	Slight to moderate limitations on executive authority
4	(Intermediate category)
5	Substantial limitations: The executive has more effective authority than any accountability group but is subject to substantial constraints by them.
6	(Intermediate category)
7	Executive parity or subordination: Accountability groups have effective authority equal to or greater than the chief executive in most areas of activity.

Influence Relations: Directiveness

This variable refers to the scope of the state's regulation and control of the social and economic activities of its citizens/subjects. It does not refer to regulation of political activity, which is reflected in the participation variables. Ideally, it would be desirable to code the extent of directiveness separately for various social and economic activities. Limited information and coding resources led us to devise a composite nine-category scale ranging from 1 for totalitarian authority structures, in which the state attempts to control all salient aspects of economic and social life, through 9 representing the minimal state. The scale is not designed to distinguish precisely between the two alternative (or complementary) means of directiveness, direct control versus regulation. The detailed coding guidelines specify that categories 1 and 2 are used for states that rely mainly on direct control. In the higher scale categories (3 through 9) the balance between control and regulation tends to follow political form, with autocracies relying more on the former and democracies on the latter.

For the nineteenth and early twentieth centuries virtually all states are coded 9, 8, or 7, reflecting the fact that, historically, the functions of the European states were limited largely to defense, the maintenance of public order, provision of justice, and some rudimentary responsibilities for economic infrastructure. Ethiopia and Pakistan in the 1950s are archetypical of countries whose states remained minimal in scope in the modern era. The Soviet Union after implementation of Stalin's economic policies and China during the Cultural Revolution define the totalitarian end of the continuum. Detailed guidelines have been used to identify thresholds among the intervening categories, taking into account information on social and economic policies, data on the proportion of school-age children in public schools, and data on central government spending as a proportion of Gross Domestic Product (Gurr, Jaggers and Moore 1989:21–26).

Recruitment of the Chief Executive

An essential part of the democratization process in Europe was the shift of executive authority from hereditary monarchs to chief ministers and presidents, individuals who at first were selected from within the political elite, later chosen in competitive elections. In contemporary autocracies some chief executives owe their position to forceful seizures of power; others are selected through a process of intra-elite bargaining. Three different dimensions of recruitment are used to represent some of the diversity of these practices. Specifically, we distinguish among the regulation, competitiveness, and openness of the processes by which chief executives are chosen.

Regulation refers to the extent to which a polity has institutionalized procedures for transferring executive power. Three categories are used:

Regulation of Recruitment

Code	Label	Characterization
1	Unregulated	Changes in chief executive occur through forceful seizures of power.
2	Designation/ transitional	Chief executives are chosen by designation within the political elite, without formal competition. Also coded for transitional arrangements intended to regularize future transitions after an initial seizure of power.
3	Regulated	Chief executives are determined by hereditary succession or in competitive elections.

Competitiveness refers to the selection of chief executives through popular elections matching two or more parties or candidates. If power transfers are coded unregulated, competitiveness is not coded. Three categories are used:

Competitiveness of Recruitment

Code	Label	Characterization
1	Selection	Chief executives are determined by hereditary succession, designation, or by a combination of both, as in monarchies whose chief minister is chosen by king or court.

Competitiveness of Recruitment

2	Dual/ transitional	Dual executives in which one is chosen by hereditary succession, the other competitive election. Also used for transitional arrangements between selection and competitive election.
3	Election	Chief executives are typically chosen in or through popular elections matching two or more major parties or candidates.

Recruitment of the chief executive is "open" to the extent that all the politically active population has an opportunity, in principle, to attain the position through a regularized process. If power transfers are coded unregulated, openness is not coded. Four categories are used.

Openness of Recruitment

Code	Label	Characterization
1	Closed	Chief executives are determined by hereditary succession
2	Dual/ designation	Hereditary succession plus selection (by the executive or court) of the chief minister
3	Dual/ election	Hereditary succession plus election of the chief minister.
4	Open	Chief executives are chosen by elite designation, competitive election, or transitional arrangements between designation and election.

Some examples may clarify. The Soviet Union's profile on these variables, since the accession of Khruschev, is Regulated/Selection/Open. Victorian Britain's profile was Regulated/Transitional/Dual:election, whereas contemporary Britain, along with other modern democracies, is coded Regulated/Election/Open. The polities of leaders who seize power by force are coded unregulated, but there is a recurring impulse among such leaders to regularize the process of succession, usually by relying on some form of selection. A less common variant, as in modern Iran and Nicaragua under the Somozas, is one in which a Caesaristic leader attempts to establish the principle of hereditary succession. We code all such attempts at regularizing succession as transitional (under regulation) until the first chief executive chosen under the new rules takes office.

The Complexity of Authority Structures

State structures are least complex in a unitary state with a single, all-powerful executive. The concentration of executive powers is coded under executive constraints. Two structural aspects of complexity also are coded: monocratism and centralization. The former refers to whether the effective chief executive is an individual or a collectivity (a cabinet, junta, politburo, or dual executive). The second refers to the familiar federal versus unitary state distinction. Neither of these dimensions is relevant to our composite indicators of democracy and autocracy. Their categories are listed here with a minimum of explanation.

Monocratism: Characteristics of the Chief Executive

Code   Category
1   Pure individual executive
2   (Intermediate category)
3   Qualified individual executive, "first among equals"
4   (Intermediate category)
5   Collective executive with full power sharing

Centralization of State Authority

Code   Category
1   Unitary state: regional units have little or no independent decision-making authority.
2   (Intermediate category)
3   Federal state: most/all regional units have substantial decision-making authority.

Indicators of Democracy, Autocracy, and State Power

The authority traits of the 155 contemporary and historical states coded in the POLITY II dataset can be analyzed in a variety of ways. Each of the dimensions of authority can be examined separately, a procedure Lichbach (1984) followed when using the POLITY I dataset to study historical sequences of political development in Europe. The scope of this initial analysis of POLITY II is limited to the countries (listed in appendix A) in which political development can be examined over the longer run: Europe (including the Anglo-American democracies and Israel), and Latin America. The patterns of institutional change are traced using two composite indicators of general properties of political systems: democracy and autocracy. These are then compared against indicators of three facets of state power: political coherence, directiveness, and military capacity. Although we do not formally propose or test hypotheses, the theoretical purpose of the exercise should be clear: we want to assess the plausibility of the historical arguments sketched at the beginning of the article.

The Indicator of Institutionalized Democracy

There are three essential, interdependent elements of democracy as it is conceived in the contemporary political culture of Western societies. One is the presence of institutions and procedures through which citizens can express effective preferences about alternative policies and leaders. Second is the existence of institutionalized constraints on the exercise of power by the executive. Third is the guarantee of civil liberties to all citizens in their daily lives and in acts of political participation. Other aspects of plural democracy, such as the rule of law, systems of checks and balances, freedom of the press, and so on are means to, or specific manifestations of, these general principles. We do not have coded data on civil liberties. Instead our operational indicator of democracy is derived from codings of the competitiveness of political participation, the openness of executive recruitment, and constraints on the chief excutive.

The democracy indicator is an additive ten-point scale, constructed, using these weights, for the traits that are conceptually associated with democracy.

Authority Coding	Scale Weight
Competitiveness of Political Participation:	
Competitive	+3
Transitional	+2
Factional	+1
Competitiveness of Executive Recruitment:	
Election	+2
Transitional	+1
Openness of Executive Recruitment:	
Dual: election	+1
Open	+1
Constraints on Chief Executive:	
Executive parity or subordination	+4
6 (Intermediate category)	+3
Substantial limitations	+2
5 (Intermediate category)	+1

This "institutionalized democracy" indicator follows a logic similar to that underlying the democracy scale used in the POLITY I studies. There is no "necessary condition" for characterizing a political system as democratic; rather democracy is treated as a variable. For example, the scale discriminates among Western parliamentary and presidential systems based on the extent of constraints on the chief executive. Charles de Gaulle as president of the French Fifth Republic operated within slight to moderate political limitations. Thus the early years of the Fifth Republic have lower democracy scores than the United States or the Federal Republic of Germany, where constraints on the executive approximate parity. Similarly, the onset of "cohabitation" in France during the second phase of the first Mitterand presidency is marked by a shift toward parity on the executive constraints scale and a concomitant increase in France's democracy score.

If the composite indicator of institutionalized democracy is inappropriate for some conceptual purposes, it can be easily redefined either by altering the constituent categories and weights, or by specifying some minimum preconditions. A mature and internally coherent democracy, for example, might be operationally defined as one in which (a) political participation is fully competitive, (b) executive recruitment is elective, and (c) constraints on the chief executive are substantial.

The Indicator of Institutionalized Autocracy

"Authoritarian regime" in Western political discourse is a pejorative term for some very diverse kinds of political systems whose common properties are a lack of regularized political competition and a lack of concern for political freedoms. We use the more neutral term autocracy and define it operationally in terms of the presence of a distinctive set of political characteristics. In mature form, autocracies sharply restrict or suppress competitive political participation. Their chief executives are chosen in a regularized process of selection within the political elite, and once in office they exercise power with few institutional constraints. Most modern autocracies also exercise a high degree of directiveness over social and economic activity, but we regard this as a function of political ideology and choice, not a defining property of autocracy. Social democracies also exercise relatively high degrees of directiveness. We prefer to leave open for empirical investigation the question of how autocracy, democracy, and directiveness have covaried over time.

The ten-point autocracy scale is constructed additively, like the democracy scale.

Authority Coding	Scale Weight
Competitiveness of Participation:	
Suppressed	+2
Restricted	+1
Regulation of Participation:	
Restricted	+2
Factional/restricted	+1
Competitiveness of Executive Recruitment:	
Selection	+2
Openness of Executive Recruitment (only if Competitiveness is coded Selection):	
Closed	+1
Dual: designation	+1
Constraints on Chief Executive:	
Unlimited authority	+3
2 (Intermediate category)	+2
Slight to moderate limitations	+1

The logic of this "institutionalized autocracy" scale is similar to that of the institutionalized democracy scale, and it is subject to the same kinds of operational redefinition to suit different theoretical purposes. Note that the two scales have no categories in common, which is consistent with conventional wisdom that (pure) democracy and autocracy are polar opposites. Nonetheless, many polities have mixed authority traits and thus can have middling scores on both the autocracy and democracy indicators. Note also that a polity's democracy score is not necessarily the inverse of its autocracy score because the coding categories of unregulated participation and unregulated executive recruitment do not enter the operational definitions of either democracy or autocracy. Polities with these authority traits were defined as "anocratic" in the POLITY I studies. Anocratic or uninstitutionalized polities are not separately analyzed in this study, but their prevalence, especially in Latin America, has implications for some of our results.

The autocracy and democracy scores for the European and Latin American countries are listed in Table 1 for 1878 and 1978. A number of pure democracies (score = 10) are listed whereas the only pure autocracy is Czarist Russia. Pure autocracy is qualified in contemporary Socialist countries (autocracy = 9, democracy = 1) by the relative "openness" of recruitment to the position of party first secretary, or its

TABLE 1
Autocracy and Democracy Scores for European and Latin American States, 1878 and 1978

Country	Autoc: 1878	Democ: 1878	Autoc: 1978	Democ: 1978
European				
Albania	—	—	9	1
Australia	—	—	0	10
Austria	5	1	0	10
Belgium	1	7	0	10
Bulgaria	—	—	7	1
Canada	3	7	0	10
Cyprus	—	—	0	10
Czechoslovakia	—	—	7	1
Denmark	4	1	0	10
Finland	—	—	0	10
France	0	7	1	6
Germany	5	1	—	—
German Dem. Rep.	—	—	9	1
German Fed. Rep.	—	—	0	10
Greece	0	9	0	8
Hungary	5	1	7	1
Ireland	—	—	0	10
Israel	—	—	0	10
Italy	5	1	0	10
Luxembourg	5	2	0	10
Netherlands	6	3	0	10
New Zealand	0	9	0	10
Norway	6	2	0	10
Poland	—	—	7	1
Portugal	7	0	0	9
Rumania	7	0	7	1
South Africa	4	3	3	7
Spain	5	5	0	9
Sweden	6	2	0	10
Switzerland	0	10	0	10
United Kingdom	3	6	0	10
U.S.A.	0	10	0	10
U.S.S.R.	10	0	7	1
Yugoslavia	—	—	7	1
Latin American				
Argentina	4	2	9	1
Bolivia	7	0	2	1
Brazil	7	1	3	4
Chile	1	4	7	0
Colombia	0	8	0	10
Costa Rica	0	6	0	10
Cuba	—	—	7	0
Dominican Republic	4	2	0	5

TABLE 1 (continued)
Autocracy and Democracy Scores for European and Latin American States, 1878 and 1978

Country	Autoc: 1878	Democ: 1878	Autoc: 1978	Democ: 1978
Ecuador	2	1	4	1
El Salvador	2	1	3	4
Guatemala	6	2	3	4
Haiti	3	0	8	1
Honduras	4	2	2	1
Jamaica	—	—	0	10
Mexico	*	*	6	1
Nicaragua	6	2	8	1
Panama	—	—	6	0
Paraguay	5	2	7	1
Peru	2	1	*	*
Uruguay	4	1	8	1
Venezuela	6	2	0	8

[—] = country not in existence for these years.

[*] = country experiencing a rapid transition from one polity to another; no autocracy or democracy scores recorded.

NOTE: The following countries were included in the analyses (see Appendix 1) but are not included in this table because (1) they were no longer independent nation-states by 1878; or (2) they were short-lived polities which fell between the two time periods under observation: Baden, Bavaria, Hanover, Saxony, Wurttemburg, Modena, Papal States, Parma, Tuscany, Two Sicilies, Estonia, Latvia, and Lithuania.

equivalent. In historical autocracies, typified by nineteenth century Russia, monarchical succession was determined by ascription; in contemporary autocracies the pool of eligible members of the political elite is quite wide.

A comparison of the coding for two contemporary polities, India and China, is provided in Table 2. The authority dimensions are shown on the left, the codings for each are given verbally, and the contribution of each of the codings to the summary democracy and autocracy scores are shown in parentheses. As explained earlier, not all the authority dimensions are relevant to these summary indicators.

TABLE 2
Polity Traits of India and China 1978 Compared

Authority Dimension	India		Peoples Republic of China	
Participation				
Regulation	Institutionalized		Restricted	(A + 2)
Competitiveness	Transitional from		Suppressed	(A + 2)
	factional	(D + 2)		
Constraints on Chief Executive				
	Parity	(D + 4)	Slight to moderate	(A + 1)
Recruitment of Chief Executive				
Regulation	Regulated		Designation	
Competitiveness	Election	(D + 2)	Selection	(A + 2)
Recruitment	Open	(D + 1)	Open	(D + 1)
Complexity of Authority Structures				
Monocratism	Qualified individual		Qualified individual	
Centralization	Federal state		Unitary state	
Democracy score	9		1	
Autocracy score	0		7	

Indicators of State Power

As suggested above in several contexts, we regard the concentration of power in the hands of state authorities to be analytically and functionally distinct from democracy and autocracy. The typical nineteenth century autocracy exercised much less effective control over its subjects than the typical activist welfare democracy of the late twentieth century. "Power" has many facets, three of which are examined in this initial study.

Coherence refers to the internal consistency of authority patterns, specifically to whether they are consistently democratic or autocratic. The POLITY I studies cited above suggest that, as a group, the "incoherent" polities—those with a mixture of democratic and autocratic traits—were somewhat less durable, and more subject to internal political change, than coherent democracies and autocracies. The reasons follow from Eckstein's congruence theory of political performance (1969), in which he contends that mixed authority traits cause dissonance in citizens' perceptions of a regime and its actions, which undermines its legitimacy in their eyes; such traits, according to this theory, also increase conflict among decision-makers about the "rules of the game," which undercuts their ability to respond efficiently to crises. Coherence therefore is an aspect of power: consistently democratic or autocratic states should be able to pursue their leaders' objectives more efficiently and with less popular resistance than incoherent or anocratic states. "Coherent" polities are operationally defined in the POLITY II study as those which score 7 or more (of a maximum of 10) on either democracy or autocracy.

Directiveness, as coded, is a measure of the extent to which a state uses its powers of regulation and command to organize and direct the social and economic activities within its own borders. Coherence is an aspect of the institutionalized potential for state power; Directiveness is a general indicator of its realization at any given time.

Military capacity is a specific dimension of state power that has both domestic and international consequences. The ability of a state to pursue its interests internationally depends in part on the size (and technology) of its armed forces. In the Third World especially, coercion is often used to implement or back up domestic policy decisions as well as to suppress violent resistance to the state's claim to authority. We index coercive capacity using an updated version of J. David Singer's "Capabilities" data on military manpower, weighted by total population.[9]

Patterns of Political Change in Europe and Latin America Since 1800

In this initial analysis we use the POLITY II dataset to trace the aggregate patterns of political change in Europe and Latin America since the beginning of the nineteenth century. Specifically, the data help give substance to the generalizations offered at the outset of this article.

The Growth of Democracy and the Decline of Autocracy. The transformation in the structures of political participation and legitimation toward democracy since the mid-nineteenth century has been particularly pronounced in Europe, as is evident from Figure 1. To construct this and subsequent figures, we calculated the average

FIGURE 1.
Trends in Autocracy and Democracy in Europe, 1800–1984.

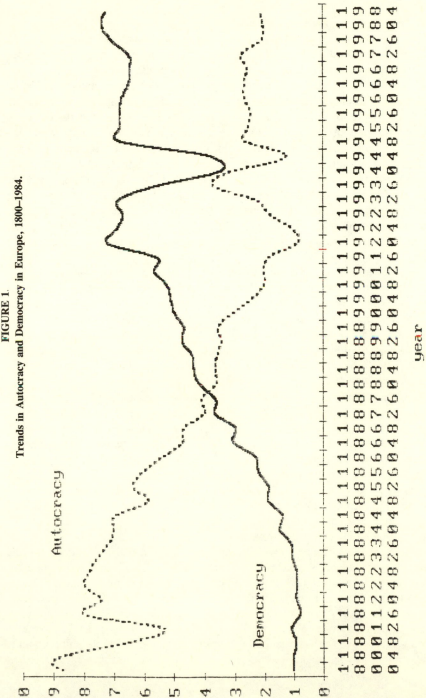

scores for democracy and autocracy for the countries in each region, then plotted the averages for every fourth year. The procedure provides a portrait of the broad trends and major fluctuations around them.

The general pattern is one of an accelerating increase in the prevalence of democracy from the 1840s to the early 1920s. In the immediate aftermath of World War I, when democratic structures were introduced among the peoples of the defeated European autocracies, democracy reached its zenith. The resurgence of autocracy in the late 1920s came about as many of the weak "new democracies" gave way to military dictatorships, Fascism, or Nazi rule, shifts precipitated in a number of countries by the impact of the global depression. In the late 1940s democracies were reestablished in Western Europe while Soviet-style autocracies were entrenched in Eastern Europe. During the cold war democratic and autocratic patterns were frozen. The indicators are sensitive to short-term changes such as the brief decline in autocracy in those parts of Europe conquered by Napoleon's armies after 1804; a lesser decline after the 1848 wave of revolutions swept continental Europe (more noticeable in the annual data than in the quadrennial data used in Figure 1); and to the political democratization in Spain and Portugal in the 1970s (which underlies the parallel shifts of increased democracy and decreased autocracy for the last three time points).

By 1984 the mean level of democratization in the European region had reached its highest point since democracy's heyday in the early 1920s, and events in Eastern Europe since then suggest that the tide continues to rise. On the other hand a major implication of the long-run pattern is that the "developmentalist" notion of a unilinear trend toward domocratization is empirically unfounded precisely in the continent that suggested the generalization in the first place. In particular, international forces, in the form of war, depression, and alliance structures, have repeatedly influenced the shape and direction of political change in Europe.

Distinctive patterns in Latin American political change are much harder to discern. As shown in Figure 2, there were slight downward trends in autocracy and a parallel increase in democracy from the 1840s to c. 1920, but the economic crisis of the 1930s and the militant anticommunism of the 1960s and early 1970s pushed a number of democratic regimes into the hands of autocratic *juntas*. The beginning of the much celebrated contemporary trend toward democratization in Latin America since the mid-1970s is evident, but in view of the historical pattern of political swings back toward autocracy, impelled as much by international as domestic factors, the "trend" should be regarded as a fragile one.

Figures 3 and 4 contrast the European and Latin trends in democracy and autocracy. It is clear from Figure 3 that, except for the first decades of independence, democratic authority traits have been less common in Latin America. Similarly, Figure 4 shows that autocratic traits have been consistently more prevalent in Latin America than in Europe throughout the twentieth century. Note that the mean level of autocracy in Latin America has varied relatively little over time by comparison with the downward trend in Europe. On the other hand, the mean level of Latin autocracy has always been substantially lower (by two to three scale points) than it was during the early nineteenth-century ascendency of European autocracy. There is

FIGURE 2

Trends in Autocracy and Democracy in Latin America, 1828–1984

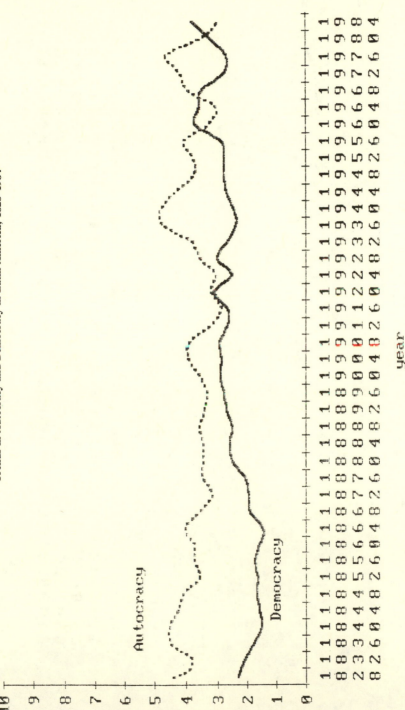

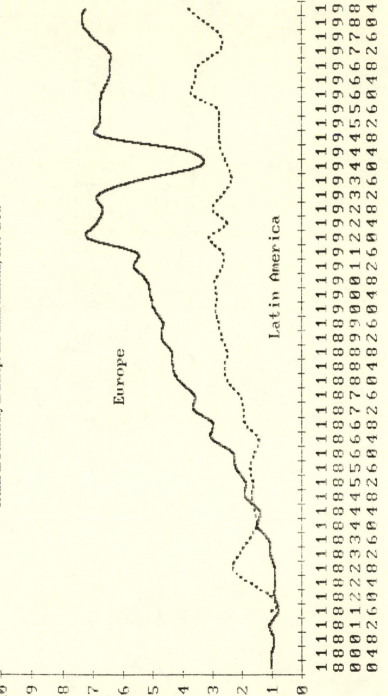

FIGURE 3

Trends in Democracy in Europe and Latin America, 1800–1984.

FIGURE 4

Trends in Autocracy in Europe and Latin America, 1800–1984.

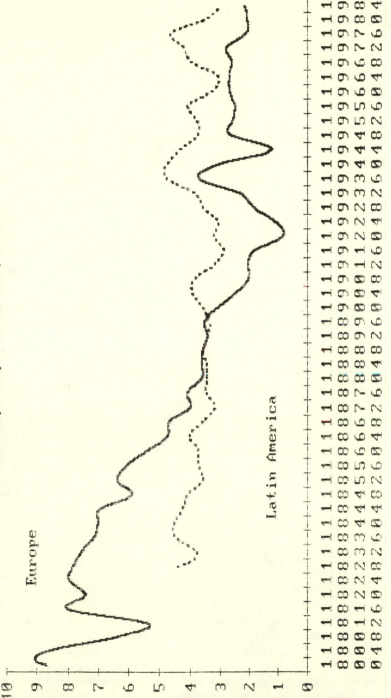

TABLE 3
Coherent Polities in Latin America and Europe, 1830–1986

	Latin America				Europe	
		No. with Coherent Polities:				No. with Coherent Polities:
Year	Number of Countries	Autoc	Democ	Number of Countries	Autoc	Democ
1830	13	2	0	25	18	1
1850	18	2	0	26	14	2
1870	18	2	1	29	8	7
1890	18	1	1	25	2	11
1910	20	2	1	25	2	12
1930	20	2	1	34	6	21
1950	20	3	1	33	11	22
1970	21	7	5	34	12	21
1986	21	2	7	34	8	24

Note: Number of countries refers to the number of independent countries in each region coded for the year shown in the POLITY II dataset.

Coherent polities are those with scores of 7 to 9 on the scales of Autocracy and Democracy defined in the text.

little support here for theories extracted from the "European experience" that states should move through "common pathways" of political development. The POLITY II patterns suggest that the transferability of the European experience to Latin America is empirically unfounded (see Tilly 1975).

Underlying the trends we have observed is the pervasive failure of most Latin American societies to establish coherent, institutionalized political systems of either democratic or autocratic type. The typical Latin polity has had "mixed" authority traits: Caesaristic transfers of power, factional-restricted participation, and executive constraints that fall between the "substantial/parity" limits characteristic of European democracies and the "slight to none" limits characteristic of European autocracies. When coherent autocracies have been established in Latin America their institutions usually were too weak to outlast the founding elite. A summary comparison of the numbers of coherent democracies and autocracies in each region is provided in Table 3. In the century that ended in 1930 there were never more than three coherent polities in all of Central and South America. In Europe, by comparison, half or more of the polities were coherent throughout the century, despite the sharp shift from autocracy to democracy. Since 1950, all but one or two of the thirty-three/thirty-four European countries have been governed by either coherent democracies or coherent autocracies. In Latin America, by contrast, about half of post-1950 polities have been and remain incoherent. And among the coherent ones autocracy was in the ascendent in the 1970s, democracy in the 1980s. This suggests that coherence is not associated with longevity, not among Latin American polities. This parallels the evidence of the POLITY I studies that coherence markedly enhanced the persistence of European polities (on the average, coherent polities outlived incoherent ones by sixty-five to nineteen years) but had no significant effect on the persistence of Latin polities (twenty-five years for the handful of coherent polities v. twenty-three years for incoherent ones).[10]

It may be objected that there remains a Eurocentric bias in our interpretation of these results. Latin political cultures are arguably different from those of Continental Europe and may be more supportive of, for example quasidemocracy on the Mexican model than either of the "pure" European types. Moreover Latin America's enduring political and economic dependency on Europe and North America have at times sharply constrained the political options of its leaders. From a more radical viewpoint it may be questioned whether "political stability" has the virtues attributed to it by social scientists working in the (bourgeois) Anglo-American tradition. Our results nonetheless reflect a core of incontestable facts: (1) For more than 150 years Latin American leaders have experimented with, and continue to experiment with, diverse variations on European models for autocratic and democratic rule. (2) Relatively few of their political systems have closely followed the blueprints of the most durable European polities. (3) The blueprints chosen haven't made any difference for durability anyway, because, coherent or not, Latin polities tend to be relatively short-lived by comparison with their European counterparts. One of a number of unanswered questions that can be explored using the POLITY II dataset is whether there are one or several distinctive Latin authority patterns—qualified democracies or qualified autocracies—that have been more persistent and adaptable than others. Another is whether the above three generalizations are equally applicable to all eras in the political history of independent Latin America. An alternative, suggested by some of the post-1945 data, is that the dynamics of Latin American political change are shifting toward those of the European democracies. There are compelling historical reasons for thinking that the outcomes of any such shift will be conditioned by what happens with regard to international debt and policies of economic development and social justice.

The Growth of State Power. Three indicators of state power have been discussed, one of which is coherence. In Europe the evidence is that coherently democratic and autocratic polities have greater capacity for managing and, hence, surviving crises and lesser challenges. Coherent polities in Latin America have been too rare to support a similar generalization. Coherence has been relatively high among European countries for the last two centuries, as is evident from Table 3. During the fifty years before World War I, slightly more than half the European countries had internally consistent authority patterns, almost all of them democratic. The interwar years saw a substantial increase in the number of coherent regimes of both types, trends that continued after World War II.

We have no direct evidence that links coherence to state power other than the coherence-longevity connection that suggested it in the first place. There is strongly suggestive evidence, though, in the impact of the two world wars on the authority patterns of the principal belligerents. Three of the four victorious allies in World War I had coherent democracies that survived the war: Britain, France, and the United States. The exception was the Italian regime, an autocratic monarchy grafted to a weak parliament, where postwar stresses led to Mussolini's seizure of power in 1922 and the establishment of a coherent autocracy. The war so devastated Imperial Russia that it precipitated revolution, a separate peace, and the founding of the new Communist autocracy. On the other side, the members of the Triple Entente—

Imperial Germany, Austro-Hungary, and the Ottoman Empire—all had polities that by our criteria featured an incoherent mix of autocratic and democratic patterns. Under external pressure, all underwent postwar changes of polity; in Germany and Austro-Hungary to democracies (the Weimar Republic falls one point short of "coherent democracy" on our indicator); in Turkey to coherent autocracy (after 1923).

In World War II the coherent democracies again were on the winning side, along with the Soviet Union (a coherent autocracy) and Nationalist China (a mixed regime). The losing Axis powers were coherent autocracies but lost nonetheless: their all-out mobilization could not overcome the military superiority of their combined opponents. Defeat meant polity change imposed by the occupying powers, leading to the establishment of three coherent democracies and one autocracy (in East Germany). In China the only incoherent regime among the combatants was overthrown in 1949 by the Communists.

In summary, the outcomes of the two wars enhanced the appeal of the winners' political systems and precipitated polity changes toward coherence in the countries that suffered most. First, in World War I the coherent democracies proved more effective than Imperial Russia or the incoherent polities—with the exception of Germany—in mobilizing resources and support for the war effort. Second, defeat in war discredited the German and Austro-Hungarian attempts to modernize traditional autocracies by grafting on weak parliaments. The postwar search for more effective and legitimate rule led to polity changes toward greater coherence, following the models of the winning democracies. Third, the inability of the Russian and Italian regimes to deal with wartime and postwar stress set the stage for revolutionary changes that culminated in the establishment of coherent autocracies. Nationalist China followed the same course after World War II. Fourth, World War II discredited one kind of totalitarian model—the militaristic imperialism of the Axis powers—and reinforced the prestige of Soviet-model autocracy. Finally, the second time around, the erstwhile Allies used their power to impose, not merely encourage, their political models on defeated peoples.

We have more discriminating indices of the other two dimensions of state power: directiveness and military capacity. The first is an annually-coded index of the extent to which the state used its powers to regulate or control social and economic activity. Increased directiveness implies, among other things, the growth of a large and technically proficient bureaucracy and expansion of the state's capacity to raise the taxes to finance it. The second is an index of military manpower proportional to population. High military capabilities also depend on state capacities to raise and manage resources and men. Sustaining them over a long period requires a public that is supportive, or at least acquiesent. The European and Latin American trends in these power indicators are compared in Figures 5 and 6. The figures are constructed in the same way as the Democracy and Autocracy indicators in Figures 1 to 4: they represent the mean values of each indicator, across all countries in each region, plotted for every fourth year.

The directiveness indicator for Europe (Figure 5) shows a steady increase in state intervention in society and economy during the last 180 years. The mean directiveness score from 1800 to 1836 was "1", in a period where the scope of government

FIGURE 5

Trends in State Power in Europe and Latin America: Directiveness, 1800–1984.

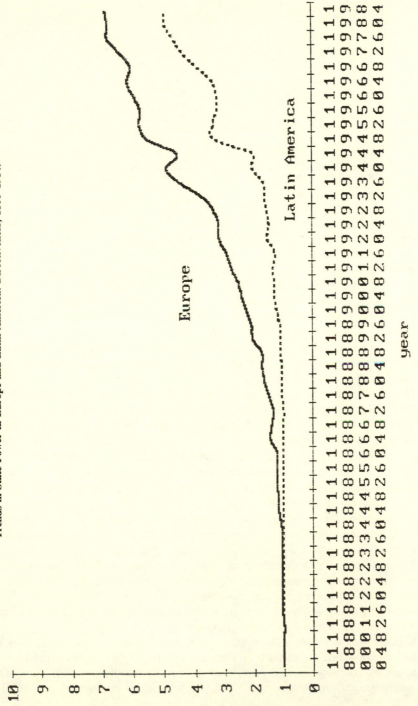

TABLE 4
The Impact of War and Depression on Indicators of State Power in Europe

	Mean Directiveness	Percent Change	Percentage of Coherent Polities(a)
1910	2.64		56%
1920	3.13	19%	72%
1927	3.16	1%	71%
1938	4.47	42%	85%
1950	5.73	28%	100%
1960	5.91	3%	97%
1970	6.18	5%	97%

a. Proportion of all countries in the region with coherent democracies or autocracies. See Table 3.

was restricted almost entirely to the provision of justice, maintaining armies and navies, and ensuring domestic order. Thereafter directiveness increased to an average of 3 at the outset of World War I. The growth of state subsidy for and intervention in the economy during these eighty years derived from the prevailing belief among European elites that a strong and expanding private economy was necessary to provide the resource base for national power. National governments also assumed new responsibilities for education and the beginnings of regulatory and welfare systems, partly to meet entrepreneurs' needs for healthy and better trained workers in livable urban environments, partly to satisfy demands from a growing industrial labor force for some minimum protection against exploitation, disability, and penurious old age.

The largest and most rapid increases in directiveness, however, occurred during and after the two world wars. The mean scores for directiveness in successive decades and the rate of decennial change are shown in Table 4, along with the percentages of countries with coherent polities. The sharp increases in directiveness during 1910–20, 1927–39, and 1939–50 are the aggregate of a variety of war- and crisis-fueled expansions of state power. A number of empirical studies have shown that involvement in global wars causes abrupt upward shifts in state resource mobilization and expenditures (see Rasler and Thompson 1985 a, b, and sources cited there). Moreover, the coherent autocracies established in Europe after the two wars were all far more directive than the regimes they replaced. In the Depression years virtually all the European and Anglo democracies expanded the scope of government action in response to socioeconomic crises. The increases in coherence closely parallel increases in directiveness, which is consistent with our theoretical assumption that coherence is a significant dimension of state power. The coherent democracies and autocracies were the ones most able to increase directiveness in response to the stresses of war and the Great Depression.

In Latin America, where most states have had fewer resources to dispose of, Figure 5 shows that the increase in directiveness has lagged well behind Europe. Whereas the first significant expansion of state activity in Europe took place in the second half of the nineteenth century, in Latin America it occurred in the 1940s. The

Depression had devastating economic effects in much of Latin America and brought about a pronounced shift toward autocracy, depicted in Figure 4, but did not stimulate a similar expansion of the state's socioeconomic role: even if Keynesian doctrine had taken root in Latin America (it had not), Latin elites lacked the will, coherent political institutions, or resources to follow the European example by expanding substantially the scope of state action. Mean directiveness in Latin America increased very little during the Depression, from a mean of 1.55 in 1927 to 1.65 a decade later.

The sharp increase of directiveness in Latin America in the 1940s (1.65 in 1937, 3.33 in 1949) reflects policies of state-sponsored development (e.g., in Argentina) and the rapid expansion of social infrastructure and welfare services, inspired in some countries by European examples and funded in part by high wartime export earnings. By the 1950s, however, conservative resistance to the "liberal" policies of economic interventionism and social welfare set in, leading to the reversal in a number of countries of the policies of the previous decade. The next upsurge in state activism, which began in the mid-1960s, included state-led economic expansion in some countries and efforts, encouraged by the U.S. government, to deal with the poverty that was widely regarded as a breeding ground for Marxist revolution. Popular demands that the state take a greater economic and social role, analogous to European practice, no doubt motivated some of the increase in state responsibilities. But most of the growth during this period can be attributed to the consolidation of the bureaucratic-authoritarian state, in response to the concerns of conservative elites. A leveling off of directiveness is evident in the 1980s, due to oil crisis, debt crisis, and some emulation of the Reagan administration's policies of privatization.

The third dimension of state power, military manpower, was originally incorporated in this analysis because of the "ratchet effect" argument that wars lead to enduring increases in military power. Once military effort has been geared up to wartime levels, a "ratchet" of bureaucratic and political-economic pressure supposedly keeps it from dropping back down to the prewar level. This phenomenon can be observed in the United States following all its major wars in the last ninety years except for Vietnam (see Russett 1970). The mean levels of manpower per 10,000 population, shown in Figure 6, provide no direct support for the argument. The peaks in European militarization are, of course, associated with major conflicts: the Crimean War (1853–56) followed by the American Civil War; World Wars I and II; and the cold war. But there is no discernible long-term trend. In the century from the end of the Napoleonic Wars to 1914, the mean manpower ratio hovered around eighty, and, in the aftermath of the "war to end all wars," fell below sixty. The post–1945 force ratios were higher, near or above one-hundred until the mid-1970s, than before either of the two world wars, but this can be more directly explained by strategic competition between NATO and Warsaw Pact powers than by a universal rachet effect.

In Latin America, the data on military personnel before the 1850s are too sparse and unreliable to support any firm inferences about common trends. Inspection of country data does suggest, though, that civil wars repeatedly spurred short-term growth in armies throughout the nineteenth century. In the late 1860s, the graph

FIGURE 6

Trends in State Power in Europe and Latin America: Military Manpower per 10,000 Population, 1816–1980.

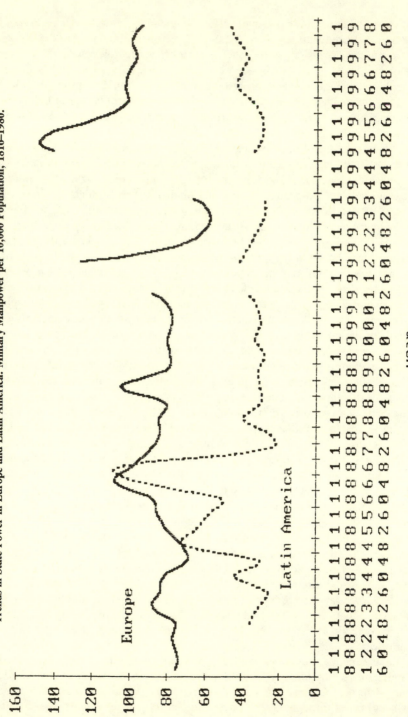

registers the most devastating war in Latin American history, in which the combined armies of Brazil, Argentina, and Uruguay virtually annihilated the Paraguayans: less than a fifth of the defeated country's male population survived the war. Also evident is the temporary militarization that accompanied the 1879–84 war of the Pacific which Chile won at the expense of Bolivia and Peru. What is not evident is any general or sustained impact of these wars on militarization in Latin America. Military force levels in Latin America during the last century have held relatively steady at one third to one half the mean European level. The one period of sustained increase began in the 1950s and continued into the 1980s. Inspection of country time-series shows that the trend has been most pronounced in military-dominated regimes.

These highly aggregated results do not necessarily invalidate all versions of the "ratchet effect" theory. The fact that European military manpower has, on average, far exceeded that of Latin America is in fact consistent with the argument. The proportional difference is not necessarily a reflection of disparities in resources. Eastern European autocracies have maintained far larger armies with less resources than those of the developed Latin American countries. The European state system is more militarized as a consequence of centuries of recurring wars and preparations by bitter rivals for future wars. International conflict within Latin America has been infrequent and has left few enduring hostilities comparable to the intensity of those between Russia and Germany or, historically, between Germany and its Western rivals. In both regions we would expect military expansion to be greatest in countries most frequently and successfully involved in wars. This suggests a different research strategy, one that examines statistically the impact of war and its outcomes on military manpower in individual countries.

One other research question is also suggested by these results: whether revolution, civil war, and military coups may have results analogous to war's ratchet effect on military manpower. Some but not all the extensive research on the effects of military coups on public policy and expenditures supports such a conclusion (see for example Zimmermann 1983). One of the authors has argued that there is a general tendency for the victors in revolution and civil war to favor coercive responses to internal and external challenges, and to maintain large military and security forces for that purpose (Gurr 1988b). This is, in turn, one aspect of the largest question raised, but not answered, by this initial study: What general conditions underlie the long-run increase in the power of modern states? In the conclusion that follows, we sketch some research strategies for dealing with this and related issues using the POLITY II dataset.

Conclusion: Issues and Strategies for Further Research

The results of this initial study suggest a number of fruitful avenues for empirical research on state growth using the POLITY II dataset. Some of the most intriguing ideas concern the complex connections among war and crisis, state power, economic performance, and the directionality of political change. Tilly has summarized one strand of research on historical Europe in the aphorism that "War made the state, and the state made war" (1975:42). Theories of the impact of class conflict, economic crisis, and revolution on the development of Western and Third-world states have been articulated by Moore (1966), Eisenstadt (1978), and Skocpol (1979) among others. The POLITY studies suggest some different perspectives on these questions, and employ a more comprehensive dataset for examining them than has been hitherto available. Work in progress makes use of the 1815–1980 "Capabilities" dataset developed by Singer and colleagues plus time-series data we have developed on central government revenues, expenditures, and national productivity.

Impact of War on State Power. Preliminary analyses of our data on fifteen states' involvement in thirteen different wars show that several dimensions of war have had significant effects on state power. Long wars generally stimulate sustained increases in productivity in the states involved. Moreover, the more prolonged the war, the greater the increases in central government revenues, total expenditures, and military expenditures. States that win wars experience more pronounced increases in the same variables. There also is a general tendency, not limited to participants in the two world wars, toward greater political coherence within the winning states (Jaggers 1989). It may be that the persisting differential we have observed between Europe and Latin America on indicators of state power and coherence is a byproduct of the absence of serious interstate warfare in Latin America during the last century. More detailed, time-series analysis of particular European countries is needed to ascertain the extent to which the power-enhancing effects of war are cumulative over time, and whether they are reversed when several successful wars are followed by one or more losses.

Revolution and State Power. There is evidence from case studies of revolutionary outcomes by Skocpol (1979) and Trimberger (1978) that internal conflicts also bring about significant changes in state power. Revolutionary regimes typically are coherent autocracies with greater directiveness, higher revenues, and larger armies than the regimes that they replaced. The POLITY II data can readily be used to test whether similar consequences follow from civil and revolutionary wars won by incumbents, and from coups: and whether the consequences have varied across regions, or between the nineteenth and twentieth centuries.

Economic Crisis and Polity Change. Similar questions are raised by economic crisis, in particular by the POLITY II evidence about the differential impact of the Depression of the 1930s on political change in Europe and Latin America. Economic crisis pushed a number of democratic and mixed regimes in both regions toward autocracy. In Europe, but not in Latin America, the crisis also led to increases in the scope of state power among regimes of both types. The general pattern is one in which coherent democracies with ample resources were strengthened through their response to economic crisis, while a number of other regimes—including weak democracies like Weimar Germany—were toppled and replaced by autocracies. The relative effectiveness of the new and more established autocracies in dealing with economic crisis remains to be assessed. These effects of the Great Depression and other historical economic crises on political stability and state power can be systematically analyzed with the POLITY II data.

Polity Characteristics and International Conflict. The connections between traits of regimes and international conflict have been studied by a number of scholars, including an analysis by Maoz using the POLITY I dataset. One issue is whether revolutionary states are more likely to be involved in war than states whose political development has been evolutionary. In a study of all the POLITY I states from 1816 to 1976, Maoz (1989) finds that states which experienced abrupt (revolutionary) polity changes were much more often involved than evolutionary states in international conflict during the following twenty years. A parallel study asks whether democracies or autocracies, as defined in the POLITY studies, are more likely than others to be involved in international conflict. The general answer, for the same 160-year timespan, is negative, but analysis of dyadic conflict linkages shows that democracies and autocracies have been substantially less likely to fight among themselves, and more likely to fight their opposites—at all levels of dispute (Maoz and Abdolali 1989). The POLITY II data can be used to replicate and extend these studies.

Economic Performance and Transitions toward Democracy. The POLITY II studies have implications for the experiments in participatory democracy now underway in some Eastern European and Third World countries. During the last generation the state Socialist model of autocracy has been discredited, to a degree, because most state-directed economies have performed far worse than the regulated market economies of the industrial democracies. The supposition is that the introduction of democratic institutions in Socialist and other autocracies will help unleash the genie of economic growth. This argument posits the same correlation but reverses the directionality of Lipset's classic thesis (1959) that material prosperity provides a strongly disposing precondition for political democracy. No one has yet demonstrated on a larger scale, globally or historically, whether the economies of democracies have consistently outperformed the economies of mixed or autocratic states. We suggest two less optimistic hypotheses: (1) that incoherent polities have weaker economic performance than either coherent democracies or autocracies; and (2) that chronic political instability over issues of participation (as in contemporary Poland) exacerbates economic problems.

The POLITY II dataset, which includes economic performance data for most countries for much of the twentieth century, provides means for testing these and some related speculations. It also should be used to determine whether, and under what circumstances, transitions toward either democracy or autocracy enhance economic performance in the longer run. We suspect that the several versions of the democracy/prosperity thesis will prove to be valid only in regions and countries with certain kinds of resource and cultural endowments. It also will be necessary to factor in the effects of international conflict and constraints. Our own findings (here and in Jaggers 1989) suggest that there are positive reciprocal relations between economic growth and successful war, and, more tentatively, negative reciprocal relations between international dependency and political stability.

The POLITY II dataset has wide but not unlimited applicability to the study of state power and the development of democracy and autocracy. It covers a far longer timespan than any other dataset except that developed by Banks (1971). Since it employs a general analytic scheme to code a wide range of authority it can be used, as demonstrated in this article, to index autocracy, democracy, state power, and some of their components.

Two potential liabilities of the POLITY II dataset are counterparts of its strengths.[11] It registers traits of institutions and power relations that are salient and discernible over the long historical run. It is not designed to register more detailed aspects of democracy, such as regimes' performance with respect to human rights or civil liberties, or to provide detailed information on patterns of state regulation and control. This suggests making time-series comparisons of POLITY II authority codings with more fine-grained measures of regime characteristics and policies developed by other scholars.[12] Second, the use of an analytic scheme with variables such as directiveness and executive constraints to characterize authority traits in general may be distracting or irrelevant for research that centers on concrete manifestations of democracy such as the extent and structure of interparty competition, the precise allocation of powers between chief executives and parliaments, press freedom, and so on. The merits of the two approaches depend on the questions asked. The POLITY II dataset is suitable for answering a wide range of macropolitical questions: there are others to which it is not well suited. Thus we conclude with a more-than-token acknowledgement of the need for pluralism in the empirical analysis of the many facets of political democracy and its competitors.

Appendix 1

Countries Utilized in the Analysis by Region

Europe and the Anglo Democracies	Latin America and the Caribbean
United Kingdom	Cuba
Ireland	Haiti
Netherlands	Dominican Republic
Belgium	Mexico
Luxembourg	Guatemala
France	Honduras
Switzerland	El Salvador
Spain	Nicaragua
Portugal	Costa Rica
Baden	Panama
Bavaria	Colombia
Hanover	Venezuela
Saxony	Ecuador
Wurttemburg	Peru
Prussia/Germany	Brazil
West Germany	Bolivia

Europe and the Anglo Democracies

East Germany
Poland
Austria
Hungary
Czechoslovakia
Modena
Papal States
Parma
Tuscany
Two Sicilies
Italy
Albania
Yugoslavia
Greece
Cyprus
Bulgaria
Rumania
Russia/USSR
Estonia
Latvia
Lithuania
Finland
Sweden
Norway
Denmark
United States
Canada
Australia
New Zealand
Israel
South Africa

Latin America and the Caribbean

Paraguay
Chile
Argentina
Uruguay
Jamaica

Appendix 2
Reliability of the Authority Codings

The reliability of the indicators developed here depends on the accuracy and consistency of the coding of the constituent authority variables. The POLITY I data were collected by a single coder, Erika B. K. Gurr, who worked with increasingly-refined versions of category definitions and coding guidelines. On three occasions all information gathered to date was reviewed and recoded by the coder, in consultation with the first author, to ensure its consistency with revised guidelines. Multiple historical sources were used for each country, along with reference to a variety of standard sources. The first step was to identify historical and social science works for each country, then to compile from them a basic political chronology. Periods of substantial political change were identified in this process and then examined in detail to determine whether events met the specified criteria for changes in and of polities. The same sources provided information for the coding of authority characteristics.

The POLITY I codebook, dataset, and narrative summaries of the political chronologies for each polity, with source lists, were deposited with and subsequently distributed by the Inter-University Consortium for Political and Social Research (Gurr and Associates, 1978). The reliability of authority codings have been taken as given by most of the investigators who have used them in secondary analyses. The principle exception is Mark Irving Lichbach (1984), who detected some ambiguities about the timing of minor changes in authority traits when he attempted to convert the European codings to time-series form. He resolved them by further reading in historical sources. The construction of POLITY II was begun by Lichbach, who converted the remaining POLITY I codings to annual data, and completed by Keith Jaggers, who recoded and extended the dataset using a wide variety of historical and contemporary source materials. The first author reviewed much of the coding, with special attention to questions of consistency, and (re)coded Directiveness for all polities. The POLITY II coding guidelines were amplified and refined in the process.

No intercoder reliability tests have been carried out. We are reasonably confident that the coding guidelines have been applied consistently, because they were developed and used by four people who worked with them intensively and over a long period of time. The fact that coding was done by four individuals also lends confidence that the judgments do not reflect the idiosyncratic interpretations of one individual—and if they do, the idiosyncracies are explicit in the coding guidelines and thus subject to revision by other scholars.

The related question is whether the sources examined prior to coding were sufficiently complete and accurate. This is a potential threat to the reliability and validity of the codings for some minor European and Latin American states during the nineteenth century for which source materials are scarce. Accurate coding of Executive Constraints, for example, requires political analyses with a depth not often included in summary histories. A few of the predecessor states of Imperial Germany that nominally qualify for inclusion in POLITY I and II were not coded for lack of adequate sources.

Notes

This is a substantial revision of a paper presented to the Conference on Measurement of Democracy at the Hoover Institution, May 27–28, 1988. Comments on the paper by Alex Inkeles, Robert W. Jackman, Seymour Martin Lipset, Kenneth A. Bollen, Mark J. Gasiorowski, and Raymond D. Gastil helped guide the revision. The study was carried out with support from National Science Foundation grant SES-8610567; institutional support from the Center for Comparative Politics at the University of Colorado, Boulder; and a 1988–89 Jennings Randolph Peace Fellowship awarded to the first author by the U.S. Institute of Peace, Washington, D.C.

1. On the growth of bureaucracies in historical European states see Jacoby (1973) and the contributions to Tilly (1975).
2. The four countries are Great Britain, Italy, Sweden, and Germany. The data and sources are summarized in Gurr and King 1987:26.
3. Unpublished data collected by the first author. On the relationship between warfare and the growth of technology and state power in Europe since the Middle Ages see, for example, McNeil (1982).
4. Two empirical studies that use longitudinal data on long-term patterns of political development are Banks (1972) and Lichbach (1984).
5. Th original analysis (Gurr 1974) did not include the polities of the "new nations" established in the aftermath of World War II. Data on these countries were later gathered and documented in the POLITY I codebook (Gurr and Associates 1978), but the conditions associated with their persistence and adaptability have yet to be analyzed.
6. Composite indicators of democracy and autocracy were constructed from the coded data on authority traits. Similar indicators are used in the present study and are described in this article. Polities with the highest three scores on the composite indicators were operationally defined as "coherent" democracies and autocracies.

7. The POLITY II study is part of the National Science Foundation-supported Data Development in International Research (DDIR) project, directed by Richard Merritt and Dina A. Zinnes of the University of Illinois, Champaign-Urbana. The new polity coding was carried out at the Center for Comparative Politics of the University of Colorado, Boulder.
8. The POLITY II codebook (Gurr, Jaggers and Moore 1989) includes more detailed operational definitions of the categories used later in this article and specific guidelines for distinguishing among adjacent categories. The codebook and dataset have been deposited with, and will be available from, the Inter-University Consortium for Political and Social Research, Ann Arbor, Michigan.
9. The original Capabilities data on military manpower (see Singer, Bremer and Stuckey 1972) were recorded annually for 1816 through 1970. Data were not collected for the years of World Wars I and II, 1914–1918 and 1939–1945 inclusive. For the years 1950–1980 we have relied on a corrected and updated version of the Capabilities dataset prepared by Michael D. Ward and Kun Y. Park at the University of Colorado (Park and Ward 1988).
10. Calculated from data in Gurr 1974:1503. Harmel's reanalysis using alternate definitions of polity change had comparable results (1980:203, 204). These results are approximately, but not precisely, relevant to the present study because, first, in the POLITY I study Spain and Portugal were included with the Latin American countries rather than Europe; and, second, because the POLITY I studies were based on data coded through 1971 rather than 1986.
11. The reliability of the authority codings may also be of concern to some scholars, as they are to us. See appendix 2 for a discussion of this issue.
12. Long-run comparisons can be made using Arthur Banks' Cross-Polity Time-Series dataset (1971). An unpublished paper by Ward (1974) used this dataset to construct roughly comparable indicators of the POLITY I authority traits and then replicated the "Persistence and Change" study of the authority correlates of polity durability (Gurr 1974). The results were inconclusive because of basic differences between the datasets. The POLITY II dataset, with its annual codings and additional dimensions, parallels the Banks dataset more closely. It now is feasible to assess the validity of the POLITY II codings, and the composite indicators of democracy and autocracy, by graphic and correlational comparisons with similar indicators constructed from Banks' dataset.

    A much wider range of post-1945 comparisons can be made between the POLITY II codings and other scholars' time—series data on regime characteristics and performance. These include Mark J. Gasiorowski's new "Political Regimes Project," see p. 109–125, this issue; Raymond Gastil's codings of political rights and liberties (annually since 1973, see Gastil 1987); and the *World Handbook* annual codings of conflict events and sanctions, 1948–1980 (Taylor and Jodice 1983).

References

BANKS, ARTHUR S.
    1971   *Cross-polity time-series data*. Cambridge, MA: MIT Press.
    1972   Correlates of democratic performance. Comparative Politics 4, 1: (January): 217–230.
BENDIX, REINHARD
    1978   *Kings or people: Power and the mandate to rule*. Berkeley: University of California Press.
ECKSTEIN, HARRY, and TED ROBERT GURR
    1975   *Patterns of authority: A structural basis for political inquiry*. New York: Wiley-Interscience.
EISENSTADT, S. N.
    1978   *Revolution and the transformation of societies: A comparative study of civilizations*. New York: Free Press.
GASTIL, RAYMOND D.
    1987   *Freedom in the world: Political rights and civil liberties, 1986-87*. Westport, CT: Greenwood Press.
GURR, TED ROBERT
    1974   Persistence and change in political systems 1800-1971. *American Political Science Review* 68, 4 (December): 1482–1504.
    1988a   The political dimension of national capabilities: Concepts and measurement. *International Interactions* 14, 2: 133–139.
    1988b   War, revolution, and the growth of the coercive state. *Comparative Political Studies* 21, 1 (April): 45–65.
GURR, TED ROBERT and ASSOCIATES
    1978   *Comparative studies of political conflict and change: Cross national datasets*. Ann Arbor: Inter-University Consortium for Political and Social Research.
GURR, TED ROBERT, KEITH JAGGERS, and WILL H. MOORE
    1989   *Polity II codebook*. Boulder, CO: Center for Comparative Politics, Department of Political Science, University of Colorado.
GURR, TED ROBERT, AND DESMOND S. KING
    1987   *The State and the city*. London: Macmillan: Chicago: University of Chicago Press.

HARMEL, ROBERT
    1980   Gurr's 'Persistence and change' revisited: Some consequences of using different operationalizations of 'change of polity.' *European Journal of Political Research* 8, 2 (June): 189–214.
JACOBY, HENRY
    1973   *The bureaucratization of the world*. Berkeley, CA: University of California Press.
JAGGERS, KEITH
    1989   War and the three faces of power: War-making and state-making in Europe and North America, 1823–1953. Paper presented at the Annual Meetings of the International Studies Association. London. March.
LICHBACH, MARK IRVING
    1984   *Regime change and the coherence of European governments*. Denver: Graduate School of International Studies, Monograph Series in World Affairs, Vol. 21. Book 1.
LIPSET, SEYMOUR MARTIN
    1959   Some social requisites of democracy: Economic development and political legitimacy. *American Political Science Review* 53,1 (March): 69–105.
MAOZ, ZEEV
    1989   Joining the club of nations: Political development and international conflict. 1816–1976. *International Studies Quarterly* 33,2 (June): 198–231.
MAOZ, ZEEV, and NASRIN ABDOLALI
    1989   Regime types and international conflict, 1816–1976. *Journal of Conflict Resolution* 22,1 (March): 3–36.
MCNEILL, WILLIAM
    1982   *The pursuit of power*. Chicago: University of Chicago Press.
MOORE, BARRINGTON, JR.
    1966   *Social origins of dictatorship and democracy: Lord and peasant in the making of the modern world*. Boston: Beacon Press.
PARK, KUN Y., and MICHAEL D. WARD
    1988   A research note on the Correlates of War national capability data: Some revised procedures applied to the 1959-1980 era. *International Interactions* 14,2.
RASLER, KAREN, and WILLIAM THOMPSON
    1985a   War and the economic growth of major powers. *American Journal of Political Science* 29,3: 513–538.
    1985b   War making and state making: Governmental expenditures, tax revenues, and global wars. *American Political Science Review* 79,2: 491–507.
RUSSETT, BRUCE
    1970   *What price vigilance? The burdens of national defense*. New Haven: Yale University Press.
SINGER, J. DAVID, STUART BREMER, and JOHN STUCKEY
    1972   Capability distribution, uncertainty, and major power war, 1820–1965. In *Peace, war, and numbers*, edited by Bruce M. Russett. Beverly Hills, CA: Sage Publications.
SKOCPOL, THEDA
    1979   *States and social revolutions: A comparative analysis of France, Russia, and China*. Cambridge: Cambridge University Press.
TAYLOR, CHARLES L., and DAVID JODICE
    1983   *World handbook of political and social indicators*, 3d ed. New Haven: Yale University Press.
THIESSEN, HEATHER, and MARTHA BAYS
    1986   A survival analysis of polity persistence and change: A reanalysis of "Persistence and change in political systems, 1800–1971." Paper presented at the Annual Meetings of the Midwest Political Science Association, Chicago (April).
TILLY, CHARLES, ed.
    1975   *The formation of national states in Western Europe*. Princeton, NJ: Princeton University Press.
TRIMBERGER, ELLEN K.
    1978   *Revolution from above*. New Brunswick, NJ: Transaction Books.
WARD, MICHAEL D.
    1974   Authority dimensions: A study of the reliability and validity of the polity data. Unpublished research paper, Department of Political Science, Northwestern University.
ZIMMERMANN, EKKART
    1980   *Political violence, crises, and revolutions: Theories and research*. Cambridge, MA: Schenkman.

5

The Political Regimes Project

Mark J. Gasiorowski

The Political Regimes Project is a comprehensive effort to study the determinants and comparative performance of political regimes. The main goal of the project is to assemble and analyze a large cross-national dataset containing indicators of the three basic political regime types (democracy, totalitarianism, and authoritarianism) and a variety of politcal regime subtypes (e.g., parliamentary democracy, bureaucratic authoritarianism). This dataset will contain yearly measures of political regime type and subtype for 117 major countries from 1946 (or a country's first full year of independence) through 1988. The author plans to use this dataset as the basis for a comprehensive study of the determinants and performance of political regimes, and will eventually make the dataset available to other researchers. The comprehensive scope of the Political Regimes Database, its time series properties, and the elaborate typology of regimes that it is based upon will enable researchers to examine political regimes in novel ways that may yield valuable new insights.

Questions about democracy and other types of political regime have been a central focus of political inquiry since the time of Aristotle. Research on political regimes has remained at the forefront of modern political science and political sociology throughout the post-World War II era, as researchers have grappled with problems such as the origins of totalitarianism (Arendt 1951; Friedrich and Brzezinski 1965), the prospects for democratization in underdeveloped societies (Lerner 1958; Lipset 1960; Huntington 1968), the emergence of authoritarianism in certain newly industrializing countries (O'Donnell 1973; Stepan 1973; Linz 1978), and the comparative performance of different regime types (Powell 1982; Weede 1983; Sloan and Tedin 1987). Recently, a number of major studies have appeared on the democratic transitions currently occurring in Latin America and elsewhere (O'Donnell, Schmitter, and Whitehead 1986; Baloyra 1987; Malloy and Seligson 1987).

Mark J. Gasiorowski is an associate professor in the Department of Political Science at Louisiana State University, Baton Rouge, LA. He has published recent articles in *Comparative Political Studies, International Studies Quarterly, International Organization,* and other journals, and is the author of a forthcoming book on U.S. foreign policy toward Iran.

Most of the literature on political regimes has focused on two basic issues. First, many of these studies have examined the *determinants* of political regime type: the social, economic, political, psychological, and cultural factors that determine what type of regime exists in a particular country. Second, a growing body of literature has examined the *comparative performance* of different types of regime in such areas as promoting political stability, resolving intrasocietal conflict, promoting economic growth, and reducing inequality. Most of the pioneering work in these two areas consisted of case studies focusing on one or a few countries. However, broad, cross-national studies utilizing quantitative data have made important contributions to this literature by enabling researchers to use comprehensive samples and employ rigorous analytical methods (e.g., Lipset 1960; Cnudde and Neubauer 1969; Bollen 1979; Powell 1982).

This article describes the conceptual foundations and data collection procedures being used by the author to assemble a cross-national dataset on political regimes called the Political Regimes Database. This dataset is similar to those already mentioned in both its conceptual and its methodological foundations. It is designed to address questions about the determinants and performance of political regimes similar to those addressed in these earlier studies. However, the Political Regimes Database differs from most of the datasets used in these earlier studies in three important ways. First, it classifies countries into three main regime types (democratic, totalitarian, and authoritarian), as well as a variety of subtypes, rather than according to a simple democracy-autocracy continuum, as most earlier studies do. Second, it employs richer definitions of regime type which yield more robust empirical measures. Third, it contains not only cross-national data on most countries in the world but also yearly time series data covering the entire post-World War II period, enabling researchers to address complex questions about the timing and dynamics of issues pertaining to political regimes.

The Conceptual Foundations of the Political Regimes Database

A dataset of this kind must be based on definitions of the main types of political regime that are both widely accepted and easily operationalized. This section discusses the basic definitions used in developing the Political Regimes Database. The next section then discusses how these definitions are operationalized and the coding procedures used to collect empirical data on the different political regime types.

A political regime is a set of rules, procedures, and understandings which govern relations between the state and society in a particular country (Macridis 1986:2). Three main types of political regime are commonly referred to in the literature: democratic, totalitarian, and authoritarian. In addition, many variations exist on each of these basic regime types, yielding a wide variety of political regime subtypes.

A democratic regime is defined by Robert Dahl (1971: 2-3) as a regime in which the state is highly responsive to the preferences of society because all adult citizens are free to formulate their preferences, to signify their preferences to other citizens and to the state, and to have their preferences weighed without discrimination in the

TABLE 1
A Typology of Political Regimes

Dimension	Democracy	Totalitarianism	Authoritarianism
1) Freedoms of Organization and Expression (2a-c, 1b)	Y	N	N
2) Representative Process for Selecting Government Officials (3a, 3b)	Y	N	N
3) Representative State Institutions (1a, 1b)	Y	N	?
4) Number and Character of Political Parties (2d)	>1	1t	?
5) "Totalist" Ideology (1c, 5b)	N	Y	N
6) State/Party Domination of Societal Organizations (5i, 5j)	N	Y	?
7) Political Repression (4a-c)	N	Y	Y

conduct of state policymaking. Dahl goes on to list eight basic requirements necessary for these conditions to hold, including freedoms of organization and expression, the universal rights to vote, run for public office, and compete for political support, the existence of alternative sources of information and free and fair elections, and the existence of institutions for making state policy responsive to public expressions of preference. Carl Friedrich (1969: cited in Linz 1975: 187-188) defines a totalitarian regime as one in which the state is guided by a "totalist" ideology, is controlled by a single, mass-mobilizational political party backed up by a pervasive secret police, and maintains monopolies on mass communications, the coercive apparatus, and other societal organizations. Juan Linz (1970: 255) defines an authoritarian regime as one in which the state is controlled by one leader (or a small group of leaders), affords very limited political pluralism, is not guided by an elaborate ideology, does not seek or permit extensive political mobilization, and exercises power in ways that are formally ill-defined, though actually quite predictable.

These definitions, with some minor modifications, suggest that the three main political regime types can be fully defined and adequately distinguished from one another with the seven-dimensional typology shown in Table 1.

The first three dimensions of this typology embody the eight essential requirements for democracy identified by Dahl. The first dimension incorporates three of these requirements: freedoms of organization and expression, and the existence of alternative sources of information.[1] The second dimension incorporates four more of Dahl's requirements: it identifies whether the process for selecting government officials is representative in the sense that it is determined by free and fair elections in which all adult citizens can vote, run for office, and compete for support. The third dimension of the typology embodies Dahl's last essential requirement for democracy: it identifies whether state institutions are representative in the sense that they are structured in a way that makes state policy responsive to public expressions of preference. As indicated in the first column of the table, democratic regimes must have affirmative values (i.e., "Y") on each of these dimensions. Although totalitarian and authoritarian regimes may possess formally representative institutions such as a parliament that are rendered nonrepresentative by the nature of the selection process or by the extralegal use of coercion by the state (''?'' on dimension three).

The next three dimensions of the typology refer mainly to characteristics of totalitarian regimes. Totalitarian regimes have a single political party with a totalitarian (i.e., vanguard, mass-mobilizational) character (''1t'' on dimension four). By contrast, democratic regimes almost inevitably have two or more nontotalitarian parties (''>1''). Although authoritarian regimes may have political parties, these parties are nontotalitarian and rarely have much political significance (''?''). Totalitarian regimes also have an official ideology that is ''totalist'' in the sense that it guides much of the activity of the state and the party, producing a ''total'' politicization of society (''Y'' on dimension five). Although democratic and authoritarian regimes may have guiding ideologies, they are never ''totalist'' in this sense (''N''). The state and/or the party also control a variety of societal organizations in a totalitarian regime, including the mass media, labor unions, schools, and productive establishments (''Y'' on dimension six). Although the state and political parties may also control such organizations in democratic and authoritarian regimes, this control is never so extensive in a democratic regime (''N'') and rarely so in an authoritarian regime (''?''). Finally, repression does not occur systematically in democratic regimes (''N'' on dimension seven), but generally does in totalitarian and authoritarian regimes (''Y'').

Most of the dimensions in this typology are clearly continuous rather than dichotomous, as depicted in Table 1. Moreover, the characterizations given in Table 1 of democracy, totalitarianism, and authoritarianism in terms of these seven dimensions clearly omit several theoretically possible political regime configurations, such as a nondemocratic regime which is not repressive. These two considerations suggest that some political regimes in practice may actually lie somewhere between the three ideal-typic regime types depicted in Table 1 and therefore should be described in such terms as ''partial democracy'' or ''limited authoritarianism'' (Wesson 1987: ix) rather than simply ''democracy'' or ''authoritarianism.'' This issue will be discussed further in the article, where more detailed measures of political regime type are introduced.

The typology shown in Table 1 also does not embody a number of other factors that are not central to the definitions of democracy, totalitarianism, and authoritarianism but which nevertheless can be important characteristics of political regimes. These additional regime characteristics identify certain *subtypes* of democratic, totalitarian, and authoritarian regimes. Exhibit 1 lists some of the more important political regime subtypes that have been identified in the literature.

One important factor that distinguishes different subtypes of democratic regime is the nature of the rules and procedures governing representation, which are typically spelled out in a country's constitution. Two key aspects of these rules and procedures have received considerable attention in the literature on democratic regimes: the distinction between presidential and parliamentary forms of executive-legislative relationship, and the distinction between majoritarian and representational electoral

EXHIBIT 1
Political Regime Types and Sub-Types

Democratic Regimes

presidential vs. parliamentary (3c)
majoritarian vs. representational (3d)
two-party vs. multi-party (2d, 2e)
distribution of power among parties (2d)
extremist multi-party (2f, 2g)
consociational (5a)

Totalitarian Regimes

type of ideology (1c)
populist (5c)

Authoritarian Regimes

traditional (5d)
military (5e)
bureaucratic (5f, 5i)
corporatist (5g)
racial/ethnic "democracy" (1c)
post-totalitarian (1c, 2d, 5b, 5f, 5h)
mobilizational (5b)
personalistic (5h)
populist (5c)

---

systems (Powell 1982: 54-73). Another important distinction among democratic regimes concerns the nature of their party systems. Three important aspects of party systems have received considerable attention in the literature: the number of significant political parties operating at the national level, the distribution of power among these parties, and the existence of extremist parties in a multiparty system (Sartori 1976: 131-216; Powell 1982: 74-110). A third important distinction among democratic regimes concerns the existence of consociational mechanisms which serve to promote compromise and consensus among societal groups, including federalist systems, special legislative practices, and state agencies that facilitate intergroup compromise (McRae 1974; Lijphart 1977).[2]

Linz (1975: 191, 230-240) has suggested that useful distinctions can be made among totalitarian regimes on the basis of differences in the nature and importance of the guiding ideology, the party, other mass organizations, and the leader or leadership group. Fundamental differences in the ideological bases of Soviet and Nazi totalitarianism and the implications of these differences for institutional structure and leadership style suggest that the distinction between "Left" and "Right" totalitarianism is quite significant. Moreover, the Khomeini regime in contemporary Iran fits the totalitarian model quite closely yet differs substantially from the Soviet and Nazi examples, suggesting that other types of ideology can provide a basis for totalitarianism (Macridis 1986: 246-249). Charismatic leadership and very high levels of mass mobilization have been important features of both the Khomeini regime and the Castro regime in Cuba, suggesting that populist totalitarianism may be a useful subtype. Unfortunately, the predominance of the Soviet model of total-itarianism has restricted the variation in this regime type, making it difficult to distinguish genuine subtypes of totalitarianism from anomalies caused by cultural and other differences.

Linz (1975: 252-350) has also developed a useful typology of authoritarian regimes.[3] The two most basic subtypes distinguished by Linz are traditional[4] and bureaucratic-military authoritarian regimes. Traditional authoritarian regimes are those in which the ruling authority (generally a single person) maintains itself in power primarily through a combination of appeals to traditional legitimacy, patron-client ties, and repression, which is carried out by an apparatus bound to the ruling authority through personal loyalties. Authoritarian regimes that are wholly or partly traditional include those in Morocco, Oman, Nepal, and Ethiopia under Haile Selassie. Linz defines bureaucratic-military authoritarian regimes as those governed by a coalition of military officers and technocrats who act pragmatically (rather than ideologically) within the limits of their bureaucratic mentality. Given the large number of military regimes and the recent prominence of "bureaucratic authoritarianism" in countries like Argentina and South Korea (O'Donnell 1973; Im 1987), it is perhaps best to distinguish simple military authoritarian regimes from bureaucratic authoritarian regimes, where a powerful group of technocrats uses the state apparatus to try to rationalize and develop the economy.

Three other well-known subtypes of authoritarian regime identified by Linz are corporatist (or organic-statist) authoritarian regimes, racial and ethnic "democ-racies," and post-totalitarian regimes. Corporatist authoritarian regimes are those in which corporatist institutions (Schmitter 1974) are used extensively by the state to coopt and demobilize powerful interest groups. Authoritarian corporatism appears in a variety of forms and is an important component of many authoritarian regimes, although it has been most widely studied in Latin America (Malloy 1977; Hammer-gren 1977). Racial and ethnic "democracies" are authoritarian regimes in which certain racial or ethnic groups enjoy full democratic rights while others are largely or entirely denied these rights, as in South Africa today. Post-totalitarian regimes are those in which totalitarian institutions such as the party, the secret police, and the state-controlled mass media have been firmly established, but where the following conditions exist: ideological orthodoxy has declined in favor of growing routiniza-tion, the use of repression has declined, the state's top leadership is less personalized and more secure, and the level of mass mobilization has declined substantially. All of the Eastern European Communist countries (except perhaps Albania) can be considered post-totalitarian in the mid-1980s.

Finally, Linz identifies several kinds of authoritarian regime that resemble total-itarianism in certain ways and can be classified together as mobilizational authori-tarian regimes. One well-known variant of this subtype is the Fascist (or post-democratic mobilizational) regime, which generally contains a single mass party that promotes a fair amount of popular mobilization and follows an ideology that is not very coherent and not really "totalist." Italy under Mussolini, and Spain in the early Franco era, are good examples of Fascist regimes. Postindependence mobilizational regimes, such as those that appeared in many African countries after decolonization, also usually have a single, mobilizational party and a guiding ideology, although neither is generally as prominent as under fascism. Pretotalitarian regimes, such as those that existed briefly in Germany and in several Eastern European Communist countries befrore the emergence of full totalitarianism, generally consist of an emerging totalitarian party in competition with one or more other parties in a highly unstable and unpredictable situation.

Two other subtypes of authoritarian regime are frequently referred to in the literature. Personalistic authoritarian regimes are those in which heads of government rule arbitrarily, exercising authority mainly through patronage networks and coercion rather than through institutions and formal rules (Jackson and Rosberg 1982: 10-12). Most political regimes in postcolonial Africa have had a highly personalistic character. Populist authoritarian regimes are mobilizational regimes in which a strong, charismatic, manipulative leader rules through a coalition involving key lower class groups (Dix 1985), in the manner of Peron in Argentina and Nasser in Egypt.

The political regime subtypes listed in Exhibit 1 are not all mutually exclusive. For example, parliamentary consociational democracies and corporatist bureaucratic authoritarian regimes can clearly exist (e.g., Belgium and Brazil in the 1970s, respectively); and personalistic and populist authoritarian regimes overlap considerably with traditional and mobilizational authoritarian regimes (respectively). Moreover, some of the subtypes associated with one of the basic regime types identified above can obviously be applied to the others, for example, traditional, corporatist, or populist democracy (Coleman 1960; Katzenstein 1984; Dix 1985). Finally, as with the typology given in Table 1, some regimes in practice may not fit clearly into any of the subtypes listed in Exhibit 1.

Variables in the Political Regimes Database

Exhibit 2 contains a list of the 35 variables included in the Political Regimes Database. Values for each variable are coded on a yearly basis from 1946 (or a country's first full year of independence) through 1988 for the 117 countries that were independent and had a population of at least one million in 1970.[5] Most of these variables are categorical rather than continuous, and most have simple ordinal properties. The permissible values each variable can assume are listed beside it in parentheses. These variables are of two basic types: variables that are used to identify the political regime types and subtypes listed in Table 1 and Exhibit 1 (variables 1a-5j), and a few variables that are included for use as dependent or independent variables in the analysis of the regime type data (variables 6a-h),

Variables 1a-c, 2a-d, 3a-b, 4a-c, 5b, 5i, and 5j embody the seven dimensions of the typology introduced here and therefore serve to distinguish the three basic political regime types. (See Table 1 for a summary of the variables associated with each dimension.) The first dimension of the typology ("freedoms of organization and expression") is embodied in variables 2a-c, which address these freedoms directly, and in variable 1b ("existence of the rule of law"), since citizens are not really free to organize or express themselves if they are not assured of protection

EXHIBIT 2
Variables Contained in the Political Regimes Database

1) Exercise of Authority

a) Representative Institutions and Law (yes, no; yes, no)
b) Existence of the Rule of Law (yes, no)
c) Type of Official Ideology (totalists, guiding, none; Marxist-Leninist, nationalist, religious, exclusionary, other)

2) Political Participation

a) Freedom of Speech and Press (yes, moderate, low)
b) Freedom of Association (yes, moderate, low)
c) Freedom of Organization (yes, moderate, low)
d) Number and Character of Political Parties (0, 1, 2, >2; totalitarian, hegemonic, predominant)
e) Party Fractionalization (index)
f) Extremist Parties (left, right, left + right)
g) Extremist Party Vote (percent)

3) Leadership Selection

a) Representative Selection Process (yes, no; yes, no)
b) Representative Government (yes, no)
c) Executive-Legislative System (presidential, parliamentary, none)
d) Electoral System (majoritarian, representational, none)

4) Fundamental Human Rights

a) Existence of Political Prisoners (high, moderate, none)
b) Abuse of Political Prisoners (high, moderate, none)
c) General Climate of Repression (high, moderate, none)

5) Other Political Regime Characteristics

a) Consociational Institutions (high, moderate, low)
b) Mobilizational Regime (high, moderate, low)
c) Populist Regime (high, moderate, low)
d) Traditionalistic Regime (high, moderate, low)
e) Military Leadership (high, moderate, low)
f) Technocratic Leadership (high, moderate, low)
g) Corporatist Institutions (high, moderate, low)
h) Personalistic Leadership (high, moderate, low)
i) State Role in Economic Planning (high, moderate, low)
J) State Involvement in Political Socialization (high, moderate, low)

6) Miscellaneous Indicators

a) Level of Popular Political Activity (high, moderate, low)
b) Degree of State Ownership of Means of Production (high, moderate, low)
c) Extent of State-Sponsored Social Welfare Programs (high, moderate, low)
d) International Alignment (east, west, non-aligned)
e) Changes of Government (0, 1, 2, >2)
f) Acts of Non-Violent Popular Unrest (0, 1, 2, >2)
g) Acts of Violent Unrest (0, 1, 2, >2)
h) Extremist Guerrilla Groups (left, right, left + right)

Note: All variable values can also be designated as "probable." See note 12.

under the law from their political opponents.[6] The second dimension ("representative process for selecting top state officials") is embodied in variables 3a and 3b.

Variable 3a asks whether an explicit set of rules exists for selecting all top state officials and, if so, whether these rules are representative in the sense that the highest such officials are chosen through free and fair elections, all adult citizens can vote, run, and compete freely for support in these elections (except under extraordinary circumstances), and all top state officials who are not elected in this way are appointed by higher officials who are.[7] Variable 3b asks whether the current government was selected through such a representative process. The third dimension of the typology ("representative state institutions and laws") is embodied in variable 1b ("existence of the rule of law") and variable 1a, which asks whether the rights of citizens and the structure of government are formally specified in a body of law, whether this body of law (if one exists) is representative in the sense that it forces state policy to reflect popular preferences, [8] and whether these laws are actually enforced by the state.[9]

Variables 1c, 2d, 4a-c, 5b, 5i, and 5j embody the remaining dimensions of the typology. The fourth dimension ("number and character of political parties") is embodied in variable 2d, which indicates the number of political parties and whether a single party is totalitarian. The fifth dimension ("totalist ideology") is embodied in variable 1c, which indicates whether state policy is guided by a totalist ideology, and in variable 5b, which indicates whether the regime is mobilizational. The sixth dimension ("state/party domination of societal organizations") is embodied in variables 5i and 5j, which indicate the degree to which the state and/or the ruling party dominate the economy and institutions like schools and the mass media. The seventh dimension of the typology ("political repression") is embodied in variables 4a-c, which ask whether political prisoners exist, how badly they are treated, and whether a more general climate of repression exists.

Table 2 shows how the three basic political regime types are operationalized in terms of the permissible values of variables 1a-c, 2a-d, 3a-b, 4a-c, 5b, 5i, and 5j. It is evident that certain configurations of these 15 variables do not correspond to any of the three basic regime types as they are operationalized here (e.g., a regime without representative institutions and law [1a = no] but where repression does not occur [4a-c = no]). A regime of this kind can be referred to as a "partial democracy," "partial totalitarianism," or "partial authoritarianism," depending on which of the three basic regime types it most closely resembles. Measures of these "partial" categories can be operationalized in terms of the 15 variables used to define the three basic regime types, much like the operationalizations of these three regime types show in Table 2. Moreover, since most of these 15 variables have simple ordinal properties, ordinal measures of the "degree" of democracy, totalitarianism, and authoritarianism can be constructed from them. Ordinal measures of this kind would make distinctions of "degree" among the partial regimes of each type and would distinguish the "degree" to which each partial regime differs from the corresponding "full" regime type, which would have the highest permissible value on the ordinal measure. For example, an ordinal measure of the "degree of democracy" could be constructed that would distinguish among the partial democracies as well as each partial democracy from a full democracy, whose value would lie at one endpoint of the measure. Although it is beyond the scope of this article to develop such measures here, it should be noted that a "degree of democracy" measure of this kind would closely resemble those developed by Dahl (1971), Bollen (1980), Coppedge and Reinicke (1988), and other scholars.[10]

Variables 1c, 2d-g, 3c-d, and 5a-i identify the political regime subtypes discussed above. (A summary of the variables corresponding to each subtype is given in Exhibit 1.) Presidential, parliamentary, majoritarian, and representational democratic regimes are identified with the appropriate values of variables 3c and 3d. Two-party, multiparty and extremist multiparty democratic regimes are identified with variables 2d and 2f, which draw on Sartori's (1976:285) classification of party systems, and alternatively with variables 2e and 2g, which provide continuous measures of party fractionalization and the percentage of the vote going to extremist parties (Powell 1982: 74-96). Consociational democratic regimes are identified with

TABLE 2
Characterizations of the Three Main Political Regime Types in Terms of the Variables in the Political Regimes Database

Variable	Democracy	Totalitarianism	Authoritarianism
1a	yes-yes	yes-no	any
1b	yes	any	no
1c	none or guiding	any totalist	none or guiding
2a	yes	low	moderate or low
2b	yes	low	moderate or low
2c	yes	low	moderate or low
2d	2 or >2	1-totalitarian	any
2e			
2f			
2g			
3a	yes-yes	no or yes-no	any
3b	yes	no	no
3c			
3d			
4a	no	any	any
4b	no	any	any
4c	no	high	high or moderate
5a			
5b	any	high	any
5c			
5d			
5e			
5f			
5g			
5h			
5i	any	high	any
5j	low	high	any
6a			
6b			
6c			
6d			
6e			
6f			
6g			
6h			

high values of variable 5a. Different ideological subtypes of totalitarianism, as well as racial and ethnic "democracies," are identified with variable 1c. Populist totalitarianism and authoritarianism are identified with high values of variable 5c. Military, corporatist, mobilizational, and personalistic authoritarianism are identified with high values of variables 5e, 5g, 5b, and 5h (respectively). Bureaucratic authoritarianism is identified with high values of variables 5f and 5i. Finally, posttotalitarian authoritarian regimes are identified with the variable values shown for totalitarianism in Table 2, except that they have guiding rather than totalist ideologies (variable 1c); they have nontotalitarian single parties (variable 2d); they are not highly mobilizational (variable 5b); they do not have highly personalistic leadership (variable 5h); they are at least moderately technocratic (variable 5f); they are usually not highly repressive (variables 4a-c); and they have succeeded totalitarian regimes chronologically.

Variables 1a-5j therefore delineate a complex typology in which political regimes are classified in two basic ways: (1) according to the three basic regime types (democracy, totalitarianism, and authoritarianism) and the "partial" categories corresponding to these three basic regime types; and (2) according to the regime subtypes listed in Exhibit 1. In the first of these classification systems, regimes can be distinguished with ordinal measures that embody the "degree" of democracy, totalitarianism, and authoritarianism. In the second classification system, regimes of each basic type are distinguished according to the qualitative criteria embodied in the corresponding sub-types.[11] As mentioned earlier, some of the subtypes associated with one basic regime type can be applied to others, providing further possibilities for classifying regimes; and variables 6b-d can be used to classify regimes further according to their international alignment and type of economic system. The research issues that will be addressed by the author with these data are outlined in the following section.

The variables listed in Exhibit 2 are coded by research assistants in a procedure designed to maximize the accuracy of the data. This procedure currently entails three basic steps for each country. First, the research assistant studies the recent history of the country by examining sources like *Keesing's Contemporary Archives, The Political Handbook of the World,* the *Encyclopedia of the Third World,* reference works published by organizations such as Amnesty International and Europa Publications, and appropriate books and articles on the country. Second, the research assistant writes a detailed yearly chronology on the country using these sources. As the research assistant writes each yearly entry in this chronology, he or she assigns appropriate values to each of the 35 variables for that year, using decision rules[12] developed by the author. The text of the chronology is written in a way that explains why each value was assigned to each variable.[13] Third, when the chronology and list of variable values have been completed for a particular country, the author examines them in detail and returns them to the research assistant for any necessary revisions. This last step is repeated until the author is satisfied with the quality of the chronology and variable list. To date, studies embodying these three steps have been completed for sixteen countries. The regime types and subtypes identified for these sixteen countries are shown in Exhibit 3.

EXHIBIT 3
Regime Types and Sub-Types for Sixteen Selected Countries

Burma
1948-1961 authoritarian
1962-1987 military authoritarian

China
1949-1978 Marxist totalitarian
1979-1987 post-totalitarian authoritarian

Cambodia
1954-1969 traditional authoritarian
1970-1974 military authoritarian
1975-1978 Marxist totalitarian
1979-1987 military authoritarian

Japan
1946-1952 partial democracy
1953-1987 parliamentary majoritarian democracy

Laos
1954-1959 traditional authoritarian
1960-1974 military authoritarian
1975-1987 Marxist totalitarian

Liberia
1946-1979 personalistic authoritarian
1980-1985 military authoritarian
1986-1987 personalistic authoritarian

Mexico
1946-1987 corporatist bureaucratic authoritarian

Nigeria
1960-1965 partial democracy
1966-1979 military authoritarian
1980-1983 partial democracy
1984-1987 military authoritarian

North Korea
1948-1987 Marxist totalitarian

North Vietnam/Vietnam
1955-1987 Marxist totalitarian

Philippines
1946-1947 presidential representational democracy
1948-1971 partial democracy
1972-1985 personalistic authoritarian
1986-1987 partial democracy

Singapore
1966-1987 personalistic authoritarian

South Korea
1949-1960 partial democracy
1961-1985 military authoritarian

South Vietnam
1955-1963 personalistic authoritarian
1964-1974 military authoritarian

Taiwan
1948-1987 personalistic authoritarian

Turkey
1946-1959 partial democracy
1960   military authoritarian
1961-1979 partial democracy
1980-1982 military authoritarian
1983-1987 partial democracy

In addition, the author hopes to hire academic specialists on each of the 117 countries to examine the chronology and variable list developed for each country and recommend any further revisions that may be necessary. These revisions will then be made by a research assistant and checked by the author. This fourth step in the data coding procedure would serve essentially as an external validity check on the three preceding steps, helping to ensure the accuracy of the data.[14]

Research Objectives

The author intends to use the Political Regimes Database to study the determinants and comparative performance of the various political regime types and subtypes contained in the Database. He also intends to make the Database available to other researchers.[15] This section outlines the main research questions of each kind that will be addressed by the author and the main advantages offered by the Database in studying these issues.

In a recent review of literature on the determinants of democracy, Samuel Huntington (1984) distinguished between two basic types of determinants: broad, structural characteristics of a society which serve essentially as preconditions for democracy, and political processes which result in the installation or breakdown of democracy. Huntington's classification provides a useful starting point for delineating the determinants of regime type more generally. The first group of determinants identified by Huntington includes factors such as a society's level of economic development (Lipset 1960: Cutright 1963; Neubauer 1967); the particular nature of its economic development (Moore 1966; O'Donnell 1973; Gasiorowski 1988); characteristics of its political system (Dahl 1971; Lijphart 1977; Diamond, Lipset, and Linz 1987); aspects of its political culture (Pye and Verba 1965; Bollen and Jackman 1985); and various international factors (Gourevitch 1978; Muller 1985; Gasiorowski 1986; Whitehead 1986). The second group includes the effect of institutionalization on democracy (Huntington 1968); cyclical and dialectical patterns of democratization (Huntington 1984: 210-211); and democratic installations or breakdowns caused by legitimation crises (Rustow 1970; Kaufman 1976; Linz 1978; Baloyra 1987).

Studies of the comparative performance of political regimes have examined whether some types of regime are more successful than others in achieving policy goals such as promoting economic growth (Weede 1983; Goldsmith 1986); reducing inequality (Jackman 1975; Muller 1988); implementing certain kinds of social programs (Moon and Dixon 1985; Sloan and Tedin 1987); reducing intrasocietal conflict and violence (Hibbs 1973; Powell 1982); and avoiding or engaging in international war (Merritt and Zinnes 1988). A large body of literature also exists on the comparative performance of military and civilian regimes, which can be regarded as aspects of political regime type (Nordlinger 1970; Jackman 1976; Remmer 1978; Ravenhill 1980).

The author intends to replicate and extend these studies using the Political Regimes Database. The conceptual framework and coding procedures used to create the Database contain a number of features that will permit this to be done in new and innovative ways. The comprehensive typology of political regimes used in constructing the Database will make possible studies of the determinants and performance of nondemocratic regimes and processes of transition among different regime types and subtypes. The large number of countries represented in the Database (117) will enable researchers to undertake comprehensive studies of these research issues. The existence of time series data for each country will facilitate analyses of processes and sequences of regime transition, the stability of regimes over time, the effect of regime change on performance, and various kinds of time-delay and cumulative effects. The multidimensional typology and the large number of component variables contained in the Database will enable researchers to study alternative conceptualizations of regime type and to use the component variables themselves as dependent or independent variables in empirical analyses.

Finally, the use of detailed historical research to assemble the Database gives the data a high degree of validity, eliminates the problem of missing values in the data,[16] and makes possible the study of regime characteristics that cannot be measured easily in any other way, such as the existence of the rule of law, populism, and personalistic leadership.

The current centrality of the concepts of democracy, totalitarianism, and authoritarianism in the fields of comparative politics and political sociology and the shortcomings of the existing empirical literature on these regime types suggest that the Political Regimes Database may make possible important new contributions in the various areas of research it touches upon. Moreover, with the growing realization that politics plays a key role in economic performance, the growing importance of political unrest in underdeveloped countries for U.S. foreign policy and for international politics more generally, and the increasing interest in the United States and elsewhere in democracy and human rights, research based on the Political Regimes Database may have considerable practical significance as well.

Notes

1. "Freedom of expression" and "alternative sources of information" are quite similar in practice and are therefore combined here and in the variables introduced below.

2. For other typologies of democratic regimes see Almond and Powell (1966: 259-271) and Lijphart (1977: 105-119).

3. For other typologies of authoritarian regimes see Almond and Powell (1966: 271-191), Huntington (1970), and Perlmutter (1981). Each of these typologies includes totalitarianism as a subtype of authoritarianism.

4. Although Linz (1975: 252-264) does not consider traditional regimes to be authoritarian (because they are not "modern"), they clearly fit the definition of authoritarianism given above.

5. Countries that were not independent by 1970 are excluded from the Database because the relatively short span of years available for them would preclude their use in many of the analyses to be undertaken in the project. Countries with a population of less than one million by 1970 are excluded because their small size is likely to introduce complicating anomalies into the analysis, and because appropriate data for them are often difficult to obtain.

6. This latter criterion implies that a country cannot be considered democratic if domestic unrest routinely prevents citizens from exercising their political freedoms. Although this criterion is not generally regarded as a requirement for democracy, it is essential for excluding cases like contemporary El Salvador and Colombia, where legitimate democratic institutions appear to exist and full political freedoms are apparently permitted by the state, but where civil war and death squad activity routinely prevent citizens from exercising these freedoms. This criterion can easily be dropped by researchers using the Database.

    For these and all other variables in the Database which identify regime types and subtypes, permissible values are defined in ways that facilitate these identifications. For example, variable 3a is defined in a way that clearly distinguishes between democratic and nondemocratic methods for selecting government officials. (See note 12.) Three permissible values ("yes," "moderate," and "low") can appear for variables 2a-c and for many other variables in the Database, enabling researchers to make simple ordinal distinctions among regimes with these variables. Only three categories are used for these variables because initial data collection efforts indicated that the use of four or more categories had an adverse effect on intercoder reliability.

7. Variable 3a asks *two* interrelated questions: whether such rules exist, and whether they are representative. (See note 12.) This variable can therefore take on three possible values: yes, such rules exist, and, yes, they are representative; yes, they exist, and, no, they are not representative; and, no, they do not exist.

8. Variable 1a also asks two interrelated questions and can take on three possible values. (See note 7.)

9. The empirical measure of democracy embodied in variables 1a-b, 2a-c, and 3a-b is based explicitly on Dahl's eight requirements for democracy. This measure is therefore *an improvement* over Dahl's (1971: 231-243)

empirical measure, which was based on component variables developed for other purposes, and is very similar to the measure recently developed by two of Dahl's students (Coppedge and Reinicke 1988). It is also quite similar to Bollen's (1980) measure of democracy, which has been used very widely by other scholars. The major difference between this measure and Bollen's is that it does not include as a component variable Taylor and Hudson's (1972) measure of the number of government sanctions, which really has nothing to do with democracy as this term is commonly conceived. For a good review of many other empirical measures of democracy see the discussion in Bollen (1980).

10. The main difference between the measure described here and those developed by these other authors is that full democracies can be explicitly identified and distinguished from partial democracies with this measure, because all full democracies receive the highest permissible value, whereas no clear distinction is made between full and partial democracies by these other authors. This implies that distinctions of the "degree" of democracy can be made only among partial democracies and *not* among full democracies, as is done by these other authors. For example, this measure could make ordinal distinctions between partial democracies such as Mexico and Turkey, and could also make ordinal distinctions between these two countries and a full democracy such as the United States, but could *not* make ordinal distinctions among full democracies such as the United States and France. This feature of the measure eliminates the ambiguity that is inherent in distinctions of the latter kind and enables researchers to identify explicitly (and therefore study) transitions between partial and full democracies.

11. Most of the political regime subtypes listed in Exhibit 1 are identified with variables that have simple ordinal properties. Ordinal distinctions can therefore also be made among regimes falling within these subtypes.

12. For example, the decision rule for variable 3a ("representative selection process") reads as follows:
Does a clearly-specified set of rules exist for the selection of all top government officials? (Yes or No).
If so, is this selection process representative in the sense that: (i) the highest offices of government are subject to free and fair elections; (ii) all adult citizens can vote, run for office, and compete freely for support in these elections, except under extraordinary circumstances; and (iii) all top government officials who are not selected through such elections are appointed by higher officials who are? (Yes or No).
All other variables in the Database have similar decision rules. If a research assistant is unable to find enough information to make a definite decision about a particular variable, that individual is instructed to assign a value based on his or her general knowledge of conditions in the country at the time and to designate that value as "probable" (e.g., "yes-probable," "no-probable").

13. Research assistants are instructed to include in the text of the chronology all factual information used to assign values to the variables. After each passage in the text where this has been done, the variable number and value assigned to it are given in parentheses (e.g., "[3a=no]"). The chronologies therefore explain all value assignments made in assembling the Database.

14. The most important task performed by these specialists would be to check any "probable" values assigned by the research assistants. See note 12.

15. This will presumably be done through the Inter University Consortium for Political and Social Research (ICPSR).

16. Missing values are obviated by permitting the data coders to code variable values as "probable." See note 12.

References

ALMOND, GABRIEL A., and G. BINGHAM POWELL, JR.
1966   *Comparative politics: A developmental approach.* Boston: Little Brown.
ARENDT, HANNAH
1951   *The origins of totalitarianism.* New York: Harcourt, Brace.
BALOYRA, ENRIQUE A.
1987   *Comparing new democracies: Transition and consolidation in Mediterranean Europe and the Southern Cone.* Boulder: Westview.
BOLLEN, KENNETH A.
1979   Political democracy and the timing of development. *American Sociological Review.* 44, 4 (August): 572-587.
1980   Issues in the comparative measurement of political democracy. *American Sociological Review.* 45, 3 (June): 370-390.
BOLLEN, KENNETH A., and ROBERT W. JACKMAN
1985   Economic and noneconomic determinants of political democracy in the 1960s. *Research in Political Sociology.* 1: 27-48.
CNUDDE, CHARLES F., and DEANE E. NEUBAUER, EDS.
1969   *Empirical democratic theory.* Chicago: Markham Publishing Co.
COLEMAN, JAMES S.
1960   Conclusion: The political systems of the developing areas. In *The Politics of the Developing Areas,* edited by Gabriel A. Almond and James S. Coleman. Princeton: Princeton University Press.
COOPEDGE, MICHAEL, and WOLFGANG REINICKE
1988   A measure of polyarchy. Paper presented at Conference on Measuring Democracy, Hoover Institution, Stanford University, May 27-28, 1988.

CUTRIGHT, PHILLIPS
    1963   National political development: Measurement and analysis. *American Sociological Review*. 28, 2
                (April): 253-264.
DAHL, ROBERT A.
    1971   *Polyarchy: Participation and opposition*. New Haven: Yale University Press.
DIAMOND, LARRY, SEYMOUR MARTIN LIPSET, and JUAN LINZ
    1987   Building and sustaining democratic government: Some tentative findings. *World Affairs* 150, 1
                (Summer): 5-19.
DIX, ROBERT H.
    1985   Populism: Authoritarian and democratic. *Latin American Research Review* (20): 29-52.
FRIEDRICH, CARL J., and ZBIGNIEW K. BRZEZINSKI
    1965   *Totalitarian dictatorship and authocracy*. New York: Praeger.
FRIEDRICH, CARL J.
    1969   The evolving theory and practice of totalitarian regimes. In *Totalitarianism in Perspective: Three
                Views,* edited by C. Friedrich, Michael Curtis, and Benjamin R. Barber. New York: Praeger.
GASIOROWSKI, MARK J.
    1986   Dependency and cliency in Latin America. *Journal of Interamerican Studies and World Affairs* 28,
                3 (Fall): 47-65.
    1988   Economic dependence and political democracy: A cross-national study. *Comparative Political Stud-
                ies* 20, 4 (January): 489-515.
GOLDSMITH, ARTHUR A.
    1986   Democracy, political stability, and economic growth in developing countries. *Comparative Political
                Studies* 18, 4 (January): 517-531.
GOUREVITCH, PETER
    1978   The international system and regime formation. *Comparative Politics* 10, 3 (April): 419-438.
HAMMERGREN, LINN A.
    1977   Corporatism in Latin American politics. *Comparative Politics* 9, 4 (July): 443-461.
HIBBS, DOUGLAS A.
    1973   *Mass political violence: A cross-national analysis*. New York: John Wiley & Sons.
HUNTINGTON, SAMUEL P.
    1968   Political order in changing societies. New Haven: Yale University Press.
    1970   Social and institutional dynamics of one-party systems. In *Authoritarian Politics in Modern Society,*
                edited by Samuel P. Huntington and Clement H. Moore. New York: Basic Books.
    1984   Will more countries become democratic? *Political Science Quarterly* 99, 2 (Summer): 193-218.
IM, HYUG BAEG
    1987   The rise of bureaucratic authoritarianism in South Korea. *World Politics* 39, 2 (January): 231-257.
JACKMAN, ROBERT W.
    1975   *Politics and social equality : A comparative analysis*. New York: John Wiley & Sons.
    1976   Politicians in uniform: Military governments and social change in the Third World. *American
                Political Science Review* 70, 4 (December): 1078-1097.
JACKSON, ROBERT H., AND CARL G. ROSBERG
    1982   *Personal rule in black Africa*. Berkeley: University of Californai Press.
KATZENSTEIN, PETER J.
    1984   *Corporatism and change: Austria, Switzerland, and the politics of industry*. Ithaca: Cornell Univer-
                sity Press.
KAUFMAN, ROBERT R.
    1976   *Transitions to stable authoritarian-corporate regimes: The Chilean case?* Beverly Hills: Sage.
LERNER, DANIEL
    1958   *The passing of traditional society*. Glencoe, IL: Free Press.
LIJPHART, AREND
    1977   *Democracy in plural societies: A comparative exploration*. New Haven: Yale University Press.
LIPSET, SEYMOUR MARTIN
    1960   *Political man*. New York: Doubleday.
LINZ, JUAN J.
    1970   An authoritarian regime: The case of Spain. In *Mass Politics: Studies in Political Sociology,* edited
                by Erik Allard and Stein Rokkan. New York: Free Press.
    1975   Totalitarian and authoritarian regimes. In *Handbook of political science, Vol. 3, Macropolitical
                theory,* edited by Fred I. Greenstein and Nelson W. Polsby. Reading, MA: Addison-Wesley.
    1978   *The breakdown of democratic regimes: Crisis, breakdown, & reequilibration*. Baltimore: Johns
                Hopkins University Press.
MACRIDIS, ROY C.
    1986   *Modern political regimes*. Boston: Little Brown.
MALLOY, JAMES M., ED.
    1977   *Authoritarianism and corporatism in Latin America*. Pittsburgh: University of Pittsburgh Press.

MALLOY, JAMES M., and MITCHELL A. SELIGSON, eds.
    1987   *Authoritarians and democrats: Regime transition in Latin America.* Pittsburgh: University of Pittsburgh Press.
MCRAE, KENNETH D., ED.
    1974   *Consociational democracy: Political accommodation in segmented societies.* Toronto: McClelland and Stewart.
MERRITT, RICHARD L., and DINA A. ZINNES
    1988   Democracies and international conflict. Paper presented at Conference on Measuring Democracy, Hoover Institution, Stanford University, May 27-28, 1988.
MOON, BRUCE E., and WILLIAM J. DIXON
    1985   Politics, the state, and basic human needs: A cross-national study. *American Journal of Political Science* 29, 4 (November): 661-694.
MOORE, BARRINGTON, JR.
    1966   *Social origins of dictatorship and democracy.* Boston: Beacon Press.
MULLER, EDWARD N.
    1985   Dependent economic development, aid dependence on the United States, and democratic breakdown in the Third World. *International Studies Quarterly* 29, 4 (December): 445-470.
    1988   Democracy, economic development, and income inequality. *American Sociological Review* 53, 2 (April): 50-68.
NEUBAUER, DEANE E.
    1967   Some conditions of democracy. *American Political Science Review.* 61, 4 (December): 1002-1009.
NORDLINGER, ERIC A.
    1970   Soldiers in mufti: The impact of military rule upon economic and social change in the non-western states. *American Political Science Review.* 64, 4 (December): 1131–1148.
O'DONNELL, GUILLERMO A.
    1973   *Modernization and bureaucratic-authoritarianism: Studies in South American politics.* Berkeley: Institute of International Studies, University of California.
O'DONNELL, GUILLERMO A., PHILIPPE C. SCHMITTER, and LAURENCE WHITEHEAD, eds.
    1986   *Transitions from authoritarian rule.* Baltimore: The Johns Hopkins University Press.
PERLMUTTER, AMOS
    1981   *Modern authoritarianism: A comparative institutional analysis.* New Haven: Yale University Press.
POWELL, G. BINGHAM, JR.
    1982   *Contemporary democracies: Participation, stability, and violence.* Cambridge: Harvard University Press.
PYE, LUCIAN W., and SIDNEY VERBA, eds.
    1965   *Political culture and political development.* Princeton: Princeton University Press.
RAVENHILL, JOHN
    1980   Comparing regime performance in Africa: The limitations of cross-national aggregate analysis. *Journal of Modern African Studies* 18, 1 (March): 99–126.
REMMER, KAREN L.
    1978   Evaluating the policy impact of military regimes in Latin America. *Latin American Research Review* 13, 2: 39–54.
RUSTOW, DANKWART A.
    1970   Transitions to democracy: Toward A dynamic model. *Comparative Politics* 2, 3 (April): 337–364.
SARTORI, GIOVANNI
    1976   *Parties and Party Systems.* Cambridge: Cambridge University Press.
SCHMITTER, PHILIPPE C.
    1974   Still the century of corporatism? *Review of Politics* 36, 1 (January): 85–131.
SLOAN, JOHN AND KENT L. TEDIN
    1987   The consequences of regime type for public policy outputs. *Comparative Political Studies* 20, 1 (April): 98–124.
STEPAN, ALFRED
    1973   *Authoritarian Brazil: Origins, policies, and future.* New Haven: Yale University Press.
TAYLOR, CHARLES LEWIS, and MICHAEL C. HUDSON
    1972   *World handbook of political and social indicators, 2d Ed.* New Haven: Yale University Press.
WEEDE, ERICH
    1983   The impact of democracy on economic growth: Some evidence from cross-national analysis. *Kyklos* 36, 1: 21–39.
WESSON, ROBERT, ed.
    1987   *Democracy: A worldwide survey.* New York: Praeger.
WHITEHEAD, LAURENCE
    1986   International aspects of democratization. In *Transitions from authoritarian rule*, edited by O'Donnell, Schmitter, and Whitehead.

II
Measuring Consequences and Concomitants

6

The Effects of Democracy on Economic Growth and Inequality: A Review

Larry Sirowy and Alex Inkeles

What effects does political democracy have on such development outcomes as economic growth and socioeconomic equality? Competing theoretical models have been proposed that represent each of the possibilities: democracy as facilitating development, democracy as a hindrance to development, and democracy as bearing no independent relationship to development outcomes. Each of these theoretical models is explicated and, then, the evidence from quantitative, cross-national tests of the effects is reviewed. Overall, the evidence provided by the approximately dozen studies for each outcome yields few robust conclusions with respect to the theoretical models. To guide in the evaluation of the evidence, the studies are in turn distinguished by such design characteristics as sample, period observed, measures used, and form of relationship specified. This procedure, while it does not produce definitive support for any of the models, does assist in interpreting the results of past research as well as generating fertile guidelines for future research.

O ver the last two decades many researchers have sought confirmation for hypotheses expressing systematic relations between characteristics of political regimes and patterns of national development. More specifically, do politics matter with respect to the pace and form of economic growth, and with respect to the distribution of economic and social benefits?

Larry Sirowy received his Ph.D. from Stanford University and is presently assistant professor of sociology at Brown University. His general research interest is in the political economy of development, and he recently completed a study of the national and global roots of the nationalization activity of Third World countries. He is currently conducting research on the development consequences of political democracy.

Alex Inkeles is currently professor of sociology at Stanford University. He is also a senior fellow of the Hoover Institution on War, Revolution and Peace, Stanford University. His most recent book is *Exploring Individual Modernity*, and his current research focusses on convergent trends in the social organization and popular attitudes and values within sets of industrial and industrializing nations.

Of the characteristics of political regimes that have been considered in theory and research, the democratic character of national political procedures and institutions has been allotted considerable attention. While we should not find this surprising, since most of us would wish to observe the simultaneous advance of democracy and economic development, the fact remains that theorists are strongly divided with respect to the compatibility of development and political democracy, particularly within the context of developing societies (though note the parallel argument as it has arisen with respect to the crises of governability and economic management in the advanced democracies as presented, for example, by Thurow 1980). Moreover, despite the lengthy and rich dialogue on the subject, many of the central questions pertaining to the developmental consequences of political democracy remain, by and large, unresolved (see also Nelson's 1987 appraisal). Instead, the relevant quantitative, cross-national research continues to be plagued by conflicting findings, a state of affairs made only more complex by conceptual, measurement, modeling, and research design differences. Together these theoretical and research-related issues have contributed to a good deal of confusion with respect to theories of how political democracy might affect development, and with respect to the empirical status of testable claims implied by such theories.

In view of the present state of affairs in this research program, this article seeks to accomplish two tasks in order to provide a firmer foundation for future research: first, to review the relevant theoretical literature in order to explicitly identify and elaborate the different sets of arguments that explain how political democracy might affect development generally, and economic growth and socioeconomic inequality more specifically; and second, to review systematically the relevant quantitative, cross-national studies that have been conducted to evaluate the consequences of political democracy for economic growth and socieconomic inequality within nations so as to assist our interpretations of their diverse results as well as to suggest fertile avenues for future research efforts.

Strikingly, the task of reexamining the development consequences of political democracy could not come at a more critical time in contemporary history. On the one hand, the presumption of a linkage between current democratic political reforms and future economic prosperity has come to inform much of the West's policy prescriptions for Eastern Europe and China. At the same time, numerous Latin American nations face critical political tests in the near future because of the severe economic problems they are experiencing, problems which may or may not be contributed to by the democratic political organization of their polities. In the final analysis, such current events point out the urgent need to reexamine the issue of the development consequences of democracy.

Theoretical Perspectives

Effects of Political Democracy on Economic Growth

Since the early 1970s, a growing body of scholars and Third World officials have come to embrace the position that difficult, sometimes cruel, choices must be made among such development goals as economic growth, socioeconomic equality, and political democracy (for example, see the works of Hewlett 1979 and Huntington and Nelson 1976). As Huntington (1987) aptly describes it, there has emerged a strong tendency to perceive the relationships among such development goals as being conflictive, even to the point of incompatibility. With respect to the particular empirical questions of interest here, the implications of this position are clear: political democracy is a luxury that can be ill-afforded by Third World countries.

In general, proponents of this perspective suggest that developing countries in today's world cannot achieve rapid economic growth through a democratic framework. In other words, developing countries are considered to face the dilemma of choosing to pursue either economic growth or democratic development, but not both simultaneously.

This position stands in stark contrast to the earlier perspective that democratic institutions and political freedom are neither peculiarly limited to Europe nor relevant only to the nineteenth century, but rather that democratic institutions are meaningful, appropriate, and potentially very satisfying programs for organizing social and economic life in the currently less-developed countries. Moreover, proponents of this alternative perspective contend that the notion of conflict between democracy and development in Third World nations only serves to legitimate the denial of basic human rights and freedoms by repressive and exclusionary regimes, and so ultimately undermines democratic political change.

As Huntington (1987) notes, this older, alternative perspective, which appears to be receiving a groundswell of support in recent years, has its roots in the works of such modernization theorists as Karl Deutsch, Daniel Lerner, and Cyril Black. For them, modernization was a systematic process, wherein such development goals as political democracy, economic growth, and equity were not only compatible with one another, but generally mutually reinforcing. All in all, it remains the case, as Huntington so perceptively points out, that this perspective continues to influence U.S. policy toward the Third World.

Following Huntington (1987) we adopt the terminological convention of labeling these theoretical positions as the "Conflict" and "Compatibility" perspectives, respectively. In the balance of this section these perspectives are more fully elaborated with respect to their implications for the effects of political democracy on economic growth and socioeconomic inequality. In addition, a third perspective, which we shall refer to as the "Skeptical" alternative, is presented. The hallmark of this latter alternative is the contention that no universal relationship exists between political democracy and the developmental outcomes under consideration here. Put simply, economic growth is held to be potentially compatible with both a more democratic framework and a more authoritarian framework.

The Conflict Perspective

Fundamental to the conflict perspective is the claim that economic growth is hindered by the democratic organization of the polity (see De Schweinitz 1964, Andreski 1968, Chirot 1977, and Rao 1985). In other words, democracy and economic growth are seen as being competing concerns; hence trade offs in the political realm are considered necessary. Moreover, in this view successful and rapid economic growth requires an authoritarian regime that suppresses or delays the extension of basic civil and political rights and the development of democratic procedures and institutions, because these latter would otherwise subvert the national development project. The reasons that have been offered in support of such a claim are basically threefold: 1) dysfunctional consequences of "premature" democracy act, in turn, to slow growth, 2) democratic regimes are largely unable to implement effectively the kinds of policies considered necessary to facilitate rapid growth, 3) the uniqueness of the present world-historical context requires pervasive state involvement in the development process, which is in turn unduly fettered by political democracy. We will consider each of these reasons in turn.

With respect to the first reason cited, two lines of theory and research on political change have been influential. The first consists of early research supporting the idea that economic development is a prerequisite of democracy (for example, Lipset 1959). And the second is the theory of political change offered by Huntington (1968). From research on the antecedents of democracy, many have drawn the conclusion that the relationship between economic development and political democracy properly conceived is sequential: first growth, then democracy. Regimes more democratic in character that emerge before the appropriate thresholds of resource availability, consonant class structure, and psychological and institutional modernity are crossed will tend to generate dysfunctional consequences that not only threaten further economic progress, but endanger the democratic character of the political institutions as well.

Chief among these dysfunctional consequences is political instability. As Huntington (1968) argues, the political institutions of developing societies tend to be weak and fragile to begin with. Add to that the enormous pressures on government created by a democratic system's participatory institutions and the sources of instability are greatly magnified. Because of the greater availability of channels through which such impatient groups as workers and the poor can express their demands and because political elites and their parties must cater, at least to some extent, to such groups in order to win support in elections, democratic regimes in less developed countries quickly become overburdened and must necessarily become preoccupied with the maintenance of internal order.

In addition, states the conflict perspective, many of today's Third World societies are so besieged by internal conflict stemming from heterogeneity of region, caste, religion, ethnicity, and class that forging a consensus by force becomes critical if these nations are successfully to undertake mobilization for rapid national development. Democratic regimes, because of the political and civil liberties they rest on, only act to inflame social division and erode the capacity of the government to act quickly and effectively. More authoritarian systems, in contrast, are held to be better able to suppress disruptive dissent and conflict.

Finally, even short of disruptive internal conflict and instability the electoral politics that are inherent in democracy may well act to distort the economy and incapacitate the government as officials shift their allegiances among policies based on short-run political expediency, rather than focusing exclusively on policies oriented toward national development in the long-run.

Overall, the implications of this reasoning for the effect of democracy on economic growth are clear. As Apter (1965) has argued, before a certain level of economic development has been attained, coerciveness is best suited to change. To deal successfully with the problems of nation-building, to contain discontent, and to control domestic pressures, a Third World regime must be able to insulate itself while having the wherewithal to impose its programs against opposition efficiently and effectively. These are needs best filled by authoritarian rule. In contrast, democracy is held to decrease the efficiency of decision making, thereby leading to inconsistent and vacillating policies, if not outright paralysis, as well as engendering higher levels of instability, all of which in turn slow economic growth.

The particular relevance of these arguments for us lies not solely in the implication that, in the Third World nations, authoritarian regimes are simply better able to govern, but that such regimes are better able to implement the kinds of policies thought critical for rapid economic growth and to create the conditions necessary to support them. In this view, the superior ability of an authoritarian regime to govern that facilitates economic growth is expressed indirectly by the social and political stability it fosters, the insulation from outside influence it allows, and the single-minded strength that it can muster. But authoritarian forms of regimes are also thought to facilitate rapid economic growth directly through a number of mechanisms. Some of these mechanisms include their ability to exert firmer control over labor and labor markets, their greater efficiency in the allocation of resources, their ability to use coercion to break traditional patterns, and their capacity to collectively organize and direct economic policies.

But perhaps the most frequently noted mechanism by which authoritarianism is thought to directly facilitate economic growth is through its effect on consumption and saving. Underlying this idea is the notion that growth is primarily the result of huge material and personnel investments. In a poor economy, total production cannot be increased rapidly without building new factories, improving education, developing infrastructure services such as communication and transportation, and introducing new productive technologies. But these goals cannot be achieved without the accumulation of capital, which in turn depends on the rate of saving.

The accumulation of a surplus for investment requires enormous sacrifices. Current consumption must be cut at the same time that savings increases. But who is to bear the burden of the sacrifices? In the authoritarian model, since the rich have a higher marginal propensity to save, the larger share of national income and of increments due to growth should be directed toward those who are already well off in order to maximize the rate of social savings. Any shifting of resources to the poorer segments of the population, in contrast, would unduly hamper the accumulation of capital because such groups tend to consume rather than save. Hence the idea that economic growth requires large distributive inequalities is assumed by proponents of this model, and is thought to be confirmed by the experience of Western European societies during their own periods of industrialization (see Kuznets 1955).

The model further holds that no democratic government can tolerate the degree of restraint in consumption necessary for maximizing the rate of growth in a developing economy (Hewlett 1979). This is the case because, for a Third World nation to successfully expand economically, the government needs to adopt policies that hold down the real wages of the working classes and favor national and foreign capital. Because of their openness and need for internal legitimacy, democratic governments fall victim to numerous claims for shares of national resources; hence they become preoccupied with issues of distribution (expansion of government benefits and welfare policies) rather than accumulation. The consequence is that the allocation of national income is likely to be biased toward consumption and away from saving (Nelson 1987). More authoritarian regimes, in contrast, because of the absence of a political mechanism through which accountability can be demanded and because of their relative freedom to act coercively, can pursue policies that benefit a minority at the expense of the majority, and thereby foster the accumulation of needed capital. Such regimes are relatively unrestricted in their ability to squeeze surplus from some domestic groups in order to finance industrialization.

Finally, with respect to the third reason cited in support of the conflict perspective, a number of writers, including De Schweinitz (1964), Chirot (1977), and Cohen (1985), argue further that the unique domestic and international conditions complicate greatly the situation facing Third World nations in their development drives today. In contrast to the development experience of most European nations in the nineteenth century, the late developers need to implement distinct strategies because of differences in demographics, class structures, level of technological development, structures of finance, rural-urban dynamics, and transnational linkages, such as the multinational corporation. Under these different circumstances, it is argued that authoritarian regimes are better able to adopt appropriate national strategies because the state necessarily must play a more initiating and direct role under these new historical conditions. Thus, more autocratic governments are assumed to be better able to resist the influences of multinational businesses and "core" governments.

Hence, in general, proponents of the conflict model argue that in the world facing developing nations after World War II, those with a more authoritarian form of government will experience more rapid economic growth than will democratic regimes. One must say "in general" because at least two kinds of qualifications can be identified in the literature. These qualifications are not inconsistent with the claim stated above; rather they identify specific kinds of authoritarian regimes that are most capable of generating economic change for different types of developing countries.

One popular qualification of the general argument revolves around the proposed effects of military rule, as opposed to civilian rule, whether the latter happens to be more or less democratic. Such theorists as Pye (1966), Shils(1964), and Levy (1966) have argued that in developing countries military rule is a progressive force in society. The reasoning behind this argument is as follows. In modernizing societies, the military is unrivaled by any other organization in its ability to combine high levels of modernization with maximum levels of stability and control. The progressive consequences of military rule stem from the fact that alternative organizations are not only weak, but that the military, as one of the few avenues available for social mobility, attracts the most talented and confers on its members substantial experience with rational organization and sophisticated modern technology. Moreover, the military regularly recruits individuals of middle class background, and such individuals are more progressive in their policies than the prior entrenched ruling elites were.

It is important to note, however, that a number of theorists, for example, Bienen (1971) and Nordlinger (1970), have argued exactly the opposite. They charge that military rulers are too obsessed with maintaining order and power to act as modernizing agents. A sort of compromise is offered by Huntington who suggests that the effects of military rule depend on the degree of backwardness of the developing country: military rule has a progressive effect only at very low levels of socioeconomic development.

A second qualification of the general hypothesis has been put forth by O'Donnell (1979). He argues that because of the associated problems of delayed dependent industrialization, late industrializers already far along on the road to modernity can be greatly benefited by a specific type of authoritarian rule, bureaucratic-authoritarianism. More specifically, bureaucratic-authoritarian regimes are necessary to deepen import substitution from final demand goods to intermediate and capital goods. Only bureaucratic-authoritarian regimes (formed by a peculiar alliance of the military and technicians) are capable of freezing consumption and creating the policy predictability and political stability necessary to generate the preconditions for the kinds of long-term investments needed. Though the necessity of bureaucratic-authoritarianism on these grounds has been seriously questioned (see the essays in Collier 1979), Cohen (1985) argues that such regimes still possess an advantage in effectively implementing the kinds of austere orthodox policies necessary for industrialization to deepen more thoroughly and quickly.

In sum, then, while there is some disagreement among these theorists over which kind of authoritarian rule is best suited for which kinds of developing countries, they still share the contention that democracy hampers economic growth.

The Compatibility Perspective

Proponents of the democratic model sharply object to the charges levied by proponents of the authoritarian model. Although the compatibility model concedes that economic development requires an authority to enforce contracts, ensure law and order, and so on, they strongly disagree with the assumption that development needs to be commanded in all respects by a central authority, an assumption that takes a heavy toll in terms of citizen rights and freedoms (see Holt and Turner 1966). Moreover, even if one accepts the argument that latecomer nations in the post—World War II era need governmental structures that perform a wider range of functions and more heavily penetrate sectors of their societies than their Western counterparts did, we can still treat as analytically distinguishable the scope of state involvement and the democratic character of political institutions.

In addition, proponents of the democratic model challenge the authoritarian model on such assumptions as the propensity of the well off to save in a manner that is beneficial to the nation (Goodin 1979), the prevalence of distortions of economies in democracies (Goodin 1979), the degree of corruption in Third World democracies (McCord 1965), the tendency of democracy to foster internal divisiveness and conflict (see the evidence in Hibbs 1973 and Marsh 1979), and the cost of political competition to the accumulation of capital and scale of investment (Goodin 1979). Finally, in this model it is assumed that the redistributive tendencies of democracies, far from fueling useless consumption and thereby being a drain on growth, actually broaden markets and promote economic expansion.

Indeed, proponents of the democratic model are quick to point out numerous weaknesses of centralization under authoritarian rule. These weaknesses include a relative deprivation of the informal sector, a distorted size distribution of enterprises (the Barton gap), a tendency toward corruption and waste, a tendency to transform conflicts normal to the development process into larger confrontations, and a limited capacity of the center to handle problems in the periphery of society. Moreover, as Nelson (1987) notes, democratic regimes have no monopoly on internally inconsistent policies, policies that vacillate over time, or policy paralysis, since sharp factional or ideological disputes within regime circles or among fairly narrow participatory groups can paralyze a regime effectively as can highly mobilized and conflicting mass groups. Finally, King (1981) charges that the kind of development strategy so frequently adopted under authoritarian rule, capital-intensive development, is unbalanced and detrimental not only to the rural sector but to the society as a whole in the long-run.

Some proponents of the democratic model, however, do not stop at simply taking issue with the assumptions of the authoritarian model. Indeed, such theorists as McCord (1965), Goodin (1979), King (1981), Goodell and Powelson (1982), and Kohli (1986) argue that it is a democratic government in the Third World that is best suited to foster sustained and equitable economic development. In their view, democratic processes and the existence and exercise of fundamental civil liberties and political rights generate the societal conditions most conducive to economic development.

Goodin (1979) and Goodell and Powelson (1982) argue that economic pluralism is essential for economic growth. In other words, a requisite of economic growth is a condition where members are free to accrue and dispense their resources within the marketplace. Only under this condition of economic pluralism will the most innovative and competitive technologies emerge.

Central to this model is the argument that political pluralism is critical to the survival and vitality of economic pluralism. Goodell and Powelson argue that economic pluralism depends on open competition and predictability. In their view, only when the political system is organized according to democratic rules and mechanisms and citizens have fundamental safeguards against governmental intrusion do conditions conducive to competition and predictability exist.

Overall, the extension and protection of civil liberties and basic freedoms are thought to generate the security of expectation necessary to motivate citizens to work, save, and invest (Claude 1976). In addition, popular political participation not only has the consequence of breaking down the privilege and vested interests of a few but also feeds a participative mentality that carries over into the economic arena and greatly increases the flow of information so essential to effective and efficient governments. In sum, political pluralism acts to release energies and foster conditions conducive to change, entrepreneurial risk, and economic development.

Proponents of the compatibility perspective hold that, at most, only limited trade offs are necessary between democracy and economic development. Indeed, proponents of this model view democracy and development as very much compatible, actually working to support one another. Among the proponents there is the sentiment that although authoritarian rule may, on some occasions, generate a more rapid rate of economic development in the short run, democratic rule is more conducive to a sustained, sectorially balanced, and equitable growth in the long run. Hence repression is viewed as not being necessary for growth, but only to protect a particular inequitable distribution of resources and power.

The Skeptical Perspective

Finally, we would like to briefly mention an alternative stance that some theorists have taken toward the issue of the consequences of democracy for economic growth. This alternative stance is skeptical that there is any systematic relationship between democracy and economic development (see Pye 1966). In other words, politics alone matter very little. Proponents of this perspective note the variable nature of levels of economic performance within groupings of more democratic and more autrhoritarian regimes and suggest that this variability indicates that we need to concentrate instead on the institutional structures that exist and the government strategies that are embraced, factors that may vary independently of the democratic character of a system, and how these can act to reconcile such development goals as democracy and development. Such factors include, for example, the nature of the political party system (two-party vs. multiparty), the level and form of state intervention into the economy, the pattern of industrialization pursued (labor-intensive vs. capital-intensive), and the cultural environment (see Huntington 1987). Hence, the skepticism in this perspective derives from the contention that additional, often intervening, factors operate to confound the direct link between democracy and development.

The Effects of Democracy on Inequality

With respect to the consequences of political democracy for socioeconomic inequality, we again find the positions of theorists divided. Regarding this relationship, the source of that division, which is obviously very much related to that of the foregoiong discussion, is the question of whether democracy operates to reduce inequality, exacerbate inequality, or simply has no systematic influence. In the following section these various positions are referred to as the ''Democratic Model,'' the ''Authoritarian Model,'' and the ''Skeptical Model,'' respectively.

Democratic Model

Oddly enough, many proponents of either the conflict or the compatibility perspectives, as discussed in reference to the consequences of democracy for economic growth, converge on the position that political democracy operates to reduce distributional inequalities. The reasoning behind this convergence is essentially twofold. On the one hand, democracy is viewed to facilitate equality indirectly because economic development itself is argued to aggravate inequalities (Kuznets 1955), at least up to a point, and democracies are argued by proponents of the conflict perspective to be less able to achieve rapid economic growth.

On the other hand, proponents of the compatibility perspective emphasize the same outcome for different reasons. Democracies are conceived to tend to neither adopt economic growth policies that directly attempt to deprive specific social groups of their relative economic shares nor are they free to ignore the voices of mobilized sectors of the population due to their legitimacy needs. Because of electoral mechanisms and rights to opposition and participation, democracies are relatively open to battles over the distribution of societal resources (Lipset 1959). And since these institutional underpinnings aid a shift in political power away from the most well-off and toward the middle classes and poorer segments of society, democratic regimes must be responsive to claims from the latter sectors as well. The consequence of all of this is the likelihood of lower distributional inequalities within democratic developing nations than within authoritarian developing nations. In short, as Lenski (1966) argues, given the existence of an egalitarian political structure, it is plausible to expect that, over time, as the more numerous poorer members of the population organize into unions and other interest groups, and as parties of the social democratic Left develop a solid electoral base, win seats in legislatures, and participate in or control the machinery of government, democracy becomes facilitative of gradual reduction of economic inequality.

Authoritarian Model

The relatively popular democratic model just presented is not, however, uniformly accepted. Beitz (1982), for one, disagrees. For Beitz, authoritarian regimes are more likely to pursue egalitarian development policies than are democratic regimes. Central to his argument is the contention that authoritarian regimes may do a better job of protecting the interests of the poor and working classes in developing societies than democracies can. Why? Because the available political rights and their expression through electoral mechanisms cannot be taken advantage of by the more disadvantaged elements of society. In other words, inequalities in the distribution of material resources are reproduced in inequalities of political influence. Thus, although Beitz accepts the view that democracies are more receptive to claims made by societal members, he contends that democracies fail to respect their members equally as sources of claims. Moreover, the disadvantaged are unable to defend their interest through democratic processes. In contrast, authoritarian regimes are more capable of protecting interests unlikely to be protected by democracies.

Huntington and Nelson (1976), while supporting the logic of Beitz' argument to a degree, nevertheless qualify his reasoning by contending that since more privileged groups usually become politically active earlier than the less privileged, then it might well be the case that at most there is a curvilinear relationship between levels of participation and equality. Still, however, this pattern of relationship depends on how much, and how effectively, the less privileged strata exercise the opportunity to participate relative to participation by the "haves." Finally, Bollen and Jackman (1985) also question whether democracies tend to be better for equality. In particular, they question whether democracies adhere to majoritarianism, whether low-income voters demand redistribution—especially given the government intervention it requires—and whether inequality is even perceived as being unjust.

Skeptical Model

The two schools of thought most frequently cited as representatives of the skeptical model are functionalists and Marxists. As Marsh (1979) argued in his review of the "skeptical model," functionalism implies that the form of government does not affect the stratification system, since any changes in the distributive outcomes are explained as a result of changes in the shape of the occupational structure brought on by the imperatives of industrialization. Any association between democracy and socioeconomic equality is spurious since both are determined by the level of a nation's economic development.

Alternatively, Marxists hold that the political system is largely of little importance. What is important is the particular configuration of the class structure, and, in particular, the economic power of the capitalist class. To understand the "why" of the distribution of inequalities and changes in distribution, one must understand the class structure and dynamics.

Finally, Nelson (1987) suggests that we should be skeptical in embracing any universal relationship between extended patterns of political participation, or democracy, and equality, since the pattern of participation may play an important intervening role. Particularly crucial may be the relative participation rates of urban versus rural populations in developing countries.

State of Empirical Research

The Effects of Democracy on Economic Development

Thirteen cross-national, quantitative studies have been reviewed in the course of our work. Each of these studies explicitly attempted to evaluate the economic consequences of differences in the democratic character of national regimes. The studies reviewed are contained in Table 1.

Out of these thirteen studies only three—Huntington and Dominguez (1975), Marsh (1979), and Landau (1986)—report findings suggesting an unqualified negative effect of democracy on rates of economic growth. Six studies—Feierabend and Feierabend (1972), Dick (1974), Russett and Monsen (1975), Meyer et al. (1979),

TABLE 1

Adelman and Morris (1967)
Feierabend and Feierabend (1972)
Dick (1974)
Huntington and Dominguez (1975)
Russett and Monsen (1975)
Marsh (1979)
Meyer et al. (1979)
Weede (1983)
Berg-Schlosser (1984)
Kohli (1986)
Landau (1986)
Sloan and Tedin (1987)
Marsh (1988)

Kohli (1986), and Marsh (1988)—report that there is no relationship between the democratic character of regimes and the pace of economic growth. Finally, each of the remaining four studies report some kind of qualified, or conditional, relationship. For example, Adelman and Morris (1967) report that democracy appears to inhibit growth, but not among the wealthier less-developed countries. Weede (1983) reports the existence of a negative relationship only when developed countries and less-developed countries are both included in the analysis (no effect when less-developed countries are examined alone), and also in those societies in which the role of the state in economic affairs is decidedly larger. Both Berg-Schlosser (1984) and Sloan and Tedin (1987), in contrast, report that the type of regime matters, that is, there are real differences among regime types, but the pattern of these differences depends on the particular measure of economic progress examined.

Hence, overall, these studies present a very mixed and confusing picture with regard to the effect of democracy on economic growth. The inconclusive results presented by these studies are further compounded by the fact that these studies are quite heterogeneous with respect to characteristics of measurement, coverage, design, and method of analysis.

One of the most systematic deficiencies to be found in these studies is the misspecification of the economic growth model. Only in the studies by Adelman and Morris (1967), Meyer et al. (1979), Weede (1983), Landau (1986), and Marsh (1988) is there any attempt to include as controls a number of factors known to affect economic growth. Indeed, clearly in seven of the studies: Feierabend and Feierabend, Dick, Huntington and Dominguez, Russett and Monsen, Marsh (1979), Kohli, and Sloan and Tedin, either no other factors were specified as influencing economic growth in the analysis or the analysis was badly underspecified. Such factors as initial level of development, the availability of human capital, the availability of internal investment, population growth, and so on must be properly specified in the analysis and thus controlled for in order for estimates of the effect of democracy to be at all meaningful. Nevertheless, even among the five studies identified as being the most adequate with respect to model specification, rather discrepant results were found.

TABLE 2
Wide Survey of LDCs

Adelman and Morris (1967) conditional	(N = 74)
Dick (1974) none	(N = 72)
Huntington and Dominguez (1975) negative	(N = 35)
Marsh (1979) negative	(N = 80)
Meyer et al. (1979) none	(N = 23)
Weede (1983) none	(N = 74)
Landau (1986) negative	(N = 65)
Marsh (1988) none	(N = 55)

Survey of DCs and LDCs

Feierabend and Feierabend (1972) none	(N = 84)
Russett and Monsen (1975) none	(N = 80)
Meyer et al. (1979) none	(N = 50)
Weede (1983) negative	(N = 93)

Survey of Select LDCs only

Kohli (1986) none	(N = 10)
Sloan and Tedin (1987) conditional	(N = 20, all L.A.)
Berg-Schlosser (1984) conditional	(N = 38, all African)

A second feature that could account for the discrepancies in the results obtained is the set of countries examined. Besides substantial variation in the number of countries examined, some looked at a set including both developed and developing nations, some surveyed less-developed countries only, and several examined only a select group of less-developed countries. The exact composition of the set of countries analyzed in each study is presented in Table 2, along with a notation on the major result found in each study for the relationship between democracy and economic growth.

As the Table 2 indicates, there has indeed been a substantial amount of variation in the number and set of countries examined. Moreover, an examination of the results reported by each of these studies indicates that there is no clear association between the population of countries observed and the major finding. Unfortunately, there has been little effort to replicate studies and thereby enhance our knowledge in the area in a cumulative fashion.

A third factor that may account for the differences in findings is the period for which economic performance was assessed. Roughly speaking, three broad periods were investigated: studies assessing economic performance for a period beginning before 1960 and ending by 1965; studies assessing economic performance for a period roughly equivalent to the decade of the sixties; and, finally, studies assessing economic performance for a period beginning in the sixties and ending in the early eighties. The exact period of each of the studies is described in Table 3.

If we categorize the twelve studies according to the appropriate period and then examine the findings reported, does any pattern emerge? Again the answer would have to be no. No systematic relationship appears between the period examined and the results.

A final feature of these studies that we can examine is how each measured democracy. How did each go about distinguishing types of political regimes? Two

TABLE 3
Period Examined Ends by 1965
Adelman and Morris (1976) conditional
Feierabend and Feierabend (1972) none
Huntington and Dominguez (1975) negative
Russett and Monsen (1975) none
Period Examined ends by 1970
Dick (1974) none
Marsh (1979) negative
Meyer et al. (1979) none
Period Examined ends by the early 1980s
Weede (1983) conditional
Kohli (1986) none
Landau (1986) negative
Sloan and Tedin (1987) conditional
Berg-Schlosser (1984) conditional
Marsh (1988) none

characteristics of the measure used seem relevant here. The first is whether the characteristic of the regime was measured at basically a single point in time for a country (''point measurement'') or was assessed for a period of time (''period measurement''). The measurement of a political characteristic such as democracy at a single point in time (or over an interval of time shorter in length than the period over which the dependent variable is observed) suffers from severe weaknesses. Most important is the fact that the point measurement method makes no allowances for subsequent changes which may necessitate substantially altering how a country is classified or rated in terms of democracy. Therefore, in order to use the strategy of point measurement one must be willing to assume that a country's political regime was accurately characterized by the same value or classification throughout the entire period during which the dependent variable is being assessed. The longer this period is, the more likely this assumption would be violated, especially in the case of Third World nations. In addition, unless one is willing to make some rather heroic assumptions about the exact length of the lag with respect to the effects of the political characteristic, the point measurement technique again falls far short of adequacy.

Overall, seven of the studies reviewed employed the point measurement technique (Adelman and Morris, Feierabend and Feierabend, Russett and Monsen, Marsh (1979, 1988), Meyer et al., and Weede). Though there is no apparent pattern to the findings of these six, the weaknesses of point measurement cast a shadow over their results. In fact, none of the authors of these seven studies make any claims about having taken political changes into account in any manner.

Period measurement of political characteristics stands in sharp contrast to point measurement. Strictly speaking, period measurement refers to the technique by which democratic characteristics are assessed for exactly the same period for which the dependent variable is assessed. This could be accomplished in either of two ways. First, one could make annual measurements of both the democratic measure and the dependent variable, as well as any other variables, and thus obtain time-series data. Alternatively, one could explicitly take steps to examine only those countries which, in terms of the investigator's rating or classification scheme, were consistent over the course of the period examined. Of these two alternatives, the first has considerably more advantages. The chief weakness of the second alternative is that it confuses stability with the characteristics of the political regime by including only those that are, for example, stable democracies or stable nondemocracies

The studies conducted by Dick, Huntington and Dominguez, Kohli, Landau, Sloan and Tedin, and Berg-Schlosser all indicate that they have employed a kind of period measurement. However, except for the effort by Sloan and Tedin, all five of the others opted for the second alternative. For example, Dick (1974) writes that his regime classification scheme, ". . . reflects the general political state of a country during the 1960s," which was the period of his analysis. Either these authors created a classification based on the average political characteristics of a nation's regime across an interval of time—as apparently Dick and Landau did—or they excluded or assigned to a distinct category those countries that substantially changed in terms of their regime characteristics. The latter is apparently the case for the efforts by Huntington and Dominguez, Berg-Schlosser, and Kohli. By pursuing the latter course, the political measures used confound democracy with stability. As Bollen (1980) notes, the problem with implicitly or explicitly including stability in the measure of democracy—something that Lipset (1959), Cutright (1963), Smith (1969), Coulter (1975), and Hewitt (1977) all do in their measures—is that it and its effects are analytically and empirically distinguishable from democracy and the latter's effects.

Only Sloan and Tedin employ the first alternative of period measurement. They classified twenty Latin American countries annually for the period 1960 through 1980. Their exact regime classification scheme will be discussed more fully in this article.

Overall, the thirteen studies examined here are fairly evenly split with respect to whether the procedure they employed to measure democracy, or a related regime attribute, was point or period. By dividing the set of studies into these two groups, it is obvious that the attribute of measurement being considered is not sufficient alone to begin to explain the disparities in findings reported. But perhaps more important is the fact that only one study adopted a procedure that, in our opinion, does not suffer from as many weaknesses as the others.

A second feature of the measures of political characteristics used in these studies relates to their operationalizations of democracy. Each of the studies reviewed here sought to identify some characteristic(s) of democracy and then to rate or classify the political regimes of a set of countries based on an operationalization of those characteristics. In terms of the methods of operationalization, either a single scale was developed consisting of numerical ratings or a typology with more or less discrete categories was adopted. This quantitative-qualitative distinction in operationalization parallels the point-period measurement distinction made earlier, with all of the studies employing point measurement also employing a quantitative operationalization. This, however, is by no means a necessary association.

TABLE 4
Scales Used by Quantitative Operationalizations

Adelman and Morris (1967)	Index of the Strength of Democratic Institutions, 1957–62 (4 pt. scale)
Feierabend and Feierabend (1972)	Index of Regime Coerciveness, 1948–60 (6 pt. scale)
Russett and Monsen (1975)	Taylor and Hudson's Electoral Regularity Scale (3 pt. scale)
Marsh (1979)	1) Bollen's Index of Democracy, 1965 2) Bank's Political Competition Index, 1962–66
Meyer et al. (1979)	1) Cutright's Formal Political Representation Index, 1950–55 2) Adelman and Morris' Index of Political Participation, 1957–62
Weede (1983)	Bollen's Index of Democracy, 1965
Marsh (1988)	1) Sum of Gastil's Political Rights Ratings, 1973–79 2) Sum of Gastil's Civil Liberties Ratings, 1973–79

With regard to the seven studies employing a scale of one kind or another, it is important to realize that each of the scales used is only ordinal in nature. This fact is important, because, in each of these studies, the scales are treated in the analysis as if they are interval-level in nature. Although it may well be the case that ordinal information is the only kind available to use in the construction of the scales, they are still ordinal-level. And no effort is made in these studies to examine what consequences this may have for the kinds of statistical analyses carried out.

The particular operationalizations used in each of the seven studies are described in Table 4.

Finally, we can consider the six remaining studies which rely on qualitative discriminations of regime types. The respective classification schemes of each of these studies are listed in Table 5.

As is made clear by Table 5, only Landau and Kohli adopted a simple dichotomy. In essence, the typologies of Landau, Kohli, and Dick are dichotomous or trichotomous breakdowns of ordinal rankings. The other three studies that employ a categorical indicator of regime type sought to discriminate among regimes in a more qualitative sense. For example, Huntington and Dominguez, Sloan and Tedin, and Berg-Schlosser each assigned Communist-Socialist nations to a distinct category. In addition, each of these also assigned to a distinct category those nations whose political regimes were unstable, though they did so in varying ways: Berg-Schlosser and Huntington and Dominguez seem to have decided, after looking at the entire regime histories for the relevant period of study for their set of nations, to assign to a separate category any nations which were judged as more or less mixed due to regime changes. In effect, this excludes these nations, and the other categories include only countries with relatively stable regimes of one kind or another. Sloan and Tedin, with their "transitional" category, took a strikingly different, and we

TABLE 5
Categorical Operationalizations

Dick (1974)	1) Authoritarian
	2) Semicompetitive
	3) Competitive
Huntington and Dominguez (1975)	1) One-party Communist
	2) One-party Non-Communist
	3) Competitive Party System
	4) Unstable System
Kohli (1986)	Dichotomization based on Bollen's Index
	of Democracy (Democratic-Authoritarian)
Landau (1986)	1) Democratic
	2) Non-democratic
Sloan and Tedin (1987)	1) Democratic
	2) Bureaucratic-Authoritarian
	3) Communist
	4) Traditional Authoritarian
	5) Transitional
Berg-Schlosser (1984)	1) Stable Polyarchic
	2) Stable Socialist
	3) Stable Authoritarian
	4) Praetorian

believe superior, approach. Since Sloan and Tedin took annual observations, a nation's regime was coded as "transitional" only for the year in which it changed. Thereafter, it was coded with the new regime code until it again changed.

In terms of the substantive distinctions among the regime types coded, each of these investigators sought to at least single out one category that conforms, more or less, to what a democracy would be. Central to nearly all of the typologies used in the six studies is the political party structure and the meaningfulness of elections (what criteria Landau used for discriminating between democracies and nondemocracies is unclear because he never formally states them nor even offers a basic conceptual distinction). This is clearly the case for the typologies constructed by Dick and Huntington and Dominguez (with the addition of a Communist-Socialist dimension). The typologies constructed by Berg-Schlosser and Sloan and Tedin also obviously consider the structure of the party system and the role of elections, though both include a number of additional dimensions. For instance, Berg-Schlosser names as other major system characteristics the following: basis of legitimacy, head of executive branch, degree of vertical and horizontal power separation, scope of regime control, and ideological orientation. The problem with Berg-Schlosser's effort, however, is that, having once stated this large number of dimensions, he employs what he describes as a "handmade factor analysis" in order to combine and reduce the dimensions down to four types of regimes. Not only does this preclude the possibility of replicating his procedure, it gives us little insight into how his dimensions were actually weighted (and it is obvious they were) in order to arrive at final classifications.

The study by Sloan and Tedin is unique because these investigators attempted to differentiate the more authoritarian end of the democracy/nondemocracy dimension by separating out not only Communist nations but also by differentiating what they label as bureaucratic-authoritarian regimes from traditional authoritarian regimes. Such an approach as this seems to possess a number of advantages, since implicitly when the claim is made that authoritarian-led nations will develop more quickly, those making the claim generally appear to have in mind the bureaucratic-authoritarian type of regime. Moreover, a good case could be made that lumping all nondemocratic regimes into a single category might well inhibit the uncovering of political effects. Unfortunately, in their article, Sloan and Tedin never formally state how they went about assigning national regimes to one or the other category, a guide which would be necessary if one wished to build on their analysis by expanding the coverage.

Before moving on to a review of the set of studies that had income distribution as their dependent variable, we would briefly like to review six studies that focused on the specific effects of military rule, a special kind of nondemocratic regime. These six studies include Nordlinger (1970), McKinlay and Cohan (1975), Jackman (1976), Dickson (1977), Pluta (1979), and Ravenhill (1980). Overall, these six studies, like the twelve discussed earlier, suffer from significant differences in coverage, measurement, and analysis technique. As a consequence, the results of these studies taken together yield few firm conclusions.

Nevertheless, these efforts are noteworthy because, besides attempting to identify significant differences between military and civilian regimes, almost without exception each of these studies examined a wide array of dependent variables (regime outputs and outcomes). In other words, they tended to go beyond a simple comparison of economic growth rates and also looked at changes in the quality of life and changes in the distribution of societal resources as indicated by government spending patterns.

If anything can be concluded from these studies, and any conclusion must be made cautiously, it is that civilian regimes as compared to military regimes appear to do better in terms of improving the basic quality of life of the masses of citizens and in improving the distribution of access to such societal benefits as health facilities and schools. Overall, this suggests that in our research effort we might be very well served by identifying different classes of outcomes and outputs for examination.

The Effects of Democracy on Inequality

Cross-national, quantitative research on the effect of democracy on societal inequality has come to form more of a research program than has research on the effects of democracy on economic growth. Surprisingly, however, the relevant studies are inconclusive. Twelve relevant studies are reviewed in this section. Included are studies performed by Cutright (1967), Jackman (1975), Hewitt (1977), Rubinson and Quinlan (1977), Stack (1979), Stack (1980), Bollen and Grandjean (1981), Weede and Tiefenbach (1981), Weede (1982), Kohli and Associates (1984), Bollen

TABLE 6

Yes	No
Cutright (1967)	Jackman (1975)
Hewitt (1977)	Rubinson and Quinlan (1977)
Stack (1979)	Bollen and Grandjean (1981)
Stack (1980)	Kohli et al. (1984)
Weede and Tiefenbach (1981)	Bollen and Jackman (1985)
Weede (1982)	
Muller (1988)	

and Jackman (1985), and Muller (1988). In each of these studies the indicator of social equality is the distribution of income.

Have these studies found support for a negative effect of democracy on societal inequality as Lenski (1966) and many other have predicted? As Table 6 shows, no clear answer to this question has emerged from these studies.

As can be seen above, seven of the studies present evidence indicating confirmation for the inverse relationship between democracy and societal inequality, where inequality is measured by the distribution of income. Their support, however, must be qualified. Cutright, after assigning nations to subgroups based upon level of economic development, found confirmation for the low and middle income subsets of nations, but not for the most advanced subset. Weede and Tiefenbach found confirmation of the inverse relationship for two measures of personal income inequality (using Paukert's data 1973), but not for four alternative measures of income inequality from two different sources. Hewitt found a negative correlation for his indicator of political democracy and income inequality, though he argues that it is social democracy (meaning the strength of Socialist parties or working-class politics within the lawmaking bodies), rather than political democracy, that is important. Finally, Muller presents results that would indicate it is the length of experience of democracy, rather than the level of political democracy as measured at one point in time, that facilitates reductions in inequality.

The five studies that indicate a disconfirmation of the proposed linkage report either that there is no significant relationship, in either a positive or negative direction, between political democracy and societal inequality or that the line of causation properly modeled actually runs in the opposite direction. The investigations of Jackman (1975) and Bollen and Grandjean (1981) each found nonsignificant effects of political democracy on societal inequality. Rubinson and Quinlan (1977) report that once the reciprocal effects between the two variables are explicitly taken into consideration, something that had not been examined before their study, the only signigicant direction of effects lies in the opposite direction (i.e., inequality affects democracy). In a more recent study, however, Bollen and Jackman (1985) reexamined the argument of Rubinson and Quinlan and found no significant effects between democracy and inequality in either direction. Muller (1988), however, reports that whereas length of democratic experience appears to facilitate significantly greater levels of income equality, he found no support for the "genesis" version of the causal impact of inequality on the inauguration of democracy.

Where do these studies leave us? It is clear that while no generalizable and robust confirmation of the thesis that democracy promotes greater equality is forthcoming from this set of studies, the issue is by no means settled. Numerous differences in design, measurement, and model distinguish these studies, which alone or in combination might account for the kinds of results they have produced.

The first of these differences that can be considered is how social equality was measured. Each of these studies attempted to measure social equality by assessing the degree of concentration of the distribution of income, or some proxy for it. The difficulties in accurately measuring the distribution of income are widely known. Information on income distribution is confounded by global heterogeneity in its standards of collection, which makes international comparisons exceedingly difficult. Some of the sources of this heterogeneity include whether the income figures are pretax or posttax, whether the data are based on households or individuals (though the efforts of Bollen and Jackman (1985) and Muller (1988) attempt to control for this confounding factor in their analyses), and whether the income figures are representative of the nation as a whole or refer only to certain regions or cities.

These data problems are yet further complicated by the fact that there are a number of data sources available (for example, Paukert, Ahluwalia, the World Bank), and these sources, although overlapping to some extent in years reported and nations covered, are still distinguishable in terms of coverage and some of the figures reported. Hence it matters whose measure one happens to be using. This has been vividly demonstrated by Weede and Tiefenbach who found confirmation using the data reported by Paukert (1973), but disconfirmation using the data of Ahluwalia (1976), though the two sources also differ somewhat in the nations covered.

Finally, one of the most serious obstacles to research on the link between democracy and income inequality continues to be the relative absence of data at more than one point in time. This forces research designs to be cross-sectional, which gives one very little leverage in addressing questions posed in dynamic terms. Efforts to piece together two points of inequality data, as only Kohli and associates attempted, to support at least a simple panel design are besieged by problems of comparability.

It is also important to remember that the dates the income inequality figures refer to in existing data banks vary across nations. Only Rubinson and Quinlan sought to explicitly match the dates for all of their variables in an effort to control for this possible weakness (they then included a control variable in their analysis, the value of which was the year the values were coded for). None of the other ten studies adopted this strategy. How much error is introduced in a cross-sectional design by having one variable measured in 1960 and another measured in 1965 is difficult to estimate, but it certainly would seem necessary in instances of discrepancies of a few years or more to make some effort to be reasonably sure that the discrepancy is not confounding the results.

In the set of twelve studies under review, only two, Cutright (1967) and Jackman (1975), did not use some measure of personal or household income distribution.

TABLE 7
Source of Personal/Household Income Distrib. Data

Paukert (1973)	Other
Stack (1980)	Weede (1982) (World Bank)
Bollen and Grandjean (1981)	Kohli et al. (1984) (World Bank)
Hewitt (1977)	Weede and Tiefenbach (1981)
	(Ahluwalia, Ballmer-Cao)
Rubinson and Quinlan (1977)	Bollen and Jackman (1985)
	(World Bank, Ahluwalia, Jain)
	(replicated with Paukert data)
Weede and Tiefenbach (1981)	Muller (1988) (Ahluwalia, Jain,
	World Bank, Lecaillon et al.,
	Paukert, Sawyer, UNECLA)

Specific Measure of Personal/Household Income Distrib. Used

Hewitt (1977)	1) Income share to top 5%: −
	2) Income share to top 20%: 0
Rubinson and Quinlan (1977)	1) Gini coefficient: 0
	2) Income share to middle 20%: 0
Stack (1979)	Gini coefficient: −
Stack (1980)	Gini coefficient: −
Bollen and Grandjean (1981)	Gini coefficient: 0
Weede and Tiefenbach (1981)	Paukert: Share to bottom 40%: +
	Share to top 20%: −
	Gini coefficient: −
	Ahluwalia: Share to bottom 40%: 0
	Share to top 20%: 0
	Ballmer-Cao: Gini coefficient: 0
Weede (1982)	1) Income share to top 20%: −
	2) Income share to bottom 40%: +
Kohli et al. (1984)	Difference (1970–1960) of ratios of income share to top 5% to share to bottom 20%: 0
Bollen and Jackman (1985)	Ratio of income share of top 20% to income share of bottom 40%: 0
Muller (1988)	1) Income share of upper quintile: −
	2) Gini coefficient: −

(symbol after the colon indicates whether negative (−) effect or no (0) effect found using that particular measure)

Instead, these two investigators used a measure of the distribution of income across industrial sectors. As Bollen and Jackman (1985) point out, this latter measure is only an imperfect proxy for personal income distribution and may well be analytically and empirically distinguishable.

The remaining ten studies used some explicit measure of personal or household income distribution, but as a set they exhibit considerable variability with respect to the source of that data and with regard to which particular measures of income distribution they examined.

As the listings in Table 7 indicate, the importance of which source of data or which particular measure was used does not seem sufficient to explain discrepancies in the findings of these studies, though they are certainly important in and of themselves. The state of data gathering on income distribution continues to be in turmoil, though Bollen and Jackman (1985) suggest that the more recent efforts and compilations of the World Bank are improving the situation.

In light of these weaknesses, a profitable area for future research is to investigate the construction of alternative indicators that have the virtue of being highly correlated with existing inequality measures, but which are available on a time-series basis and are based on information gathered according to standards that are much more comparable internationally. Such a measure might be along the lines of Morris' (1979) physical quality of life index.

Along these lines two additional studies are particuarly noteworthy. Williamson (1987) examined in cross-sectional analysis the effect of the level of political democracy, using Bollen's measure, on the physical quality of life index for eighty developing countries. He found only very weak, insignificant effects of political democracy on such an alternative indicator of welfare outputs broadly conceived. Similarly, Williamson and Pampel (1986) when estimating the lagged effects of a host of variables on still yet another welfare output indicator—in this case social security effort as measured by the percentage of GNP expended on five categories of social security programs—found that the level of political democracy, again indicated by Bollen's measure, significantly facilitated the expansion of a nation's social security effort for a sample of industrialized nations (N = 26), but found no effect within the only subsample (N = 32) of developing countries. Williamson and Pampel interpret this pattern of findings as substantiating the ideas of Lenski (1966): Democracy will have a greater effect on the distribution of societal resources in those nations with a greater economic surplus. A more recent effort on their part (Pampel and Williamson 1988), which is limited to examining the effect of two indicators of democracy—percentage of the eligible population actually voting, and electoral competition—on change in the social security efforts of eighteen advanced societies, found further support for their conclusions.

These results, however, stand in conflict with those of Moon and Dixon (1985). In their cross-sectional analysis of the correlates of physical quality of life levels in approximately 115 nations (both MDCs and LDCs), they found that the level of political democracy (as measured by an average of Bollen's 1960 and 1965 codings of political democracy) had a strong, positive impact on the PQLI index net of such other factors as level of economic development, government expenditures as a proportion of national product, and the ideological norms of the ruling regime. On the basis of their finding, Moon and Dixon argue that the provision of basic needs as policy outputs responds to representational processes.

Beyond the factors already considered, what other factors might be affecting the discrepant findings evident in the set of a dozen studies under consideration? Three issues which have been noted in the literature (see Weede 1982; Bollen and Jackman 1985) are the model specification of the relationship between level of economic development and the measure of inequality, the possibility of reciprocal effects between democracy and inequality, and the composition of the sets of nations included in the respective data bases. We will turn briefly to each of these.

First both Kuznets (1955) and Lenski (1966) have argued that the relationship between economic development and inequality follows a nonlinear (inverted U) form. However, only five of the studies have specified this form of the relationship in the models they have tested (Bollen and Grandjean, Weede and Tiefenbach, Weede, Bollen and Jackman, and Muller). Though it is obviously important to include the correct specification, the presence or absence of a nonlinear relationship cannot alone explain the discrepant findings: two of the five studies that did specify a curvilinear relationship report a negative relationship between democracy and income inequality; two report no relationship; and one, Muller, reports a negative effect of democratic experience on inequality but no independent effect of the mere level of political democracy, as measured by Bollen's indicator, on inequality.

With regard to the possibility of reciprocal effects between democracy and inequality, only three studies, those by Rubinson and Quinlan, Bollen and Jackman, and Muller, have explicitly tested this possibility. In the kind of cross-sectional research being conducted on this issue, it is important to estimate a simultaneous-equations model in order to be relatively certain that a simple recursive model, where the only allowed effect is from democracy to inequality, is not yielding misleading results. Both of these studies found no effect of democracy on income inequality

A third characteristic of these studies that must be considered in both interpreting the contradictory results of existing studies and developing an alternative indicator is that of sample composition. Because of the general scarcity of data on inequality, most of the studies examined here performed their analysis on an average of about a third of existing nations. The details of the composition of the sets of countries analyzed are presented in Table 8.

TABLE 8
Sets of Countries Examined in the Studies

DCs and LDCs

Stack (1980) negative	(N = 37)
Weede (1982) negative	(N = 21)
Bollen and Jackman (1985) none	(N = 60)
Jackman (1975) none	(N = 60)
Bollen and Grandjean (1981) none	(N = 50)
Rubinson and Quinlan (1977) none	(N = 32)
Weede and Tiefenbach (1981) negative	(N = 34–46)
Cutright (1967) negative	(N = 44)
Muller (1988) negative	(N = 50–55)

DCs only

Stack (1979) negative	(N = 18)
Hewitt (1977) negative	(N = 25, 2 LDCs)

LDCs only

Kohli et al. (1984) none	(N = 20)

TABLE 9
Used Bollen's Index of Democracy

Bollen and Grandjean (1981) none
Weede (1982) negative
Kohli et al. (1984) none
Bollen and Jackman (1985) none (replicated with a voter turnout measure)
Muller (1988) none

Used Jackman's Index of Democratic Performance

Jackman (1975) none
Rubinson and Quinlan (1977) none
Stack (1980) negative
Weede and Tiefenbach (1981) negative

Other Measures

Cutright (1967) negative (Cutright's Political Represen. Index, 1945–54)
Hewitt (1977) negative (yrs. of full democracy)
Rubinson and Quinlan (1977) none (Cutright's Political Represen. Index, 1945–54)
Stack (1979) negative (voter turnout as % adult pop.)
Weede (1982) negative (voter turnout as % adult pop.)
Muller (1988) negative (length of experience of democracy)

How far does the variation in composition of the sets of countries analyzed go toward explaining the pattern of results found? The answer is largely unknown. Obviously the differences in the sizes of the sets of countries analyzed could have had profound consequences for the results found. The sizes of many of these studies make them extremely sensitive to the inclusion or exclusion of just a few cases. Although Bollen and Jackman (1985) undertook the only effort to estimate whether their results would hold up under a check for outliers and replications with random subsamples, the fact remains that their sample was neither a random sample of all countries nor is its size large enough for us to place complete confidence in it. In addition, the issue remains as to whether the analysis should contain both developed countries and developing countries or only the latter.

A final feature of the studies being reviewed in this section that warrants attention is how democracy was measured in each. Table 9 lists the different measures used.

Again, as made obvious by Table 9, differences in the particular measure used cannot alone begin to explain the discrepancies on findings. Indeed, as is pointed out in the following section, most measures of political democracy tend to be fairly strongly intercorrelated.

Before leaving this topic, however, it must be noted that the use of voter turnout measures as an indicator of political democracy may well be quite unsatisfactory. Voter turnout data were used by both Stack and Weede in two of the studies above, and voter turnout is a component of Jackman's Democratic Performance Indicator which, in turn, was used in four studies. The problems with voter participation data are many-fold and are aptly described by Bollen (1980). Indeed, Bollen found that a measure of the percentage of the adult population who voted was either not related to or inversely related to a number of other dimensions of political democracy. Hence, its use probably only further confounds the results.

All in all, the twelve studies on the relationship between democracy and inequality reviewed here are striking in the fact that they provide us with a very weak foundation for concluding anything about the theoretically interesting link. Perhaps the best work to date is that of Bollen and Jackman (1985). Nonetheless, even this study does not escape the problems caused by the quality of the income distribution data, the lack of fuller global coverage, the validity of their measurement of democracy, and, perhaps, most important, the lack of a dynamic form of analysis.

Summary

When all is said and done, what can we conclude with confidence about the development consequences of political democracy? Even though the theoretical literature on the subject is rich and exciting, cross-national quantitative efforts to test the various hypotheses have fallen far short in their effort to yield clear grounds for rejecting or accepting many of the claims made. Almost twenty years of research efforts on the issues of economic growth and socioeconomic equality have produced few if any robust conclusions.

A. Democracy and Economic Growth

With respect to those studies where national differences in rates of economic growth have been examined, the evidence, as presented in the studies reviewed, would seem to suggest that political democracy does not widely and directly facilitate more rapid economic growth, net of other factors; hence, the compatibility perspective finds little support.

Beyond this, however, very little else seems clear. The studies examined are divided nearly equally with respect to whether a negative relationship or no relationship was found between democracy and economic growth. Our examination of such study characteristics as sample composition, use of controls in analysis, method and substance of the democracy measure used, period analyzed, and so on, unfortunately provides us with little leverage to discriminate among the conflicting findings since these characteristics tend to bear no particular relationship to the findings reported in the studies examined.

Even if we acknowledge that not all of these studies are created equal in terms of the appropriateness of their measures, research design, and methodology, something that might warrant the weightier treatment of one or a few of these studies, the sad fact remains that each of the studies reviewed suffers from one or another serious shortcoming. Ideal standards aside, perhaps the strongest analyses consist of the efforts of Marsh, Landau, Meyer and Associates, and Weede. But again we find no consensus within this subset of the studies. Therefore, in light of these weaknesses, even the conclusion that political democracy does not facilitate economic growth is at best a tentative one. Even if one were to embrace such a conclusion, the existing body of research has little to say about the form and balance of that growth.

B. Democracy and Inequality

With respect to those studies where national differences in levels of income inequality have been examined, the evidence appears to allow us to conclude that political democracy does not widely exacerbate inequality, net of other factors; hence the authoritarian model as discussed finds little support.

The debate, therefore, reduces to the issue of whether or not political democracy bears a systematic relationship to lower levels of income inequality. With regard to this question, the existing evidence suggests that the level of political democracy as measured at one point in time tends not to be widely associated with lower levels of income inequality. The validity of this conclusion rests upon an assessment of the differential quality of the studies reviewed. Clearly the efforts of Bollen and Jackman and Muller are superior to the others in terms of such considerations as their sample composition, assessment of simultaneity, and controls for the source of income data, and these two studies both support the above conclusion.

Caution must be interjected here, however, because, as Muller argues, political democracy may well act to reduce inequality in the long run. Moreover, none of the studies reviewed here are beyong reproach with respect to their coverage, model specification, research design, or measurement of democracy and inequality.

C. Conclusion

In the final analysis, the worth of our review lies in its clarification of the theoretical issues at hand and in its careful scrutiny of the studies that have been performed so as to guide our evaluations of the theoretical implications and to inform future research with the hope that such efforts will not repeat past mistakes. All in all, lively debate continues along the lines of the theoretical perspectives we have identified. When these alternative theories are confronted with the evidence as generated through quantitative, cross-national investigations, only a few basic insights appear to have been gained. In other words, much empirical work remains to be done.

In light of this state of affairs, a few remarks are in order. First, carefully designed replications of the kinds of studies reviewed are of utmost importance. In these studies special attention needs to be paid to the issues of sample composition, method of analysis, model specification, and measurement of the central variables. Moreover, assessments of robustness are crucial with respect to differences in sub-samples of countries, measures, and periods examined.

Second, before this program of research can move forward in a fertile fashion, numerous measurement issues must be addressed. Of these, none is more central than the valid and reliable measurement of political democracy. Should political democracy be assessed on a point or period basis? Which dimensions of political procedures, practices, and institutions are relevant to our classifications of national societies in terms of political democracy, and which are not? Should our measure of political democracy be continuous (ordinal) or discrete in form? All of these are critical issues that have only begun to be addressed (for a noteworthy exception, see Bollen (1980).

Along these lines our own review of existing measures of political democracy has identified ten, each of which is based upon the coding of at least two properties of a nation's political system deemed indicative of political democracy, each of which yielded ordinal rankings on some combined final index of political democracy, and each of which possesses a coverage of at least forty nations around the world. With respect to these ten indices, several points are worth noting. First, of the ten, five are basically point measured and five are period measured. Hence, at least half explicitly incorporate information on political form stability into the final index scores. Second, regardless of whether the index is point or period, all but two of the ten are based on observations made of national political systems before the start of the seventies. To some extent this is due to the fact that a considerable number of these measures are based on a small set of cross-national raw data files that were compiled during the sixties. In contrast, very little effort appears to have been undertaken to develop explicit measures of political democracy, especially annual assessments, after 1970.

Third, with respect to information about the national political systems covered by these measures, the measures differ from one another with regard to whether information on system stability, extent of franchise, and degree of exercise of the franchise are included. Nonetheless, nearly all of the measures surveyed are anchored in the notion that distinguishing systems in terms of political democracy rests ultimately on the degree to which political elites are selected by citizens via elections that are regular and meaningful. Obviously, the meaningfulness of elections of political elites is a slippery concept to operationalize. Thus, how it is exactly observed and coded is of great interest and importance. Judging from the all too frequently brief and cryptic annotations associated with the existing measures, it would appear that evidence for making "meaningfulness" judgements rests most commonly on two pieces of information: 1) was the election conducted under circumstances that would have been conducive to the presentation of real electoral choice? and 2) were the elections in fact competitive or contested?

Relevant information examined to assess the first of these prerequisites of meaningfulness, while by no means universally examined, includes such factors as the status of press freedom, freedom from government acts to suppress opposition, and the health and vitality of intermediary interest groups such as parties and unions. The degree to which elections were indeed actually competitive is most frequently inferred from an examination of the outcomes of the elections observed, particularly those elections for positions in the national legislative body, namely in terms of the proportional representation of the party memberships of those in office.

All in all, although the presence, regularity, and meaningfulness of elections are central to the assessment of political democracy in each of the measures we have scrutinized, on the whole, the set of ten remain a fairly heterogeneous lot in terms of specific pieces of information included. Some are biased in such ways that they may be designated as more democratic, including those systems that are more stable, or those systems wherein mass participation is greater, or those systems wherein interparty competition is greater than intraparty competition, or those systems wherein the parties are of generally equal size and power. Hence, the adequacy of any one of these ten measures depends not only on coverage or timing of observation, but also on the degree to which it best captures and indicates political democracy as the investigator conceives it to be. Too often little attention is paid to this linkage between concept and indicators, an issue which becomes critical for validly testing one's arguments about the development consequences of democracy.

Nonetheless, our own review of existing measures of democracy indicates that generally they correlate fairly strongly with each other, if we limit our attention to those of the ten that were measured basically around the same period of time. The average level of intercorrelation is $r = .75$, with a range of the specific correlations running from around $r = .60$ to $r = .90$. This level of intercorrelation suggests that a diverse set of measurement efforts have yielded a fair amount of agreement in discriminating systems with respect to political democracy. The task remains to extend the coverage of our measurement efforts and to assess the robustness of the conclusions we arrive at in such analyses as discussed earlier, given the use of alternative existing measures as well as new ones.

A third critical point is as follows. It is painfully clear that in order for the relevant theoretical debates to move forward, considerable attention must be allocated not just to evaluating the overall relationship between political democracy and development outcomes but also to evaluating the relationships between political democracy and a host of intervening factors through which democracy is considered to have its ultimate effects on such development outcomes as rate of economic growth and inequality. For example, some speculate that democracy hinders growth because the former engenders higher levels of instability. Huntington (1987) notes, however, that this connection is less clear than we assume. In light of Hibbs's (1973) finding that there is little systematic relationship between mass political violence and economic growth, Huntington suggests that there is perhaps a threshold effect of political violence on economic growth. Couple this with Marsh's (1979) finding that among less-developed countries there is little difference in the level of conflict between those with democratic and those with authoritarian political institutions; then even a general negative relationship between democracy and rate of economic growth offers little support to a theory that is grounded in the linkages between democracy and political instability, and, in turn, instability and economic growth.

Fourth, clearly more attention needs to be paid to specifying the conditions under which the relationships of interest hold and under which they do not. This point derives from the arguments of those who embrace what we have referred to as the "skeptical" perspectives. Clearly, even the conclusions put forth here—that democracy does not widely lead to rapid economic growth and that authoritarianism is not widely associated with lower levels of inequality—must be necessarily tempered in light of such obvious countercases as Taiwan, Republic of Korea, and Japan.

Considering quantitative, cross-national research, Weede's (1983) investigation of the effects of political democracy on economic growth under different degrees of state involvement in the economy illustrates the kind of avenue that new research could pursue.

Fifth and last, we would wholeheartedly recommend that new outcome measures be pursued in future research. Along these lines it would be most worthwhile to move beyond simple measures of rate of economic growth and on to measures that indicate features of the type of economic growth and the pattern of industrialization. Income inequality, with its widely acknowledged shortcomings, needs to be supplemented by other indicators of the general social and economic welfare of the population, indicators that likewise tap into the issue of distribution. Such indicators exist in the form of measures of fulfillment of basic human needs and welfare provisions. But as of yet, and as briefly noted earlier, only a handful of studies have begun to look at such alternative indicators of development outcomes and their relation to democracy. Obviously, much work remains to be done.

References

ADELMAN, IRMA and CYNTHIA TAFT MORRIS
  1967   *Society, politics and economic development: a quantitative approach*. Baltimore: Johns Hopkins University Press.
AHLUWALIA, M. S.
  1976   Inequality, poverty, and development. *Journal of Development Economics* 3:307–42.
ANDRESKI, STANISLAV
  1968   *Military organization and society*. Palo Alto: Stanford University Press.
APTER, DAVID E.
  1965   *The politics of modernization*. Chicago: The University of Chicago Press.
BEITZ, CHARLES R.
  1982   Democracy in Developing Societies. In *Freedom in the World: Political Rights and Civil Liberties*, edited by Raymond Gastil, 145-66. New York: Freedom House.
BERG-SCHLOSSER, DIRK
  1984   African Political Systems: Typology and Performance. *Comparative Political Studies* 17:121–51.
BIENEN, HENRY
  1971   *The military and modernization*. Chicago: The University of Chicago Press.
BOLLEN, KENNETH
  1980   Issues in the comparative measurement of political democracy. *American Sociological Review* 45:370–90.
BOLLEN, KENNETH and BURKE D. GRANDJEAN
  1981   The dimensions(s) of democracy: Further issues in the measurement and effects of political democracy. *American Sociological Review* 46:651–59.
BOLLEN, KENNETH and ROBERT W. JACKMAN
  1985   Political democracy and the size distribution of income. *American Sociological Review* 50:438–57.
CHIROT, DANIEL
  1977   *Social change in the twentieth century*. New York: Harcourt Brace Jovanovich.
CLAUDE, RICHARD
  1976   The classical model of human rights development. In *Comparative Human Rights*, edited by Richard Claude, 6-50. Baltimore: The Johns Hopkins University Press.
COHEN, YOUSSEFF
  1985   The impact of bureaucratic-authoritarian rule on economic growth. *Comparative Political Studies* 18:123–36.
COLLIER, DAVID
  1979   *The new authoritarianism in Latin America*. Princeton, NJ: Princeton University Press.
COULTER, PHILIP
  1975   *Social mobilization and liberal democracy*. Lexington, MA: Lexington Books.
CUTRIGHT PHILLIPS
  1967   Inequality: a cross-national analysis. *American Sociological Review* 32:562–78.

1963   National political development. *American Sociological Review* 28:253–64.
CUTRIGHT, PHILLIPS and JAMES A. WILEY
    1970   Modernization and political representation: *Studies in Comparative International Development* 5(2):23–
        44.
DAHL, ROBERT
    1971   *Polyarchy: participation and opposition.* New Haven: Yale University Press.
DE SCHWEINITZ, K.
    1964   *Industrialization and democracy.* New York: Free Press.
DICK, G. WILLIAMS
    1974   Authoritarian versus nonauthoritarian approaches to economic development. *Journal of Political
        Economy* 82:817–27.
DICKSON, THOMAS, JR.
    1977   An economic output and impact analysis of civilian and military regimes in Latin South America.
        Development and Change 8:325–45.
FEIERABEND, IVO K. and ROSALIND L. FEIERABEND
    1972   Coerciveness and change: Cross—national trends. *American Behavioral Scientist* 15: 911—28.
GOODELL, GRACE and JOHN P. POWELSON
    1982   The Democratic prerequisites of development. In *Freedom in the World: Political Rights and Civil
        Liberties, 1982,* edited by Raymond Gastil, 167-76. New York: Freedom House.
GOODIN, ROBERT E.
    1979   The development-rights trade-off: Some unwarranted economic and political assumptions. *Universal
        Human Rights* 1:31–42.
HEWITT, CHRISTOPHER
    1977   The effect of political democracy and social democracy on equality in industrial societies: A cross-
        national comparison. *American Sociological Review* 42:450–64.
HEWLETT, S. A.
    1979   Human rights and economic realities—Tradeoffs in historical perspective. *Political Science Quar-
        terly* 94:453–73.
HIBBS, DOUGLAS A.
    1973   *Mass political violence.* New York: Wiley.
HOLT, ROBERT T. and JOHN E. TURNER
    1966   *The political bases of economic development.* Princeton, NJ: Van Nostrand.
HUNTINGTON, SAMUEL P.
    1987   *Understanding political development: An analytic study.* Boston: Little Brown.
    1968   *Political order in changing societies.* New Haven: Yale University Press.
HUNTINGTON, SAMUEL P. and JORGE I. DOMINGUEZ
    1975   Political development. In *Handbook of Political Science, Vol. 3. Macropolitical Theory,* edited by
        F. Greenstein and N. Polsby, 1–114. Reading, MA: Addison-Wesley.
HUNTINGTON, SAMUEL P. and JOAN NELSON
    1976   *No easy choice: political participation in developing countries.* Cambridge, MA; Harvard University
        Press.
JACKMAN, ROBERT W.
    1976   Politicians in uniform: Military governments and change in the Third World. *The American Political
        Science Review* 70:1078—097.
    1975   *Politics and social equality: A comparative analysis.* New York: John Wiley and Sons.
KING, DWIGHT Y.
    1981   Regime type and performance. *Comparative Political Studies* 13:477–504.
KOHLI, ATUL
    1986   Democracy and development. In *Development strategies reconsidered,* edited by John Lewis and
        Valeriana Kallab, 153-82. New Brunswick: Transaction Books.
KOHLI, ATUL, MICHAEL ALTFELD, SAIDEH LOTFIAN, and RUSSELL MORDON
    1984   Inequality in the Third World. *Comparative Political Studies* 17:283–318.
KUZNETS, SIMON
    1955   Economic growth and income inequality. *American Economic Review* 45:18–30.
LANDAU, DANIEL
    1986   Government and economic growth in the LDCs: An empirical study for 1960–1980. *Economic
        Development and Cultural Change* 35:35–76.
LENSKI, GERHARD
    1966   *Power and privilege: A theory of social stratification.* New York: McGraw-Hill.
LEVY, MARION
    1966   *Modernization and the structure of societies.* Princeton, NJ; Princeton University Press.
LIPSET, SEYMOUR M.
    1959   Some social requisites of democracy: Economic development and political development. *American
        Political Science Review* 53:69–105.

MARSH, ROBERT M.
    1988   Sociological explanations of economic growth. *Studies in Comparative International Development*
                23(4):41–77.
    1979   Does democracy hinder economic development in latecomer developing nations? *Comparative Social
                Research* 2:215–48.
MCCORD, WILLIAM
    1965   *The springtime of freedom.* New York: Oxford University Press.
MCKINLAY, R.D. and A.S. COHAN
    1975   A comparative analysis of the political and economic performance of military and civilian regimes.
                Comparative Politics (October):1–30.
MEYER, JOHN W., MICHAEL HANNAN, RICHARD RUBINSON, and GEORGE THOMAS
    1979   National economic development, 1950—70: Social and political factors. In *National development
                and the world system,* edited by John Meyer and Michael Hannan, Chap.6. Chicago: University of
                Chicago Press.
MOON, BRUCE E. and WILLIAM J. DIXON
    1985   Politics, the state, and basic human needs: A cross-national study. *International Studies Quarterly*
                29:661–94.
MORRIS, MORRIS
    1979   *Measuring the condition of the world's poor: the physical quality of life index.* New York: Pergamon
                Press.
MULLER, EDWARD N.
    1988   Democracy, economic development, and income inequality. *American Sociological Review* 53:50–
                68.
NELSON, JOAN
    1987   Political participation. In *Understanding political development: An analytic study,* edited by Myron
                Weiner and Samuel P. Huntington, 103-159. Boston: Little Brown.
NORDLINGER, ERIC
    1970   Soldiers in mufti: The political impact of military rule upon economic and social change in non-
                western states. *American Political Science Review* 64:1131–148.
O'DONNELL, GUILLERMO
    1979   *Modernization and bureaucratic-authoritarianism: Studies in South American politics.* Berkeley:
                University of California Press.
PAMPEL FRED C. and J. B. WILLIAMS
    1988   Welfare spending in advanced industrial democracies, 1950-80. *American Journal of Sociology* 93:
                1424–456.
PAUKERT, F.
    1973   Income distribution at different levels of development: A survey of evidence. *International Labour
                Review 108:97–125.*
PERRY, CHARLES S.
    1980   Political contestation in nations: 1960, 1963, 1967, and 1970. *Journal of Political and Military
                Sociology* 8:161–74.
PLUTA, JOSEPH
    1979   The performance of South American civilian and military governments from a socio-economic
                perspective. *Development and Change* 10:461–83.
PYE, LUCIAN
    1966   *Aspects of political development.* Boston: Little Brown.
RAO, VAMAN
    1985   Democracy and economic development. *Studies in Comparative International Development* 19 (4):
                67-81.
RAVENHILL, JOHN
    1980   Comparing regime performance in Africa: The limitations of cross-national aggregate analysis. *The
                Journal of Modern African Studies* 10:99–126.
RUBINSON, RICHARD and DAN QUINLAN
    1977   Democracy and social inequality: A reanalysis. *American Sociological Review* 42:611–23.
RUSSETT, BRUCE M. and R. JOSEPH MONSEN
    1975   Bureaucracy and polyarchy as predictors of performance: A cross-national exam. *Comparative
                Political Studies* 8:5–31.
SHILS, EDWARD
    1964   The military in the political development of new states. In *The Military and Society in Latin America,*
                edited by John Johnson, 7-67. Palo Alto, CA: Stanford University Press.
SLOAN, JOHN and KENT L. TEDIN
    1987   The consequences of regime type for public policy outputs. *Comparative Political Studies* 20:98–
                124.

SMITH, ARTHUR K. JR.
  1969   Socio-economic development and political democracy: A causal analysis. *Midwest Journal of Po-
            litical Sociology 13:95–125.*
STACK STEVEN
  1980   The political economy of income inequality: A comparative analysis. *Canadian Journal of Political
            Science* 13:273–86.
  1979   The effects of political participation and socialist party strength on the degree of income inequality.
            American Sociological Review 44:168–81.
THUROW, LESTER C.
  1980   *The zero-sum society: Distribution and the possibilities for economic change.* New York: Basic
            Books.
VANHANEN, TATU
  1984   *The emergence of democracy: A comparative study of 119 states, 1850–1979.* Helsinki: The Finnish
            Society of Sciences and Letters.
WEEDE, ERICH
  1983   The impact of democracy on economic growth: Some evidence from cross-national analysis. *Kyklos*
            36:21–39.
  1982   The effects of democracy and socialist strength on the size distribution of income. *International
            Journal of Comparative Sociology* 23:151–65.
WEEDE ERICH and HORST TIEFENBACH
  1981   Some recent explanations of income inequality. *International Studies Quarterly* 25:255–82.
WILLIAMSON, JOHN B.
  1987   Social security and physical quality of life in developing nations: A cross-national analysis. *Social
            Indicators Research* 19:205–27.
WILLIAMSON, JOHN B. and FRED C. PAMPEL
  1986   Politics, class, and growth in social security effort: a cross-national analysis. *International Journal
            of Comparative Sociology* 27:15–27.

7

On the Political Capacity of Nation States: Institutionalization and Legitimacy

Robert W. Jackman

Other contributions to this volume address the definition and measurement of political democracy (or polyarchy). This article examines the political capacity of nation states in a more generic sense, in a manner that is intended to supplement rather than replace questions of democracy. It proposes a definition and measures of national political capacity conceived in terms of institutional capacity and legitimacy. The former is measured in terms of the chronological age of the juridical state and the current constitutional form, along with the number of national executives in the prevailing constitutional period. The measurement of legitimacy is informed by a distinction between power and force; legitimate regimes are those that can induce compliance without resort to force and that are not confronted with violent challengers.

Three decades ago, Lerner (1958), Lipset (1959), and Cutright (1963) pioneered the cross-national empirical study of political democracy. These studies examined the social and political "conditions associated with the existence and *stability* of democratic society" (Lipset, 1959: 69, emphasis added). Thus, Lipset developed his well-known fourfold classification of European and Latin-American states (ranging in turn from most to least democratic): stable European democracies, unstable European democracies and dictatorships, Latin American democracies and unstable dictatorships, and stable Latin American dictatorships. Four years later, Cutright constructed a continuous measure of representativeness, which involved a classification of the methods by which national legislatures and executives were chosen, counted over a period of years in order to penalize nations for instability. Common

Robert W. Jackman is professor of political science at the University of California, Davis. His areas of interest include comparative politics and political sociology. He is author of *Politics and Social Equality* (1975) and coauthor of *Class Awareness in the United States* (1983). His contribution to this volume is from a longer project he is completing on the political capacity of nation states.

to these and related efforts (e.g., Eckstein 1966) was an emphasis on stable democracies.

Subsequent work has argued for separating questions of stability from questions of democracy (e.g., Jackman 1975; Bollen 1980), on the grounds that each concept addresses a distinctive phenomenon. Stability can be seen as reflecting political capacity in a generic sense that is independent of regime type. In contrast, democracy is customarily taken to refer to the provision of political liberties and popular control, which means that it refers to a specific type of regime. When stability is explicitly and directly built into measurements of democracy, the two are necessarily confounded and it becomes impossible to distinguish the effects of one from the other.[1] This is why the two concepts should be treated separately.

At the same time, it is important that we address both general concepts. Other contributions to this volume focus on the definition and measurement of political democracy (or polyarchy). My purpose is to examine the capacity of nation states, in a manner that is intended to supplement rather than replace questions of democracy. What follows draws on material from a larger project in which I am currently engaged; here, I devote most of my attention to issues of measurement. To keep this presentation manageable, I have summarized the broader argument radically.

Background

My approach builds on and extends some of the themes common to the analysis of political development in the 1960s. Those ideas were presented by a variety of writers, including Almond and Coleman (1960), and Deutsch (1961). They were perhaps most completely treated by Huntington (1968), who argued that institutionalization is the key ingredient to political capacity. That Huntington was concerned with political capacity in some generic sense was clear from the opening sentence of his book: "The most important political distinction among countries concerns not their form of government but their degree of government" (1968: 1).

During the 1970s the whole idea of national political development came under attack from a variety of quarters, among which two stand out. First, there was a populist attack which argued that the term "development" was itself ethnocentric, teleological, and conservative with its emphasis on order (see e.g., Hopkins 1972; O'Brien 1972; Kesselman 1973). Second, the dependency/world systems perspective asserted that the focus on nation states was inordinately narrow and misguided (see, most notably, Wallerstein, 1974).

Within the last decade, these criticisms appear to have lost much of their force, and have come increasingly to be displaced by a new focus on states (see, e.g., Krasner 1984; Evans, Reuschmeyer, and Skocpol 1985; Nordlinger 1987). Nation states are increasingly seen as important arenas, and a good deal of attention has been devoted to the issue of state "strength." Although seldom acknowledged, this new statism—especially with its emphasis on state strength—has returned us to many of the issues that motivated the original literature on political development. State strength, after all, has to do with considerations of national political capacity. However, recent writings on the state have failed to define the state in unambiguous terms, and hence the notion of state strength is also undefined. Some analysts describe state strength in terms of the size of the public sector, but this approach rapidly becomes mired in the problems of differentiating the public and private sectors (consider the cases of Japan and South Korea). Others broach the question in a more general way, casting states as "actors." However, this raises more issues than it resolves. Not only does the concept of the state (and hence state strength) remain poorly defined, but when the state is cast as an actor, the perspective faces overwhelming problems of reification.

Insofar as it has reaffirmed the importance of nation states as political units, the new statism is an encouraging beginning. What is needed now is a return to fundamentals if we are to make any progress in identifying the political capacity of nation states.

The Issues

When considering political capacity, it is useful to begin by considering what politics entails. Politics fundamentally consists of the production, consumption, and distribution of power (or influence, or authority). Unlike the use of force, the exercise of power involves a relationship between those who exercise it and those who are subject to it. The threat of force is of course central to power relations, and force is often used in poorly defined political situations. However, my argument is that a primary and sustained reliance on force reflects a loss of political power, and is in this sense apolitical. As Merriam once put it, "Rape is not an evidence of irresistible power in politics or in sex" (1934: 180).

Given this, political capacity involves *institutions* that are surrounded with some aura of *legitimacy*. Institutions reflect the structures necessary for the exercise of power, which assumes a degree of continuity and regularity in the relationship between the participants. But these structures must also be seen as legitimate; that is, consent has to be manufactured. While the distinction between persuasion and manipulation is inherently ambiguous, it is essential that "authorities" are recognized as such, by most people for most of the time. Because institutions are always somewhat fragile, and given that legitimation is an ongoing process, political capacity is never an all-or-nothing phenomenon, but rather a matter of degree.

My treatment of institutions draws heavily on Weber, who argued the importance of rules based on convention and law. Weber, of course, devoted much attention to rational-legal and traditional forms of authority. A central feature of these forms is that they take considerable time to develop, which immediately draws our attention to the *age* of institutions. Weber also considered the phenomenon of charismatic authority at some length. His argument was that this is a transitory, revolutionary form that has to be routinized immediately, and this directs our attention to problems of leadership *succession*.

My analysis of national political institutions accordingly focuses on their age, conceived in both chronological and generational terms. The emphasis on the former ties in which the extensive evidence in the organizational literature on the liability of newness. With age comes the formalization of routines, and the goal becomes organizational survival. By increasing the adaptability of institutions, age increases the probability of survival (although age of course does not guarantee survival). Generational age directs our attention to the process of leadership succession and the routinization of authority, both of which are central to routinizing new institutional orders, as Machiavelli and many others have pointed out.[2] As will become clear in the next section, capacity is not a simple linear function of (chronological or organizational) age: differences among relatively young institutions are much more important than differences between older organizations.

Questions of legitimacy are partly but incompletely addressed by the age of national political institutions. While age increases the odds of survival, it hardly precludes extinction; issues of legitimacy therefore need to be addressed explicitly. Drawing on the earlier distinction between power and force, a regime (or state) is legitimate to the extent that it can resolve problems (i.e., make them go away) by exercising power without resorting to force or provoking a forceful challenge. Legitimacy need not (and is unlikely to) involve active or unanimous consent; like political capacity, it is always a matter of degree.

Because the exercise of power involves a relationship between authorities and subjects, we need to focus on the behavior of both groups. There are thus two components to legitimacy. First, to what extent do "officials" rely on force rather than persuasion to advance their interests? Second, to what degree do challengers to authorities use "irregular" channels to pursue their interests? Specifically, do challengers employ violent tactics instead of employing normal channels? Note that I am assuming that challengers and authorities act rationally (rather than anomically); since violence is a potentially costly tactic for those who employ it, its use indicates that regular channels are inefficacious.

Measuring National Political Capacity

The preceding outline discussion of organizational age and political legitimacy is cast in terms that have clear implications for measurement. However, the fact that political concepts are designed with measurement in mind does not signify that all possible empirical ambiguity has been resolved.

For example, the statement that political orders should be dated from the period of their establishment does not in itself identify that date. In many cases, reasonable people will disagree over the exact date despite the clarity of the measurement *principle* involved. Similarly, asserting the importance of the generational age of the national political leadership sounds relatively straightforward, but the argument leaves unresolved the identity of the "real" (as opposed to titular) leaders. The problems are amplified when we turn our attention to the measurement of legitimacy. One tactic commonly employed by regimes to maximize their legitimacy is to conceal information about the use of physical force to repress challenges, along with details about the extensiveness of the challenges themselves. For obvious reasons, this tactic hampers the collection of systematic data on legitimacy.

It is important to acknowledge that these are real problems—indeed, they are quite familiar to students of political conflict. However, it is equally important that we not allow ourselves to become paralyzed by these obstacles. The fact that relevant information is sometimes obscured means that measurement may not be as precise as we would like. But it does not follow that efforts to gauge phenomena like political legitimacy should be abandoned. Indeed, to endorse such a conclusion would be tantamount to conceding that the phenomena are inconsequential simply because they are difficult to evaluate empirically.

Even with inexact measurement, much valuable information is available about the political capacity of modern nation states. Although it is subject to error, this material can usefully be employed to make comparisons across states of institutional capacity and political legitimacy. These comparisons involve general orders of magnitude for each case, but national political capacity is always a matter of degree.

Institutional Age

I have suggested that age impinges directly on political capacity and that two components of age are critical in this regard. The first refers to the chronological age of institutions, and the second centers on the generational age of leaders. I address these in turn.

The Chronological Age of Institutions. Longevity has often been linked to stability and political performance (e.g., Black 1966; Rustow 1967; Huntington 1968; Eckstein 1971). Even so, different solutions have been proposed to the problem of how to identify the most appropriate start-up date for national institutions. Two treatments help define the issues.

For Black, the critical period is that time in which there is a "consolidation of modernizing leadership" (1966: Chapter 3)—that time when traditional leaders lose their power in struggles with newer elites. These struggles have three distinctive attributes. First, they include an assertion of a "determination to modernize," often manifested in violent revolution, and emanating either from disaffected elements of the traditional leadership or from those representing new political interests. Second, there is a decisive break with institutions representing agrarian interests in favor of industrial economic forms. Third, there is an expansion of political authority and organization. All three

TABLE 1
Organizational Age of Selected Nation States as Estimated by Black and Rustow

	Consolidating Period (Black)	Independence Year (Rustow)
Argentina	1853–1946	1816
Brazil	1850–1930	1822
China	1905–1949	before 1775
Cuba	1898–1959	1901
Egypt	1922–1952	1922
France	1789–1848	before 1775
India	1919–1947	1947
Indonesia	1922–1949	1949
Italy	1805–1871	before 1775
Japan	1868–1945	before 1775
Nigeria	1960–	1960
Russia	1861–1917	before 1775
Tanzania	1961–	1961
United Kingdom	1649–1832	before 1775
United States	1776–1865	1776

Sources: Black (1966: 90–94); Rustow (1967: 292–94).

elements of this consolidation take time (at least a generation) and all are conflictual. Further, this is a *political* consolidation that predates economic and social transformation.

The first column of Table 1 displays the period in which Black estimates modernizing leadership was consolidated, for selected states. It is clear that this consolidation occurred over a lengthy period in most cases; of those judged to be complete, the process took the longest in the United Kingdom (183 years) and was shortest in Indonesia and India (17 and 28 years, respectively). Among the older states, the process is often associated with revolution (e.g., China, France, and Russia). In some cases it is coded as beginning with revolution (e.g., France and the United States) while in others it is said to end with revolution (e.g., China and Russia). Among the newer states, a similar pattern obtains around the date of independence from colonial rule: contrast Nigeria and Tanzania (where the process was judged to have just begun with independence) with India and Indonesia (where it is coded as having been completed by the date of independence).

In contrast to Black's identification of a period of modernizing leadership, Rustow (1967) dated nation states from the time that they achieved independence as sovereign political units. His figures for the same illustrative set of countries are displayed in the second column of Table 1. For the newer states, this procedure is straightforward since the date of decolonization is readily identified. Among the older states, the date in which sovereignty was achieved is often more difficult to determine, and Rustow codes 22 states as having gained independence before 1775 (including the five so listed in Table 1).

Although it may not be immediately apparent from the cases displayed in this table, the approaches adopted by Black and Rustow have much in common. Indeed, when computed for all 124 countries for which data are available on both measures, the rank-order correlation (Spearman's rho) between the indices developed by Black and Rustow is .79. The size of this correlation is due in part (but not exclusively) to the fact that countries with extreme (high or low) scores on one measure tend to have a similar score on the other. Thus, for most of the countries of sub-Saharan Africa, both measures refer to the date of independence. At the other end of the scale, most industrialized Western countries are coded as old by both analysts. However, there are cases in which the acquisition of political sovereignty predated Black's period of consolidation by a substantial margin. These include, but are not restricted to, states in which there were major political revolutions; consider the figures for China, Japan, and Russia as noted in Table 1. In other cases, independence preceded the period of consolidation by a smaller margin (e.g., Argentina and Brazil). What are the implications of these differences for the measurement of organizational longevity?

To address this question, it is useful to employ the distinction between the state as a juridical entity and the state as a potential entity (Jackson and Rosberg 1982a). It is evident that, construed as legal units, states have proved in recent years to be very durable (that is, they have continued to exist), and this is true for even those cases whose lack of political capacity is perhaps their most striking characteristic. Once we conceive of the problem in these terms, it becomes clear that approaches like Rustow's employ a juridical definition, while procedures like that adopted by Black reflect more of an interest in states as political units.

The distinction is important because the durability evidenced by states as legal units has not been matched by a corresponding longevity of constitutional orders. This fact is obvious where there have been major political revolutions, but it is also apparent where such revolutions have not occurred. While most of the states of Latin America, for example, achieved their current sovereign status in the early nineteenth century, many of them have experienced considerable political instability since then, typically in the form of military coups d'etat. While falling short of full-scale revolutions, these coups have generally included the suspension and abrogation of constitutions, whose weakness was already evidenced by the occurrence of the successful coups themselves. In a parallel vein, while it was perfectly reasonable for scholars of sub-Saharan Africa in the middle 1960s to equate date of independence with the beginning of the current constitutional order, the years since have seen much evidence of a similar type of political instability (see, e.g., Jackman 1978; Jackson and Rosberg 1982b; Londregan and Poole 1990), again involving the abrogation of constitutional orders.

Such patterns indicate that the state as a juridical unit recognized in international law should not simply be equated with the state as an entity that demonstrates some political capacity. On the other hand, it is important to understand that the former is a prerequisite of the latter, and that longevity on both dimensions needs to be considered in the evaluation of national political development. Specifically, there is good reason to believe that in comparing two states which have both experienced recent major political upheavals, that state which is juridically older has more political capacity (both states would, of course, have less capacity than a third state that had experienced both juridical and constitutional longevity).

As many have noted, the problem for states that are young on both counts is that they are confronted simultaneously with the processes of state building and the creation of political institutions (e.g., Rustow 1967; Linz 1978). In the terms used by Weiner (1965), this involves territorial *and* political integration, and it is the fact that they are faced concurrently that reduces the odds that either process will be successful. The creation of Pakistan in 1947 and events in many countries in sub-Saharan Africa after independence are often taken to illustrate the problem that this generates.

By contrast, issues of territorial integration centering on the state as a juridical unit were encountered and largely (but never completely) resolved in the earlier developers *before* questions of political integration. The decoupling of the two issues increases the probability that they will be resolved. At the same time, the consolidation of the juridical state helps provide a national history, which is a key symbolic ingredient in the generation of political legitimacy.

On a more mundane note, with the creation of the juridical state comes the gradual emergence of a bureaucratic order that is likely to persist in some form even in the face of apparently major political transformations. This provides that measure of continuity to the political life of older juridical states that is lacking in their younger counterparts. As a result, the impact of upheavals involving the suspension and replacement of constitutional orders is less severe in older than it is in the youngest juridical states.

Weber made the argument some time ago with his insistence that "once it is fully established, bureaucracy is among those social structures which are the hardest to destroy" (1946: 228). But bureaucracies persist even when they fall short of being "fully" established. Thus, Weber commented that

> With all the changes of masters in France since the time of the First Empire, the power machine has remained essentially the same. Such a machine makes "revolution," in the sense of the forceful creation of entirely new formations of authority, technically more and more impossible. . . . In classic fashion, France has demonstrated how this process has substituted coups d'etat for "revolutions:" all successful transformations in France have amounted to coups d'etat (1946: 230).

A similar view is represented in Siegfried's (1956) description of the "stable instability" of the Fourth French Republic. The label was not intended to identify a paradox, but rather to show that even with the apparent instability of politics as reflected in cabinet turnovers, there remained a considerable underlying continuity in personnel, at both cabinet and civil-service levels. Hence the stability of the instability. Most recently, Veliz has argued the same case with respect to Latin America. Despite chronic instability involving coups and suspensions of constitutions throughout the area, centralist bureaucracies have survived and grown, even in periods in which there was apparent consensus that the role of the state should be minimized. "Perhaps with the arguable exception of Cuba, none of the other bureaucratic establishments of the region has been dismantled in ways that would prove the Weberian thesis wrong" (Veliz 1980: 288).

None of this should be taken to minimize the importance of recent political upheavals and the abrogation of constitutional orders for the capacity of political orders. Instead, I am suggesting that of the states that do undergo such upheavals, the experience is less incapacitating for those that are older in juridical terms. At the same time, such upheavals are consequential for all states. It follows that the measurement of the chronological age of nation states should have two components that reflect their age in both juridical and constitutional terms.

To gauge the chronological age of juridical states, I employ an updated version of the figures provided by Rustow (1967: 292–293). Adopting his convention, those states that achieved political sovereignty before 1775 are treated as a single group and coded as if 1775 were the year in which they became independent. This procedure is predicated on the view that the first few years (or decades) are the most important in evaluating the longevity of institutions. I shall return to this issue below.[3] For those states that became independent between 1776 and 1966 (the last year included in Rustow's survey), I rely generally on Rustow's figures. Temporary interruptions to sovereignty, such as those experienced by several Western European countries during the Second World War, are disregarded. The measure amends Rustow's survey by including the data in which sovereignty was achieved by former colonies in the years from 1967 through the end of 1985.

As many have observed, states conceived in juridical terms have been relatively stable and clearly defined in the modern era. In conjunction with the fact that I am ignoring temporary interruptions to sovereignty, this means that determining the age of such states is unambiguous for most cases. But some troublesome cases do remain. For example, Rustow dates both Germanys and Italy as having been independent prior to 1775. While this is reasonable at one level, unification came much later in both cases and I have adopted the later date. Even my modification does not address the issue raised by the partition of Germany after the Second World War and subsequent reunification in 1990.

This raises the more general matter of how changes in the unit of analysis are best treated. Following normal procedure, I have dated Pakistan's independence at 1947. But with the creation of Bangladesh in 1972, Pakistan's territorial definition underwent a fundamental transformation and the state of Pakistan lost more than half its population. Similarly, the age of the Vietnamese state is somewhat unclear. One could treat the French colonial period in Indochina and the subsequent military intervention by the United States as temporary interruptions to Vietnamese sovereignty, but that stretches unacceptably the everyday meaning of the adjective "temporary." Alternatively, one could trace the current Vietnamese state back to the North Vietnamese state founded by Ho Chi Minh. This would acknowledge the military victory of the North, but would by the same token overlook the approximate doubling in size and population of that "state" effective in 1975.

Finally, juridical statehood implies recognition by at least a large proportion of the international community of states. I therefore ignore the "unilateral declaration of independence" from Britain made in 1965 by the white minority regime in Rhodesia in favor of the recognized state of Zimbabwe created in 1980. The case of Taiwan is more difficult to resolve, given its recognition by a large number of other states in 1949. The difficulty here stems from the withdrawal of that legal recognition that came with the dialogue between the People's Republic of China and the United States.

Such instances, with their disputes over territory and sovereignty, remind us that even though juridical states (our units of analysis) have been relatively well delineated in recent years, some definitional uncertainty remains. Moreover, these cases are widely recognized because the disputes that have centered around them have been highly visible. But the problem should not be overstated. For the vast majority of modern nation states, estimating the year in which sovereignty was achieved is straightforward.

My measure of the age of the current political order—or, to use Jackson and Rosberg's (1982a) term, the age of the empirical state—is the year in which the constitutional form in effect as of the end of 1985 was introduced. The construction of this variable is similar to (and the result updates) figures on the age of the current constitutional form as of 1970, computed earlier by Hudson (Taylor and Hudson 1972). In those cases where no constitutional form has been formally adopted, but where a previous constitution has been explicitly suspended, this measure refers to the date of introduction of the extra-constitutional rules effective at the end of 1985.

As was true with the first variable, identifying that year in which the current rules became effective is uncomplicated in most instances, but some cases require more judgment. After all, procedures and the constitutions in which they are embodied typically evolve through processes of amendment. The problem, then, is to differentiate fundamental changes in the rules governing political life from less substantial amendments, and to date the current arrangement as having begun when the last fundamental change became effective.

The general rule I have adopted distinguishes fundamental changes as those induced either when a new juridical state is created or when the prior set of political rules is overturned and suspended. In the first case, the age of the juridical state is identical (or close) to the age of the empirical state. In the second case, abrogation of constitutional orders is most commonly manifested through effective revolutions or through successful coups d'etat. The changes are fundamental because they entail relatively abrupt breaks with the past political order, in contrast to the more evolutionary and gradual patterns of change normally associated with amendments to constitutions. The classification rule involved here is clear from the following examples.

The People's Republic of China was established in 1949, and its first constitution was adopted in 1954. In the years since, three new constitutions have been promulgated (in 1975, 1978, and 1983). While these more recent documents have introduced several major changes, none of them can be taken as a fundamental and abrupt break with the past, as was the constitution of 1954. The current (as of 1985) set of political rules for China is therefore dated as beginning in 1954. A new constitution was approved in the Republic of South Africa, effective in 1981. However, because the changes it initiated cannot be interpreted as fundamental modifications to the document of 1961, the earlier date is taken for this case. Finally, the original Republican constitution in Yugoslavia under Tito became effective in 1946. Three new constitutions were subsequently introduced (in 1953, 1963, and 1974), but since the fundamental political change was associated with the 1946 document, that date is taken as the relevant date for Yugoslavia, as of 1985.

In contrast, the constitution adopted in Greece in 1975 came after the military juntas that lasted from 1967 to 1974. Since the 1967 coup had included the explicit suspension of the 1952 constitution, the age of the current constitutional form in Greece is set at 1975. For similar reasons, Argentina and Spain are assigned the dates of 1983 and 1978, respectively, on this variable. In 1961, General Park Chung Hee mounted a successful coup d'etat in South Korea. After the end of his regime (which came with his assassination in 1979), a new constitution was adopted in 1980, which serves as the date in which the current political form was adopted in Korea. In June 1985, elements of the Ugandan government staged a successful coup. Although no constitution was formally adopted by the end of that year, 1985 serves as the date when the political rules in effect as of the end of 1985 were established in Uganda (yet a newer set of procedures was introduced early in the following year).

The general rule here, then, distinguishes upheavals according to their origins. Temporary interruptions to sovereignty brought about by *external* forces are ignored in the calculation of constitutional age. But internally induced, forceful abrogations of the political order are treated as events that reset the clock and thereby mark the beginning of a new political era.

Country values for both measures of the chronological age of nation states are reported for selected countries in Table 2. I postpone an examination of these measures to introduce the data on generational age.

The Generational Age of National Political Leadership. I argued earlier that chronological age provides us with only part of the picture, and that the measurement of organizational age should also address the nature of top leadership. The specific issue here is whether leadership is primarily personal and institutions are secondary, or whether institutional procedures have primacy. To evaluate this process, we need to focus on leadership succession, which is especially problematic in newer states.

Consider two countries which have the same current chronological age but different generational ages. In case A, there has been no leadership succession and the founder continues to rule, while case B has experienced several rel-

TABLE 2
Chronological and Generational Age of Selected Nation States

	Year of Independence	Year of Constitution effective at end of 1985	# of Leaders in Current Constitutional Period
Argentina	1816	1983	1
Brazil	1822	1984	1
China	1775	1954	2
Cuba	1901	1959	1
Egypt	1922	1971	2
France	1775	1958	4
India	1947	1950	5
Indonesia	1949	1949	2
Italy	1861	1948	16
Japan	1775	1947	14
Nigeria	1960	1984	1
Soviet Union	1775	1936	8
Tanzania	1961	1965	1
United Kingdom	1775	1832	20
United States	1776	1787	39

Sources: The two measures of chronological age are based initially on information available in Rustow (1967) and Taylor and Hudson (1972). Modifications are derived from information in the following compendia, as is the count of the number of national political leaders in the constitutional era effective at the end of 1985: Banks (1986); Jackson and Rosberg (1982b: 288–304); Spuler (1953); and Spuler, Allen, and Saunders (1977). Materials from these compendia were supplemented by data from the following yearbooks: *Europa Yearbook* (London: Europa Publications, various years); *Information Please Almanac, Atlas and Yearbook*, 40th ed. (Boston: Houghton Mifflin, 1987); *Keesing's Contemporary Archives* (London: Longman's Group, various years); *The Statesman's Yearbook* (New York: St. Martin's Press, various years).

atively orderly transfers of leadership involving a series of individual leaders. Although each has the same chronological age, case B has more political capacity (or institutional structure) simply because of its *demonstrated* history of successful transfers of leadership. Operationally, this raises three questions: to which period should estimates of the number of leadership transfers refer; which leaders should be included in the calculations; and how should multiple terms of office be counted?

On the first matter, counts of the number of leadership transfers should be made within constitutional eras. If we are concerned with the current constitutional period, the relevant quantity is thus the number of successions since the beginning of that period, as defined in the last section. If we are interested in earlier eras, then we would examine the number of successions within those eras. In other words, we need to exclude leadership transfers associated with extra-constitutional revolutions or coups because these reflect political upheavals and institutional collapses that restart the clock for leadership transfers. After such upheavals, the important issue is whether the individual who toppled the old order was able to establish a new political order. This is the sense in which the succession process must be judged to be relatively orderly before it can be included in estimates of generational age.

The second question is which leaders should be counted. In principle, the answer is straightforward: we should include the single individual who wields the most political power. This criterion directs us toward that individual who is the head of state in many instances, especially where presidential systems are involved. But in many other cases, the head of state is no more than a

TABLE 3
Summary Statistics for Measures of Age of 124 Nation-States as of 1985

	# Years Independent by 1985	# Years by 1985 since Constitution Adopted	# National Leaders since Constitution Adopted
Minimum value	6	1	1
Maximum value	211	199	61
Mean value*	59.3	16.2	2.4

* Antilog of the mean calculated from the (natural) log-transformed country scores.

figurehead. At the end of 1985, for example, President Gromyko as head of state of the Soviet Union was less significant politically than Gorbachev as general secretary of the Communist Party, and this pattern has been emulated by many other states. Similarly, prime ministers are more influential than heads of state (presidents or monarchs) in parliamentary systems. It is obvious that the title of the office held by the top political leader varies from one state to another. In gauging the number of leadership transfers, it is therefore important first to distinguish the relevant office and then to identify the individuals who have held that office.

Finally, I have emphasized the number of *individuals* who have held leadership positions rather than the number of terms that the office has been held. Individual leaders who have held the office for more than one term are thus counted once only, whether the terms involved were consecutive or nonconsecutive. Among other things, this procedure reflects the underlying continuity of top political leadership despite cabinet instability in systems like that of postwar Italy.

Country values on the generational age of national leaders for selected countries are displayed in the third column of Table 2. These figures identify the number of individuals who have held the top political position in each country during its present constitutional era, which refers to the years from the creation of the current constitutional (or extra-constitutional) arrangement through the end of 1985.

Characteristics of the Data on Institutional Age. Country values are summarized in Table 3, which shows the ranges and means for each of the three measures.[4] Two interrelated features of these data are immediately apparent.

First, most nation states are very young. In almost all instances, of course, juridical age exceeds that of the current constitutional form, but even so it is youth that is conspicuous. At one level, this is not surprising given the pace of decolonization after the Second World War and the concomitant expansion in the sheer number of sovereign states. But evidence of youth in terms of constitutional age is also striking, even among many of those states that became independent in the last century. Since the measure of the generational age of the top political leadership refers to the current constitutional period, it follows that most states should be young on this count too, and indeed they are. While the number of leaders ranges from one to sixty-one, the mean value is only 2.4.

TABLE 4
Mean Age of 124 Nation States as of 1985 by Wealth*

	# Years since Independence	# Years since Constitution	# National Leaders
Low-income economies (N = 35)	32.6	9.2	1.3
Lower middle-income economies (N = 39)	53.7	11.7	1.6
Upper middle-income economies (N = 23)	72.0	13.4	2.1
East European nonmarket economies (N = 8)	91.1	38.9	3.4
Industrial market economies (N = 19)	144.6	77.9	15.7

* Means are antilogs of the means calculated from the (natural) log-transformed country scores. Countries are grouped by wealth following the classification employed by the World Bank (1986: Annex), except that I have included "high-income oil exporters" (Kuwait, Libya, and Saudi Arabia) with upper middle-income economies.

Second, for all three indicators, the distribution of country values is heavily skewed toward low scores. This skewness is, of course, consistent with the liability of newness argument, particularly with respect to constitutional age. It also suggests that the differences among low-scoring countries are more interesting than differences among those with higher scores. There is good reason to expect that the severity of the liability of newness should decrease with organizational age, since the first few years or leaders are the most critical for institutionalization. This implies that differences between lower values ought to be weighted more heavily than differences between higher-scoring cases, which is most readily achieved by examining the logarithms (rather than the raw scores) of the organizational age of nation states.[5]

Additional perspective is gained on these data when we inspect differences in organizational age by wealth and geographic region. Table 4 displays the mean age on all three measures by level of national wealth, where the latter is indexed by the classification of per capita GNP for 1984 employed by the World Bank (1986). For each measure, there is a pronounced monotonic relation between wealth and age. Taking age as the criterion, the Western industrial states as a group have more political capacity than others by a considerable margin. Indeed, the size of that margin increases from the first to the third column of the table, so that the contrast in generational age between industrial states and all others is substantial.

Setting to one side the industrial economies, Table 5 reports mean organizational age by geographic region for Third World countries. The figures on the number of years since independence in the first column reflect patterns of decolonization, where the countries of Latin America as a group became independent first, while those of sub-Saharan Africa were decolonized last (with the average date for African states being 1960). But the figures in the second and third columns of the table indicate that regional contrasts in juridical age do not translate neatly into differences in constitutional or generational age. Most notably, despite their juridical age, the states of Latin America are, taken together, more similar in terms of constitutional age to those of sub-Saharan Africa than they are to those of the other two regions

TABLE 5
Mean Age of 92 Nation States in the Third World as of 1985 by Geographic Region*

	# Years since Independence	# Years since Constitution	# National Leaders
Asia (N = 21)	41.2	14.4	1.7
Latin America (N = 22)	126.0	10.2	2.0
Middle East & North Africa (N = 16)	47.4	13.8	1.8
Sub-Saharan Africa (N = 33)	26.5	8.5	1.2

* Means are antilogs of the means calculated from the (natural) log-transformed country scores. Calculations exclude countries in the East European nonmarket and industrial market economy categories of the last table, along with Greece, Madagascar, Mauritius, Portugal, and Yugoslavia.

TABLE 6
Regressions of Age of Nation States as of 1985 on Wealth and Geographic Region (N = 122)*

Dependent variable	# Years since Independence	# Years since Constitution	# National Leaders
Log energy consump. per capita, 1984	.31* (.07)	.34* (.08)	.31* (.07)
Asia	−.26 (.22)	.04 (.26)	−.32 (.22)
Latin America	.50* (.20)	−.29 (.24)	−.16 (.20)
Middle East & North Africa	−.25 (.23)	−.53 (.28)	−.66* (.23)
Sub-Saharan Africa	−.22 (.18)	−.22 (.22)	−.44* (.19)
Constant	2.17* (.56)	1.00 (.68)	−.59 (.57)
R²	.31	.39	.48
Restricted R² (energy consumption only)	.22	.35	.41

* Main table entries are metric regression coefficients, and numbers below them in parentheses are their standard errors. Starred coefficients are more than twice the size of their standard errors. With the exception of Chad and Lesotho (for which energy consumption rates are unavailable), these estimates are based on the same cases as the figures in Table 4. Thus, the regional effects represent contrasts between the region indicated and non-Third World countries, net of energy consumption rates.

of the Third World. Further, the last column indicates that there are no major regional differences in generational age as reflected by the number of national political leaders in the current constitutional period.

While instructive, the figures in Tables 4 and 5 ignore the systematic association between geographic region and national wealth. Table 6 accordingly reports regression estimates for all three measures of political age on wealth and region, where regions are defined as in the last table and wealth is measured by per capita energy consumption rates for 1984.[6] No causal argument is implied by these estimates; instead, they are presented simply as a way of summarizing the data in general terms.

Despite the apparent regional differences in chronological age suggested in Table 5, these regression analyses indicate that only the Latin American states have, on the average, been independent longer than one would anticipate given their wealth. For other states, juridical age is most closely related to wealth. In terms of constitutional age, there are no striking regional differences with wealth controlled, although the coefficient for the Middle East and North African states suggest that they are somewhat younger than one would expect on the basis of their wealth (this coefficient falls just short of being twice the size of its standard error). The estimates for generational age are somewhat different. Where the raw figures in Table 5 suggested little regional variation, the regression results indicate that, with their wealth held constant, the states of sub-Saharan Africa and of the Middle East and North Africa have experienced fewer leadership successions than have states in other regions.

These patterns are noteworthy because they indicate that organizational age (one key ingredient of political development) is not a simple function of economic development, and therefore cannot be reduced to the latter. First, although there is a pronounced association, the coefficients of determination show that this association is far from perfect; the figures in the bottom row of the table range from .22 for juridical age to .41 for generational age. Second, the table reveals that there are striking regional differences in the association. In other words, the argument I have made about the importance of organizational age is not a brief for the proposition that political development is an unadorned "unilinear" function of wealth.

That the regional patterns vary according to the specific element of organizational age under consideration has a second implication. The three different components cannot be treated as interchangeable indicators of development. Further evidence on this point comes from the correlations among the three components: that between juridical and constitutional age is .28; for juridical and generational age the correlation is .42; the correlation between constitutional and generational age is .78.[7]

The first two of these correlations are quite low, which underscores the distinction between juridical and constitutional age that was also clear from the regression estimates in Table 6. I argued earlier that both of these components are analytically distinct but central to the evaluation of organizational capacity. That this difference is also manifested empirically means that each of these components needs to be considered separately in the appraisal of national political performance.

In contrast, the third correlation is considerably higher. This stems in good part from the construction of the measure of generational age, which reflects the number of leaders in the current constitutional period. Such a design obviously builds a relationship into these two measures, especially for those states with older constitutions. Even so, the correlation is not perfect, and its size masks considerable variance in constitutional age among chronologically young political systems. Given my argument that the youngest states are the most fragile, this discrepancy between the two measures indicates that they are identifying different aspects of institutional age precisely in the most important range of country values. This discrepancy was already apparent in the regression estimates in the second and third columns of Table 6.

Legitimacy

The analysis of legitimacy addresses the nature of the relationship between rulers and ruled. It is therefore essential to examine the behavior of both groups. With this in mind, there are two critical ingredients to political legitimacy: to what degree do authorities rely on physical coercion, and to what extent to challengers to those authorities employ violent tactics to advance their interests?

The Official Use of Physical Force. The large-scale analysis of the ways that states and governments repress challenges has grown in recent decades. Organizations as diverse as Amnesty International, the Freedom House, and the U.S. Department of State routinely collect data that bear on this general problem. These data are thus sometimes generated by extra-governmental groups that seek in a watchdog capacity to mobilize general awareness of the use of coercion, while at other times they are developed by governments, to be used presumably in the policymaking process. Attention to the issue increased substantially with the publicity afforded human rights in the late 1970s by the Carter administration.

My emphasis on the use of physical force parallels this interest in many ways, but it is not motivated by human rights concerns. Such considerations are too broad for present purposes and divert attention away from the use of power as I have defined it. For example, the Universal Declaration of Human Rights endorsed by the United Nations in 1947 stressed the provision of such factors as food, clothing, housing, and medical care sufficient to maintain a minimal living standard along with political rights. These are, of course, important and interesting issues in their own right, but they do not bear directly on the problem at hand.

Even when attention is confined to the use of physical force, my approach diverges from a political "rights" orientation in the following way. Questions of legality necessarily bear on any evaluation of rights, and all regimes can legally employ physical force, albeit in varying degrees. Accordingly, the imposition of martial law or the detention of political opponents is usually justified as legal, and statutes bearing on "security" are typically invoked to advance such claims. Whether these proclamations are widely accepted is, of course, another matter, since it is generally unclear whose security is at issue. However, the important point is that if such justifications can be sustained, then it is not clear that political rights have been violated, even though physical force has been employed. In contrast, questions of legality have no bearing on the interpretation of the use of physical force within the power framework that I have adopted. If officials employ force, that fact directly reflects a loss of power (and thus diminished political capacity) regardless of any legal justification that they might offer. This distinguishes my approach from a human-rights perspective.

There are different ways of measuring the amount of force employed by officials. One might focus on the size of the state repressive apparatus and count either expenditures on internal security forces or the size (in terms of personnel) of those forces. The assumption here would be that states with larger internal security forces (standardized by population) rely more heavily on those forces. While this approach has much to recommend it, there are major practical difficulties in distinguishing internal from external security budgetary and personnel allocations. For example, although the imposition of martial law is typically defended on the grounds that it is an action designed to maximize internal security, martial law itself is usually administered by the military whose publicly announced purpose is to provide security against external threats to the state. The internal/external distinction is further clouded by the common use of appeals to internal security as a cover for the use of physical force against challengers and by the familiar claim by authorities that the challengers so acted against are agents of external forces.[8] Coupled with the political sensitivity of the information, these considerations make the relevant data hard to obtain.

But even without these problems of definition and information, it is important to recognize that measures of the size of internal security forces can never be more than incomplete proxies because they do not directly address the official *use* of force. Instead, on the presumption that size reflects strength, and leaving to one side questions of efficiency, they indicate at best the propensity of governments to employ force.

As an alternative gauge of the official use of force, one could transform the qualitative judgments of country experts into rankings of national differences. Perhaps the best known efforts along these lines are the evaluations compiled by the Freedom House (Gastil 1985), which include ratings of political liberties, such as rights of political expression and organization. Although this series bears more on issues of liberal democratic performance than it does on legitimacy as I have defined it, data of this type would seem in principle to offer a more clear-cut measure of repressiveness than does the first approach. However, the major practical difficulty is that ratings like Gastil's do not directly address the use of force.

Information that appears more directly linked to this question is available in the annual series on the application of official violence against the citizens of Third World countries, assembled by World Priorities (Sivard 1986: 24–25). Activities included in this classification are "torture, brutality, disappearances, and political killings." The classification itself is based on the publications and files of such organizations as Amnesty International, the Washington Office on Latin America, Americas Watch, the U.S. Department of State's *Country Reports on Human Rights Practices*, and Human Rights Internet (Sivard 1986: 42). While this coverage of sources is broad, the fact that the kinds of activities included under the rubric of official violence are not clearly defined limits the value of the measure. Further, the classification has only three categories of official violence ("none," "some," and "frequent"), and again the criteria for assignment of a country to a particular category are somewhat obscure.

In light of these difficulties, the most promising approach is to focus on *events* that involve the official use of force. As I will make clear below, this does not resolve all of the practical obstacles to measurement. But because it does make an explicit distinction between those occasions in which governments employ physical force from those occasions in which they do not (regardless of the rationales they offer), if affords the most fruitful basis from which to proceed, given the available alternatives.

When considering the use of force, governments have an extensive menu of options at their disposal. The declaration of martial law is one stratagem to which I have already alluded. It is perhaps the broadest tactic under the rubric of which a host of more specific actions are commonly included, and which is typically invoked to rationalize and provide a semblance of legality (if not the acceptance that comes with legitimacy) to those actions. But it is also the case that the use of force does not require a general proclamation of martial law, especially when governments are targeting particular groups rather than the population as a whole. A curfew may instead be imposed in selected geographic areas where specific opposition groups are the target. Even smaller groups or individuals may be targeted, in which case there is no purpose in designating geographic areas. Instead, political arrests are made, opponents are exiled, or newspapers are closed in apparently isolated fashion without resort to more general action by authorities.

The extensiveness of the menu of options available to authorities means that the set of activities one might designate as evidence of their use of physical force is necessarily heterogeneous. There is clearly a considerable variety in the *size* of the target groups. The range of forceful tactics (preemptive and reactive) employed against challengers is equally variegated. In other substantive settings, this heterogeneity might be a source of concern. For example, were one interested in tracing through a sequence of events in a given country, then the targets of particular actions, why they are targets, or the success of the action itself would become important considerations. Such an analytic focus might also require that attention be restricted to more homogeneous sets of activities. Despite their intrinsic significance and their manifest bearing on other analytic concerns, these issues are secondary in the evaluation of the general legitimacy of a regime. In any such evaluation, the question is not why a government decided to employ force in a given instance or how efficacious that action may have appeared to its initiators. The more fundamental issue centers on whether states do actually employ physical force over a specified time interval, so that they can be compared according to the pervasiveness of their reliance on coercion.

The most extensive set of data that address the frequency with which states employ physical coercion is reported in the *World Handbook of Political and Social Indicators* (Taylor and Jodice 1983, vol. 2: 61–77). Under the rubric of state coercive behavior, this compendium lists figures on "government sanctions," which identify censorship of individuals or institutions, general restrictions on political activity, and other restrictions on social and political behavior.

> Censorship includes actions by the authorities to limit, curb, or intimidate the mass media, including newspapers, magazines, books, radio, and television. Typical examples of such action are the closing of a newspaper or journal, or the censoring of articles in the domestic press or dispatches sent out of the country. . . . Restrictions on political behavior include general restrictive measures by authorities, such as the declaring of martial law, mobilizing troops for domestic security, and instituting a curfew. They also include actions specifically directed against an individual, a party, or other political organizations. Such specific actions include the removal of a government official reportedly because of his or her political beliefs and activities, the banning of a political party or acts of harassment against it, the arrest of opposition leaders on grounds of state security, the exiling or deportation of persons for engaging in political actions or for expressing opposition regarded as detrimental to the national interest, and the arrest or deportation of persons reportedly involved in political protest actions, including protest demonstration, riots, political strikes, armed attacks, and assassination attempts. Finally, restrictions on political behavior also encompass actions by the authorities against foreign espionage. (Taylor and Jodice 1983, vol. 2: 62–3)

Because this measure pertains to coercive behavior by the state, it refers only to events initiated by a formal government agency. Thus, in cases like Lebanon, where there has been little central authority since 1975, the coercive actions taken by the various private militia are not counted. Similar considerations apply to the activities of the death squads in various Latin American countries, since despite apparent associations with governmental elements, these do not constitute official agents.

In addition to this information on government sanctions, Taylor and Jodice report a separate series on political executions.

> A political execution is an event in which a person or group is put to death under orders of the national authorities while in their custody. Excluded are assassinations, even if known to have been arranged by the authorities, and persons killed in riots, armed attacks, strikes, and the like. Also excluded are executions for criminal offenses, such as murder, that are not reported to have political significance. Typically, a political execution is one in which the person executed is charged with activities threatening the security of the state, the regime, the government, or the leadership. (Taylor and Jodice 1983, volume 2: 63)

With respect to geographic and temporal coverage, the *World Handbook* data constitute the most comprehensive available collection. It includes information for over 140 countries for the thirty-five years starting in 1948 and ending in 1982.[9] In its complete form, this information is available in two series for each country. The first reports a daily count of political events, and the second is based on annual counts. For reasons that will become clear below, the data that I employ are based on aggregations of the annual series.

The country values for (a) the imposition of government sanctions and (b) political executions from 1948 through 1982 can be arranged in a variety of ways. First, for present purposes they are most usefully aggregated into five-year intervals. This smooths out short-run fluctuations in the official use of physical coercion. At the same time, comparing across the 35-year period provides some information on longer-term trends within countries.

Second, I have argued that we need to focus on differences of orders of magnitude. In addition, there is reason to place more emphasis on differences between lower scores and to discount differences between higher ones. For example, the differences between (a) 0 and 10 and (b) 50 and 100 political executions are not of equivalent significance, even though each involves a doubling of the raw scores. Going from none to ten executions is of more momentous import because it involves crossing the threshold between zero and one event. While the movement from fifty to 100 executions is certainly profound for the additional individuals involved, the score of fifty indicates that authorities were already employing force in a massive manner. Given this, the most interpretable metric for the government sanctions data is generated by applying a natural logarithmic transformation to the raw scores.[10] As I pointed out earlier, this transformation of the data preserves the original rank ordering, but attaches much more significance to differences between low values and minimizes differences between higher values.

I postpone a fuller evaluation of the properties of these data and turn to the question of how the severity of challenges to states is best measured.

The Violence of Challenges. Over the last twenty-five years, the systematic empirical analysis of domestic political conflict in a comparative context has received a good deal of attention (see, e.g., Gurr 1970 and Hibbs 1973 for two well-known studies). Although different scholars have often employed distinctive explanatory arguments, their investigations have all shared a central concern with understanding the conditions under which those who challenge authority resort to violence. Further, these studies have devoted considerable effort to questions of measurement, from which we can profitably draw.

Hibbs (1973: 7) argued that to be counted as challenges, the activities must meet three interrelated conditions. First, the behaviors in question need to have an anti-system nature, a condition that antigovernment protests meet, but pro-government parades do not. Second, they must have a clear and direct political significance, so that they "pose a threat of at least severe inconvenience to the normal operation of the political elite." This criterion excludes such incidents as "ordinary labor strikes," but includes "strikes with at least mildly threatening political objectives." Third, the behaviors must involve a collective endeavor, which stipulation is intended to exclude criminal activities like murder and armed robbery.

Employing these criteria in a dimensional analysis with data from over 100 countries for the years 1948 through 1967, Hibbs concluded that "mass political violence" has two general components: collective protest and internal war. The first of these reflects milder forms of violence, and includes antigovernment demonstrations, political strikes, and riots. Internal war refers to the escalated form, and encompasses deaths from political violence, "armed attacks," and political assassinations. Since it more clearly addresses variations in the severity of the violence with which challenges to regimes are mounted, internal war appears to be the more suitable general component for present purposes.

Even so, it is not clear all three of the variables identified by Hibbs bear equally on the question of internal war. As Hibbs himself points out (1973: 11), a good case can be mounted against including assassinations under the rubric of *mass* violence. At best, there is considerable uncertainty surrounding the political meaning, anti-system character, and collective significance of assassinations (Taylor and Jodice 1983: 43), which means that they do not necessarily meet the criteria specified for inclusion. I believe that a similar ambiguity surrounds the interpretation of the events labeled as "armed attacks," and indeed Hibbs's empirical results suggest that these events do not load cleanly on the internal war dimension.

These considerations suggest that the violence or severity of challenges is best measured by a single variable: the number of deaths from political violence. This approach has at least three advantages. First, a single variable is more readily interpretable than a composite variable. Death counts are less subject to the ambiguities just discussed because they reflect the severity of collectively based events with clear political significance. While some of these deaths stem from intergroup violence, many of them are caused by official or unofficial government agents. Second, if we conceive of violent challenges as activities with high potential costs to the participants, death counts provide the most direct available estimate of the costs that were actually incurred. Finally, and on a more practical level, there is a variety of evidence to indicate that, because of their visibility, deaths are much more likely to be considered newsworthy than the more specific events (riots, armed attacks, etc.) considered by Hibbs. They consequently tend to be more completely reported (on this point, see especially Snyder and Kelly 1977; Rosenblum 1981; Weede 1981).[11]

As was the case with the use of state physical coercion, the most comprehensive set of data on deaths from domestic political violence is reported in the *World Handbook of Political and Social Indicators* (Taylor and Jodice 1983, vol. 2: 48–51). These figures refer to the deaths that occurred in different kinds of specific events, including protests, riots, and armed attack events. "The category includes nationals who are casualties of foreign interventions in the country, but excludes deaths of foreigners. Also excluded are political executions, deaths in enemy prisons, deaths in international war, and deaths in border incidents with other countries, as well as homicide victims" (Taylor and Jodice, 1983, vol. 2: 43). Information is available for over 140 countries covering the thirty-five years from 1948 through 1982.

Paralleling my use of the information about coercion, these values are best treated in terms of the natural logarithmic values of the raw country scores. As I indicated earlier, this transformation places declining weight on country values as they increase. For instance, there were more reported casualties in the Nigerian civil war than in Indonesia in the 1960s, but the important point is that fatalities were massive in both countries.

Characteristics of the Data on Legitimacy. How well do these data reflect the official use of violence and the severity of challenges to authorities? In evaluating this question several issues need to be addressed. I consider, in turn, problems of reliability and validity, issues of aggregation, and possible standardizations of the data.

The compilers of the *World Handbook* data devoted a good deal of attention to the reliability of the conflict data they collected. Indeed, their concern in this regard is exemplary (see especially Taylor and Jodice 1983, vol. 2: chaps. 1 and 6). Information for each country was coded from two sources, *The New York Times* and one other (where possible, this second source as a regionally specific one). This procedure is reasonable because the evidence indicates that additional sources tend to yield little new information (see, e.g., Jackman and Boyd 1979). Further, Taylor and Jodice provide considerable information on inter-coder reliability. Of course, neither they nor I would claim that the data are without error. But the reliability of these data appears to be good, in the sense that they reasonably reflect the information available in the original documents.

Turning to the issue of validity, it is important to understand that these data reflect *reported* behavior; that is, events and casualties that the press deemed newsworthy. Even where there are no restrictions on the press, it is evident that news typically stresses the extraordinary and downplays the routine. Although some believe that this reflects a preference for "bad" over "good" events, nothing sinister or mysterious is involved. Just as fires are plainly more newsworthy than everyday trips to the market at the local level, assassinations attract more attention than, say, minor revisions to national budgets. In other words, there is every reason for the press to be more likely to cover and report events that assume a more spectacular form (Rosenblum 1981). In this connection, the counts I am employing are relatively dramatic. Deaths from violence are much more likely to be reported than minor peaceful protests. Similarly, there is considerable evidence to indicate that the imposition of repressive measures is more widely covered than their relaxation (Rosenblum 1981; Taylor and Jodice 1983).

Even so, attention paid by the press to different countries does vary in the absence of severe restrictions on the press. Some countries receive more attention because they are viewed as more strategically important or problematic. Thus, reporting on El Salvador (a small country) increased notably after 1981 with concern that the country might become another Vietnam (Taylor and Jodice 1983, vol. 2: 178–179). And national governments can take steps to increase at least minimally the volume of coverage accorded their country in the international press (Manheim and Albritton 1984).

The problem is of course exacerbated when governments systematically conceal information and restrict the press. Such efforts are common in states as diverse as the Soviet Union and South Africa. During the middle 1970s they gained momentum and apparent respectability in some quarters of the Third World with the UNESCO-sponsored effort to create a "New International Information Order." Among other things, this was described by its proponents as an attempt to place limits on Western control over the international media and to place more emphasis on "positive" rather than "negative" news.[12] The complaints of many non-Western participants are well summarized in the statement by Narinder K. Aggarwala (an official in the UN Development Program at the time) that rights to information are "fundamental but not absolute" (in Richstad and Anderson 1981: xvii). Aggarwala continued:

> The process of establishing equations and corelationships between various fundamental rights is going on throughout the world all the time, much more so in the Third World where the concepts of fundamental rights are being defined and interpreted *by the powers that be* in terms of each country's own national, historical, and cultural needs. While the media leaders are justified in striving for the maximum freedom of the press, the degree of freedom enjoyed by the press in a given country *will depend entirely on its leaders' perception of the country's political and security needs*. Examples can be found in the Western world as well. Media freedom is treated differently by various Western countries, according to their own historical development. (emphasis added)

The relativism and authoritarianism of this argument is self-evident. Given that the way in which leaders perceive their country's political and security needs is inextricably bound up with their own aspirations to retain office, the purpose of the proposed changes is also transparent.

Obviously, data on legitimacy are sensitive and therefore difficult to collect, and the obstacles increase with governmental efforts to conceal those data. But while we should be aware of these difficulties, their existence is hardly a brief for abandoning the available data. We need to remember that governments attempt to conceal information on the use of violence precisely because that information bears directly on their legitimacy. And, of course, material on censorship is included in the measure of government sanctions. While there is always room for refinement, I conclude that these data provide important information on the use of force by both officials and challengers.

Beyond the issues of reliability and validity, the data are aggregated summaries of events and casualties. It is difficult to draw inferences about the motivational forces behind the use of violence or about sequences of violence from information of this form. That fact may be a real constraint in some settings, as Snyder (1978), Tilly (1978), DeNardo (1985), and others have pointed out. For example, data like these cannot be used to analyze tactical calculations made by those who decide to engage in violence, whether officials or challengers.

But my focus is on variations in the overall legitimacy of regimes or states, not on issues having to do with tactics of those who employ violent tactics. The question then is not why or how violence was used in one particular setting and not in another, but the degree to which violence was employed, if at all. Aggregated data would seem both necessary and desirable for comparisons along these lines, because the question of interest is itself cast in aggregated terms. Further, I earlier emphasized the importance of examining the *use* rather than the threat of force, since all governments (states) have the capacity to employ violence. These data reflect that emphasis, because they deal with counts of events and causalities.

Of course, the manner in which I have aggregated the data is not the only possible way in which they could be assembled. Two issues are of interest here. First, I have already pointed out that the measure of the use of government sanctions includes a relatively heterogeneous set of events, which reflects among other things the variety of repressive techniques that is available to governments. But it may be useful for some purposes to disaggregate these data further, by distinguishing repression aimed at individuals (e.g., arrests) from that targeted at groups (e.g., declarations of martial law or censorship). Repression against individuals tends to be more discrete, while that against groups is generally more open-ended in terms of its duration. While recognizing the onset of repression targeted at groups is relatively straightforward, identifying the completion of the event is more difficult. Distinguishing repression according to the two basic kinds of target involved would reduce the heterogeneity in the measure of government sanctions.[13] The resulting series on sanctions against the individuals would also more closely parallel the separate series on political executions.

Second, I have aggregated the data into five-year intervals so that they reflect reasonably long-term trends. Nothing mystical is implied by this choice (as opposed, say, to a four-or six-year interval), and other analysts have used different periods (for example, Hibbs [1973] employed ten-year intervals). However, Sanders (1978; 1981) has claimed that any such intervals are excessively long, proposing instead that the data should be aggregated over monthly intervals. Once this is done, he reports that very few general patterns emerge. While I am not arguing that five-year aggregations are optimal for all purposes, Sanders' specific proposal is unsatisfactory.

In choosing a decent interval, it is important to understand that with very short intervals, analyses become extremely sensitive to short-term fluctuations of little substantive significance. Indeed, the shorter the interval, the less reliable the measure (Allison 1977). As a result, the analyses come increasingly to reflect noise, which implies Sanders' conclusion that there were few general patterns to report. That reliability should decrease with the length of the time period over which the data are aggregated will come as no surprise to those who have coded conflict data. Even a cursory examination of the sources will reveal that press reports often date events in a very general way, with statements like "It is estimated that 200 civilians were killed in ethnic conflict in the past several months." In the case of the *World Handbook* data, this is why the annual series are to be preferred over the daily series (used by Sanders).[14]

Finally, although they have been transformed logarithmically, the data under discussion are based on total scores that have not been standardized in any manner. This usage is not meant to suggest that they should never be standardized, however, and for some purposes certain adjustments may be useful. Consider three of the alternatives.

First, some might argue that these data could be profitably standardized by population size, given the wide variability in the latter across nation states. On closer inspection, however, the case for a population control is hardly overwhelming. There is little to recommend the procedure with the data on government sanctions targeted against groups, because events such as proclamations of martial law are typically directed at whole populations or subsets of them, defined for example by geographic region. The case for standardization by population size remains ambiguous when applied to official violence against individuals. Would the significance of the summary executions after the 1980 coup in Liberia have been appreciably altered had they occurred in the same number in much more populous Nigeria? Would the detention of twenty individuals for political activities be regarded as more momentous in New Zealand than in the United States? The ambiguity persists with the data on deaths in domestic political violence. Even though the population at risk of death in violence expands in some sense with population size, it is not clear that the political significance of deaths increases in the same manner. Where there may be reason to anticipate that population size is germane, that variable is best treated as a separate control variable whose effects can then be estimated rather than assumed a priori.[15]

Second, Bollen (1980; 1986) raises an interesting issue concerning the measure of government sanctions. That series, of course, includes repression against groups, in the form of press censorship, declarations of martial law, and the like. Where restrictions on the press were severe *before* the beginning of the series, however, there may be few further restrictions that could afterward be placed on the press, even if authorities were inclined to do so. Similarly, if a state of emergency had been declared prior to the beginning of the series, there would be no need for a repressive regime to impose martial law subsequently. Given these possibilities, the official use of force may be underestimated for some countries in this series unless further adjustments are made, and Bollen adjusted the series directly.[16] An alternative approach is to include appropriate adjustments as control variables, and estimate their effects. While the specific nature of any such controls will depend on the nature of the empirical model under consideration, the general goal would be to include the pervasiveness of restrictions in place at the beginning of the data series.

The third possible standardization that has been suggested (in assorted guises) stems from the proposition that raw counts of events cannot be compared directly because different political systems have differing traditions of violence. For example, Duvall and Shamir (1980) generated a measure of the coercive propensity of states from the residuals obtained by regressing the use of coercion on antigovernment protests. The official use of force is thus standardized by the extensiveness of challenges to regimes to yield a measure of the degree to which authorities over- or underreact to challenges. A very small residual is presumably taken as evidence that severe sanctions are justifiable because they were a response to a severe challenge. Sanders has made a parallel argument that levels of violence need to be "contextualized," because "'normal' patterns of political interaction vary from country to country" (1981: 74). He therefore proposed that the use of violence (by officials or by challengers) be standardized by prior levels of violence. Sanders' premise seems to be that violence loses much of its import if it is common or habitual. The implication is odd. Because it has a history of violence, high current levels of violence in country A do not signify a notable degree of instability; although it has much lower current levels of violence, country B is deemed more unstable simply because it has a history of even lower rates of violence.

Whether we consider the suggestion by Duvall and Shamir or that by Sanders, this third standardization is perverse. Indeed, these proposals come very close to a justification of the use of force.[17] They also confuse the use of force with the exercise of power. True, violence may beget violence, but such patterns are best modeled explicitly as has been done in many studies (e.g., Hibbs 1973; Duff and McCamant 1975; Weede 1981). There is no basis for normalizing various forms of violence against either each other or their own prior levels.

To summarize briefly, the way I have organized the data on legitimacy does not exhaust the possibilities. Decisions about the optimal manner in which they should be aggregated will depend on the goals of specific analyses. The same is true for decisions concerning standardization, whether by population size or by prior degrees of legitimacy. While they are not immune to error, these data offer a reasonable representation of the use of force by national governments and their challengers in the period. Of course, it is possible to envisage improvements that might be made to the series, but it should be recognized that such improvements will require a major effort. Part of my present purpose has been to offer substantive justification for this endeavor and to underscore the payoffs it will yield.

Implications

I have proposed a definition and measures of national political capacity conceived in terms of institutional capacity and legitimacy. The former is measured in terms of the age of the juridical state and the current constitutional form and the number of national executives in the prevailing constitutional period. The measurement of legitimacy is informed by a distinction between power and force; legitimate regimes are those that can induce compliance without resort to force and that are not challenged with violence. Measurement is necessarily inexact, of course, but the data I have introduced do allow broad comparisons of national political capacity across states.

I repeat that the approach outlined here is not intended as a substitute measure for democratic performance. The latter is not synonymous with national political capacity, and it is important that the two not be confounded empirically. Nonetheless, political capacity does have implications for democratic performance.

First, insofar as capacity bears on effectiveness of regimes whatever their form, relatively democratic regimes with higher levels of capacity should be more effective democracies. For example, there are more grounds for optimism about the prospects for democracy in India in 1990 than there were in 1947, given the routinization of political procedures over the past forty years. But the emergency of the 1970s coupled with ongoing communal violence remind us that those procedures are not completely institutionalized.

Second, my emphasis on legitimacy has some parallels with democratic theory. It is noteworthy that the measures of government repression that I have used are also employed in somewhat different form as part of a measure of political democracy by Bollen (1980). But the approach is not identical. When employed to reflect democracy, repression can be taken as an abrogation of political liberties. In my usage, the use of repression simply reflects a failure to find a political solution; that is, a failure to make the problem go away by any means (including co-optation and the like) excluding force.

Finally, the notion of capacity helps explain the failure of political democracy in the overwhelming majority of states that were decolonized after World War II. This failure was not generally anticipated around 1960. It is easy to forget that the ideological justification for decolonization was democratic. Colonial rule was denounced because it did not derive from or represent the people it governed (Emerson 1960: 243), and nationalist leaders themselves regarded self-government and democratic government as identical (Shils 1964: 103). In retrospect, it is clear that a major problem with this optimism was that it neglected the institutional youth of the "new" states. I believe that the only way to avoid that problem is to consider the implications of political capacity for democratic performance.

Notes

This research was materially aided by a fellowship from the Center for Advanced Study in the Behavioral Sciences, Stanford, California, with financial support provided by the National Science Foundation (BNS 84-11738). Additional support has been provided by the Political Science Department, Michigan State University, and by the Committee on Research and the Institute of Governmental Affairs, University of California, Davis. For helpful comments and advice on aspects of this research, I would like to thank Gabriel Almond, Kenneth Bollen, Michael Bratton, Bruce Bueno de Mesquita, Mary Jackman, Terry Moe, and Brian Silver.

  1. Unfortunately, the problem persists in some of the current literature (see, e.g., Muller 1988). For more extensive discussion, see Bollen and Jackman (1989).
  2. "There is nothing more difficult to take in hand, more perilous to conduct, or more uncertain in its success, than to take the lead in the introduction of a new order of things" (*The Prince*, VI).
  3. Alternative conventions could, of course, be followed. For reasons that will become clear below, these alternatives do not generate measures that can be distinguished in meaningful empirical terms from the one that I have adopted here.
  4. The two measures of chronological age have been rearranged in Table 3 and those following to reflect the number of years that had elapsed by the end of 1985 since sovereignty was achieved and the current constitutional arrangement was adopted, respectively. Thus, country scores like those in Table 2 have

been subtracted from 1986. No such modifications are necessary for the measure of generational age, for obvious reasons.

5. The logarithmic transformation, of course, substantially discounts the weight of extremely high country scores. This is why I argued earlier in this chapter that different conventions in coding the date of sovereignty for older states have no discernible impact on the empirical results (I adopted 1775 as the earliest date for this variable). By the same token, the distinction between having one or two leaders is more heavily weighted than the distinction between forty and sixty leaders. The mean values displayed in Tables 3 through 5 are calculated from the log-transformed distributions, but reported in their original, more interpretable metric.

6. Data on rates of energy consumption are from the World Bank (1986: 194–95), and are employed to maximize the number of cases. The World Bank does not report estimates of GNP for the nonmarket economies. While Summers and Heston (1984) do report estimates of real GDP for those economies, their coverage of other states is less complete. Energy consumption figures are available for all but two (Chad and Lesotho) of the countries included in Table 6. For the 108 countries for which estimates of both real GDP and energy consumption rates are available, the simple correlation between the two (using logged scores) is .95.

7. These correlations are again calculated from the logarithms of the country scores for the 124 states included in Table 4.

8. The idea of a national interest is difficult to sustain, especially when it is applied to domestic politics. This is what makes terms like "internal security threats" inherently ambiguous. That this ambiguity is recognized by many governments is reflected in recurrent attempts to discredit challengers by casting them as agents of external interests.

9. Taylor and Jodice (1983, vol. 2) report the data for the thirty years from 1948 to 1977. An updated version extending the series through the end of 1982 is available from the Inter-University Consortium for Political and Social Research. Here (and later in this chapter), I rely on the updated version.

10. Since there are several instances where the raw score is zero, and since the logarithm of zero is undefined, 1 was added to all raw scores prior to the transformation.

11. This is not, of course, to suggest that they are recorded without error. Instead, I am making the more modest claim that deaths from violence are more likely to be reported than the other events under discussion. It is interesting to note that in his original analysis Hibbs suggested death counts as the single variable most representative of his internal war dimension.

12. For a discussion of the issues involved and the views of the major protagonists, see the essays in Richstad and Anderson (1981).

13. Such a disaggregation would also alleviate the problem of the boundary in time of the sanctions events discussed by Taylor and Jodice (1983, vol. 2: 76).

14. For the deaths from domestic violence data, the annual series is also superior because it includes information from summary reports in addition to the daily reports (Taylor and Jodice 1983, vol. 2: 47).

15. This is the procedure employed by Hibbs (1973). For a useful recent survey of the use of ratio variables and their alternatives, see Firebaugh and Gibbs (1985).

16. Bollen used the government sanctions data as one component of his well-known index of political democracy. The adjustment he applied (1980: 376) involves subtracting the number of negative sanctions from a liberties index, formed by averaging measures of press freedom and the ability of groups to organize opposition groups.

17. Official coercion is reasonable if officials were challenged; in fact, if there is a negative residual (little coercion/high challenge) they underreacted and presumably should have coerced more. High civilian casualties are not particularly momentous in countries with a history (culture?) of violence.

References

ALLISON, PAUL D.
     1977   "The reliability of variables measured as the number of events in an interval of time." Pp. 238–253 in Karl F. Schuessler (ed.), *Sociological Methodology 1978*. San Francisco: Jossey-Bass.

ALMOND, GABRIEL A. AND JAMES S. COLEMAN (eds)
     1960   *The Politics of the Developing Areas*. Princeton: Princeton University Press.

BANKS, ARTHUR S.
  1986   *Political Handbook of the World*. Binghamton, NY: C.S.A. Publications.
BLACK, C. E.
  1966   *The Dynamics of Modernization: A Study in Comparative History*. New York: Harper and
            Row.
BOLLEN, KENNETH A.
  1980   "Issues in the comparative measurement of political democracy." *American Sociological
            Review* 45 (June): 370–390.
  1986   "Political rights and political liberties in nations: An evaluation of human rights measures,
            1950 to 1984." *Human Rights Quarterly* 8 (November): 567–591.
BOLLEN, KENNETH A. AND ROBERT W. JACKMAN
  1989   "Democracy, stability, and dichotomies." *American Sociological Review* 54 (August):
            612–621.
CUTRIGHT, PHILLIPS
  1963   "National political development: Measurement and analysis." *American Sociological Review*
            28 (April): 253–264.
DENARDO, JAMES
  1985   *Power in Numbers: The Political Strategy of Protest and Rebellion*. Princeton: Princeton
            University Press.
DEUTSCH, KARL W.
  1961   "Social mobilization and political development." *American Political Science Review* 55 (Sep-
            tember): 493–514.
DUFF, ERNEST AND JOHN MCCAMANT
  1975   *Violence and Repression in Latin America: A Quantitative and Historical Analysis*. New York:
            Free Press.
DUVALL, RAYMOND AND MICHAEL SHAMIR
  1980   "Indicators from errors: Cross-national, time-serial measures of the repressive disposition of
            governments." Pp. 155–182 in Charles L. Taylor (ed.), *Indicator Systems for Political, Eco-
            nomic, and Social Analysis*. Cambridge, MA: Oelgeschlager, Gunn, and Hain.
ECKSTEIN, HARRY
  1966   "A theory of stable democracy." Pp. 225–288 in Harry Eckstein, *Division and Cohesion in
            Democracy*. Princeton: Princeton University Press.
  1971   *The Evaluation of Political Performance*. Beverly Hills: Sage Publications.
EMERSON, RUPERT
  160   *From Empire to Nation: The Rise to Self-Assertion of Asian and African Peoples*. Cambridge:
            Harvard University Press.
EVANS, PETER B., DIETRICH RUESCHEMEYER AND THEDA SKOCPOL (eds)
  1985   *Bringing the State Back In*. New York: Cambridge University Press.
FIREBAUGH, GLENN AND JACK P. GIBBS
  1985   "User's guide to ratio variables." *American Sociological Review* 50 (October): 713–722.
GASTIL, RAYMOND D.
  1985   *Freedom in the World: Political Rights and Civil Liberties, 1984–1985*. Westport, CT: Green-
            wood Press.
GURR, TED ROBERT
  1970   *Why Men Rebel*. Princeton: Princeton University Press.
HIBBS, DOUGLAS A., JR.
  1973   *Mass Political Violence: A Cross-National Causal Analysis*. New York: Wiley-Interscience.
HOPKINS, RAYMOND F.
  1972   "Securing authority: The view from the top." *World Politics* 24 (January): 271–292.
HUNTINGTON, SAMUEL P.
  1968   *Political Order in Changing Societies*. New Haven: Yale University Press.
JACKMAN, ROBERT W.
  1975   *Politics and Social Equality: A Comparative Analysis*. New York: Wiley-Interscience.
  1978   "The predictability of coups d'etat: A model with African data." *American Political Science
            Review* 72 (December): 1262–1275.
JACKMAN, ROBERT W. AND WILLIAM A. BOYD
  1979   "Multiple sources in the collection of data on political conflict." *American Journal of Political
            Science* 23 (May): 434–458.

JACKSON, ROBERT H. AND CARL G. ROSBERG
    1982a   "Why Africa's weak states persist: The empirical and juridical in statehood." *World Politics*
           35 (October): 1–24.
    1982b   *Personal Rule in Black Africa: Prince, Autocrat, Prophet, Tyrant.* Berkeley and Los Angeles:
           University of California Press.
KESSELMAN, MARK
    1973   "Order or movement? The literature of political development as ideology." *World Politics*
           26 (October): 139–154.
KRASNER, STEPHEN D.
    1984   "Approaches to the state: Alternative conceptions and historical dynamics." *Comparative*
           Politics 16 (January): 223–246.
LERNER, DANIEL
    1958   *The Passing of Traditional Society.* New York: Free Press.
LINZ, JUAN
    1978   *The Breakdown of Democratic Regimes.* Baltimore: Johns Hopkins University Press.
LIPSET, SEYMOUR MARTIN
    1959   "Some social requisites of democracy: Economic development and political legitimacy."
           American Political Science Review 53 (March): 69–105.
LONDREGAN, JOHN B. AND KEITH T. POOLE
    1990   "Poverty, the coup trap, and the seizure of executive power." *World Politics* 42 (January):
           151–183.
MANHEIM, JAROL B. AND ROBERT B. ALBRITTON
    1984   "Changing national images: International public relations and media agenda setting." *Amer-*
           ican Political Science Review 78 (September): 641–657.
MERRIAM, CHARLES E.
    1934   *Political Power.* New York: McGraw Hill.
MULLER, EDWARD N.
    1988   "Democracy, economic development, and income inequality." *American Sociological Review*
           53 (February): 50–68.
NORDLINGER, ERIC A.
    1987   "Taking the state seriously." Pp. 353–390 in Myron Weiner and Samuel P. Huntington (eds.),
           Understanding Political Development. Boston: Little, Brown.
O'BRIEN, DONAL CRUISE
    1972   "Modernization, order, and the erosion of a democratic ideal: American political science
           1960–70." *Journal of Development Studies* 8 (July): 351–378.
RICHSTAD, JIM AND MICHAEL H. ANDERSON
    1981   *Crisis in International News: Policies and Prospects.* New York: Columbia University Press.
ROSENBLUM, MORT
    1981   *Coups and Earthquakes: Reporting the World for America.* New York: Harper and Row.
RUSTOW, DANKWART A.
    1967   *A World of Nations: Problems of Political Modernization.* Washington, D.C.: Brookings
           Institution.
SANDERS, DAVID
    1978   "Away from a general model of mass political violence: Evaluating Hibbs." *Quality and*
           Quantity 12 (June): 103–129.
    1981   *Patterns of Political Instability.* New York: St. Martin's.
SHILS, EDWARD
    1964   "The fortunes of constitutional government in the political development of the new states."
           Pp. 103–143 in John H. Hallowell (ed.), *Development: For What?* Durham, NC: Duke
           University Press.
SIEGFRIED, ANDRE
    1956   "Stable instability in France." *Foreign Affairs* 34: 394–404.
SIVARD, RUTH LEGER
    1986   *World Military and Social Expenditures*, 11th edition. Washington, D.C.: World Priorities.
SNYDER, DAVID
    1978   "Collective violence: A research agenda and some strategic considerations." *Journal of Con-*
           flict Resolution 22 (September): 499–534.

SNYDER, DAVID AND WILLIAM R. KELLY
   1977   "Conflict intensity, media sensitivity and the validity of newspaper data." *American Socio-
             logical Review* 42 (February): 105–123.
SPULER, BERTOLD
   1953   *Regenten und Regierungen der Welt.* Wurzburg: A. G. Ploetz Verlag.
SPULER, BERTOLD, C. G. ALLEN AND NEIL SAUNDERS
   1977   *Rulers and Governments of the World*, vol. 3. London: Bowker.
SUMMERS, ROBERT AND ALAN HESTON
   1984   "Improved international comparisons of real product and its composition, 1950–1980." *Re-
             view of Income and Wealth* 30 (June): 207–262.
TAYLOR, CHARLES L. AND MICHAEL C. HUDSON
   1972   *World Handbook of Political and Social Indicators*, second edition. New Haven: Yale Uni-
             versity Press.
TAYLOR, CHARLES L. AND DAVID A. JODICE
   1983   *World Handbook of Political and Social Indicators*, third edition. New Haven: Yale University
             Press.
TILLY, CHARLES
   1978   *From Mobilization to Revolution.* Reading, MA: Addison-Wesley.
VELIZ, CLAUDIO
   1980   *The Centralist Tradition in Latin America.* Princeton: Princeton University Press.
WALLERSTEIN, IMMANUEL
   1974   *The Modern World System: Capitalist Agriculture and the Origins of the European World
             Economy in the Sixteenth Century.* New York: Academic Press.
WEBER, MAX
   1946   "Politics as a vocation." Pp. 77–128 in H. H. Gerth and C. Wright Mills (eds.), *From Max
             Weber: Essays in Sociology.* New York: Oxford University Press.
WEEDE, ERICH
   1981   "Income inequality, average income, and domestic violence." *Journal of Conflict Resolution*
             25 (December): 639–653.
WEINER, MYRON
   1965   "Political integration and political development." *The Annals* 358 (March): 52–64.
World Bank
   1983   *World Tables*, third edition. Baltimore: Johns Hopkins University Press.
   1986   *World Development Report 1986.* New York: Oxford University Press.

8

Measures of Government Change: Indicators of Democracy from Mass Media Reporting

Charles Lewis Taylor

Events of transition in the exercise of central governing power are insufficient to measure democracy in all of its complexity and color, but peaceful change undertaken by legally established means on a regular basis is a prerequisite for democracy. Hence careful observation of the processes by which power is transferred, shared, or maintained is essential for the measurement of democracy. Several measures of regular and irregular, major and minor, successful and unsuccessful government change have been developed and are presented here for nine countries.

‘‘**M**ore governments are changed by coups d'etat than by elections" runs the blurb on a little book on violence (Luttwak 1969). This popular belief, encouraged by armchair analysts, is simply wrong. Coups and earthquakes get our attention, but a careful reading even of the mass media provides a considerable amount of data on many other political events. Actual counts from these sources make it clear that considerably more changes in governments take place by regular means of one kind or another than by coups d'etat and other violent events.

The purpose of the indicators of governmental change reported in the *World Handbooks of Political and Social Indicators* (Taylor and Hudson 1972; Taylor and Jodice 1983) is to document the events of transition in the exercise of central governing power. Taken alone, they are not sufficient to measure democracy in all of its complexity and color. Peaceful change regularly undertaken by legally established means is surely a prerequisite for democracy,

Charles Lewis Taylor is professor of political science and international studies and chair of the Department of Political Science at Virginia Polytechnic Institute and State University. He is author of the *World Handbooks of Political and Social Indicators* and editor of *Aggregate Data Analysis, Why Governments Grow*, and *Indicator Systems for Political, Economic and Social Analysis*.

but it is possible for these conditions to be present in political systems operating with other nondemocratic bases of legitimacy. Even so, the processes through which power is transferred, shared, or maintained are basic for the measurement of democracy. Distinctions between regular and irregular transfers, between adjustments and fundamental changes, and between successful and unsuccessful attempts at change help us to discriminate among political systems with regard to their responsiveness toward their populations. While democracy may be more than responsive change, it must at least be that.

This conception implies measurement of behavior at the institutional level. Political institutions as objects of scholarly examination were casualties of the behavioral revolution forty years ago. As attention was directed to what individuals did and thought, and as individual and group behavior became the focus for the creative edge in political science, the more traditional concerns with the state and its actions and structures tended to appear old-fashioned and irrelevant.

So the state tended to get left out of the measurement movement that accompanied the behavioral revolution. As serious measurement of political phenomena got underway, interest centered on individual behavior, and on the attitudes and values underlying that behavior. Party affiliation and voting choice seemed easier to measure than the degree of democracy or the responsiveness of government to popular need. This may be innately so, but it is also surely true in part because not enough theoretical attention has been devoted to the measurement of institutions and institutional change. The emphasis on political institutions as important for social and economic outcomes and as mediating variables between a changing socio-economic environment and varieties of political performance argues for a return to a systematic observation of executive, constitutional, and administrative political arrangements within societies.

Concepts Needed for Measurement

Diamond, Lipset, and Linz (1983: 3) define democracy as a political system that (a) has "meaningful and extensive *competition* among individuals and organized groups . . . for the major positions of government power," (b) "a 'highly inclusive' level of political participation in the selection of leaders and policies" and (c) "a level of *civil and political* liberties . . . sufficient to insure the integrity of political competition and participation." Added to these requirements of competitive participation within a free environment is their concern for stability, i.e., the endurance and persistence of regimes over time in spite of periods of intense conflict, crisis, and strain. The most responsive of governments is of little lasting value if it cannot be responsive over a reasonable period of time.

This definition of democracy concentrates upon the conditions and actions of the populations within a society. What are the conditions that allow ordinary people to have a say in the running of their government? What must they do to give effect to their interests? What in fact is the democratic society? And how does it remain stably democratic over time?

The same problem can also be viewed from a governmental or institutional point of view. How do the institutions of government operate so that they are responsive to the democratic elements within society? Does change at the institutional level take place in response to relatively low-level demands stated within the context of the regular political process so that periodic crises of violent pressure are not required to make things happen? Or does even violent pressure have no effect in producing changes desired by the general population?

These two approaches to the measurement of democracy are not in conflict with one another. In the best and most complete of measurement systems, they need to complement one another. Competition among individuals and organized groups can be observed through the number of active political parties and the intensity of action, dispersion of interests, and degree of support for political interest groups. It is also reflected in changes of government on a more or less regular basis. The periodicity of elections, relatively frequent executive adjustments, and regular transfers in executive power all indicate a competitive political process.

The inclusivity of participation can be measured by the proportion of population voting in elections, although the meaning and significance of the vote varies so widely from place to place and from time to time that great care needs to be exercised in the creation of control variables to use with voting percentages. One of these controls should be the proportion of population legally able to vote or the identification of groups within society whose participation is restricted by more informal, but effective, cultural and social restraints. To some extent, these restrictions are reflected in the number and intensity of sanctions imposed by governments on their populations. There are appropriate reasons even for political sanctions, but governments that must resort frequently to such sanctions are governments that are not perceived as very responsive by those who are being sanctioned.

The degree of political and civil liberties can be estimated from data of this sort, collected directly from the mass media or from other research groups such as Amnesty International and Freedom House. These data, while rather personal in their effects, are nevertheless societal or even institutional in their nature. Liberties, particularly political ones, are directly reflected in a low ratio of imposition to relaxation of sanctions and the incidence of few successful or unsuccessful attempts at irregular executive power transfer. Institutional change that does not require intervention from the military, the police, or other similar groups is more likely to be characteristic of systems with high levels of personal liberty than of those with high levels of personal restriction.

Diamond's, Lipset's, and Linz's linking of stability with the concept of democracy is essentially a system-level concern. Various indicators have been used to measure stability. Perhaps foremost among these have been differing ways to count, in years, the length of time that particular constitutional or institutional arrangements have been in place or that modernizing leadership has been in control. Another, more direct method is to track the regularity of government change within a selected period of time. Countries with few if any external interventions, with periodic executive transfers undertaken by duly constituted means, and without irregular transfers are more stable than others. To be sure, in the historical measurement of political stability—perhaps more so than with most other event indicators—one is implicitly making a projection from past to future. But then such a projection is relatively well founded on historical experience.

Stability, or at least consistency over time, is important to the measurement of government change through the indicators reported in the *World Handbooks*. In creating them, we believed that a system, if it is to be democratic, i.e., if it is to be responsive to popular demand, must be subject to frequent challenge, and that this challenge and its response must take place within the context of some previously prescribed, understood, and commonly accepted set of rules.

We did not assume that stability is the same thing as democracy. It is entirely possible to have a fully stable government that is in no way responsive to its population. In the old days that was called a traditional system. Whether through tradition, reactionary fundamentalism, or a radical ideology of government centralism, it is possible to have legitimacy for a wide range of government actions, leaders, and procedures for decision making. So the *World Handbook* indicators measure more than stability. They attempt to catch the means by which this stability is effected.

Diamond, Lipset, and Linz make use of a series of categories into which they place a sample of Third World countries. Their categories are determined essentially by two dimensions: "democrativeness" and "stability." Undoubtedly, underlying these two dimensions are a number of other less than perfectly correlated variables. With a sample of only twenty-eight polities, however, and with six to fifteen categories already available in only two dimensions, the problem quickly becomes obvious. There are too many relevant variables and too few cases, a problem that always characterizes cross-national comparative research.

At some point in the analysis, the dimensions must be collapsed. Perhaps there are no cases in some set of categories or the potential variations are irrelevant to the real world. Or perhaps each case is perceived as unique so that comparatively based theoretical statements are impossible. At some point the analyst must become the scholar and take some risks in an effort to say something wise and useful. Before that point, it is still helpful to measure as carefully as possible as many of the underlying dimensions as we can. We are not entirely sure which will turn out to be the essential ones.

The *World Handbook* measures of governmental change then are efforts to get at and to put specific numbers on at least some of the underlying dimensions. They do not directly measure competition among individuals and organized groups, levels of participation in the selection process, and the degree of political and civil liberties (although other series in the *World Handbooks* do), but they measure institutional consequences of these. These indicators of change in government allow a systematic quantitative comparison of nation-states at an institutional level.

The classification of government changes is complex; the kinds of change are many and patterns among them infinite. The event definitions were developed interactively with the sources as we tried to reflect what actually happened in the real world. Even so, others looking at particular changes may find our abstractions of specific historical events at variance with their understandings, but their interpretations have already taken series of events that originally took place within a matter of hours or even of minutes and have aggregated and arranged them into some more complex, explanatory whole. The purpose of the measurement is to arrive once again at the identification and cataloging of the original component events in order that alternative stories can be told.

The effort to measure the extent and frequency of government change, of whatever sort found, led to the construction of the categories that turned out to be needed, given the events reported in the sources employed. Unfortunately, this method was limited to formal executive power changes; "real" or informal power holders may have been ignored. Moreover, events of a similar type may have very different consequences. We are able to perceive and record only the immediate and manifest attributes of the event. These are measures for further analysis, not the analysis itself.

Indicators

The first dimension in the measurement of government change is regularity. A change in the national executive from one person or group to another that is accomplished through conventional legal or customary procedures unaccompanied by actual or directly threatened physical violence is said to be regular. Irregular changes are those that are characterized by the presence of violence or by its immediate threat or that are undertaken by abnormal procedures, i.e., by means that do not conform to the prevailing conventional procedures of the political system. The latter include not only spectacular, bloody depositions but also bloodless coups d'etat. They may be initiated by groups, cliques, cabals, parties, or factions either inside or outside a government and its agencies. They are carried out sometimes by elements within the population and sometimes by foreign conspirators.

Implicit in this measurement is an institutional understanding of democracy. Unless there is a circulation of elites in power through means that are generally accepted as appropriate, it is difficult to think of a government as responsive. This position is consistent with either a classic pluralistic view or the elite competitive view. What it does not accept is forceful change brought about by groups who have physical power but who do not command majority support within the regularly constituted legal system.

The absence of irregular change is a necessary but not sufficient condition for democratic government. Regular change may also be absent or changes may take place within constitutional and legal structures that allow the continued dominance of a small elite based upon ideological understandings. Therefore, *World Handbook* indicators of government change must be supplemented by other information for a complete picture of the conditions of governing within a country. These indicators also do not speak to some of the issues raised by more radical critiques of pluralist democracy. They do not consider "structural" violence whether by the left or the right. This is not because such consideration is unimportant. It is essential, but not everything is possible simultaneously.

A second dimension for indicators of government change is degree of change. Executive transfers may involve the replacement of one primary leader or ruling group with another. Such a transfer is a major change in power, although it may represent either a movement from one group to another closely aligned ideological or programmatic group or a movement between radically different groups. Other changes may be of a lesser degree. The modification in the membership of a national executive body may not signal a transfer of formal power from one leader or ruling group to another, but such reshuffles or shake-ups indicate at least minor shifts in power. Frequent occurrences of this sort indicate a system that is quickly responsive to political pressures. Not too much should be read into this indicator, however, since it may be a matter of style as to whether a system responds fully on a periodic basis, or partially in small but frequent adjustments.

The third dimension for government change indicators is success. Some changes are attempted but are not accomplished. These may be attempted either through the legal and conventional procedures or through the use of physical force. These events of "non-change" are important for analysis because they tell us something about efforts at change that significant groups in the population would like to make.

Using these dimensions, we constructed the following indicators:

1. A *successful regular executive transfer* is a change in the office of national executive from one leader or ruling group to another that is accomplished through legal or customary procedures and is unaccompanied by actual or directly threatened physical violence. The office of national executive refers both to individual leaders, such as presidents or prime ministers, and to collegial executive bodies, such as cabinets composed of one or more parties or groups. In the latter case, a change is recorded if a constituent element is added or if a new element replaces an old one. Chief executives include monarchs, presidents, prime ministers, and party chiefs in countries where single parties exercise decisive power, paralleling as supervising the affairs of government. Also included are all other analogous offices and titles that may not enjoy general usage. In some political systems, there are two chief executives. To avoid qualitative judgments about the relative significance of prime ministers and presidents, changes in both offices were coded. In con-

stitutional or traditional monarchies, however, only changes of prime minister were coded.

For a transfer to be scored, it was necessary that the office of chief executive actually change hands, although the new recipient of power could have held office previously. The extension of an executive's tenure through elections, however, was coded as a renewal. (See below.)

On occasion, the consummation of a power transfer took more than a single twenty-four hour period. In these cases, the date of the completion of the power transfer was recorded as the date of the event. For example, in the restructuring of a cabinet, the event is recorded as of the day the new coalition of parties took office, not the day of the precipitating resignations. In the case of a newly elected president or prime minister, the executive transfer is recorded when office was taken, not when the election results were announced.

2. An *unsuccessful regular executive transfer* is an abortive attempt by persons not holding national executive office to obtain such office through legal or conventional procedures. Such an event may occur when an incumbent executive has already lost or relinquished formal authority (although he or she may still hold the office in a caretaker capacity). The confirmation of a ruling individual or group in power is not coded as an unsuccessful regular executive transfer but rather is called a renewal.

A recurring example of this type of event is the appointment of a premier who fails to form a coalition government or who fails to have a proposed government approved by the legislature. Confidence votes initiated by the government are not coded, but successful votes of nonconfidence initiated by the opposition are.

3. A *renewal of executive tenure* is a non-change in government. It is a renewal of formal power for those who hold it by means of regularly constituted channels. The reelection of a president or of a majority party in parliament that supports an incumbent prime minister are examples. The reappointment of an incumbent who has resigned, the defeat of a vote of censure, and the passing of a vote of confidence that is initiated by the opposition are also examples.

4. An *executive adjustment* is a change in the composition of the ruling elite and its most prevalent example is the cabinet coalition shift. More formally, an executive adjustment is a modification in the membership of a national executive body that does not signify a transfer of formal power from one leader or ruling group to another. National executive bodies include cabinets, councils of ministers, presidential offices, military juntas, and ruling party councils in states where authoritative power is exercised by a single party. The simple redistribution of ministerial portfolios among the same individuals does not constitute an executive adjustment. There must be a movement in or out of the executive body or the creation or elimination of cabinet posts.

Executive adjustments are considered minor in the power process because only one or two positions change hands and the control exercised by the leader or ruling group is not transferred or lost. Indeed, it is usually strengthened.

5. A *successful irregular executive transfer* is a change in the office of national executive from one leader or ruling group to another that is accomplished outside the conventional legal or customary procedures for transferring power that are in effect at the time of the event. No qualitative assessment of subsequent political and social significance is built into this indicator. Such an event may precipitate a fundamental change in the political system, or the system may continue substantially unchanged except for the irregularity of the power transfer event itself. Again the single indicator does not tell us everything that we wish to know.

Irregular power transfers are conceptually close to the conventional notion of a coup d'etat. Some events that historians could consider a single coup d'etat, however, are represented in our coding scheme as two or more discrete irregular change events. Our only criterion for success in an irregular power transfer is that there be a report stating that the new leadership has actually replaced the old, arrogating to itself the titles and functions of chief executive. No minimum tenure limit could be imposed without being unduly arbitrary. The indicator is more sensitive to maneuverings and countercoups than a more general definition would allow.

6. An *unsuccessful irregular executive transfer* is a reported failed attempt by an organized group to remove and to replace the incumbent national executive by means outside the conventional procedures for transforming formal power. It is important that such an event be an actual attempt at seizing power. The potential for misrepresentation in a "plot" discovered by the authorities is too great to allow the inclusion of all of these. An attempt must also take place in the capital or in the center of actual government. A revolt or mutiny in a province or another city is considered only an armed attack against the government.

The criterion for success is whether or not the incumbent executive is effectively removed from exercising his or her powers and the challenger is installed in his or her place. There is no time condition; a challenger who displaces the incumbent executive even for a period of a few hours has effected a successful irregular power transfer. Unsuccessful attempts are those that do not get even that far. (Definitions for these indicators are taken from the *World Handbooks*, published by Yale University Press.)

These six indicators make up the government change measurements used in the *World Handbook* data collections. They are designed to map out the institutional history of power transfers in the countries of the world since 1948. Other indicators relevant to the measurement of democracy are also included. Among these are government sanctions, age of national institutions, party fractionalization, press freedom, voter turnout, electoral irregularity, political and civil rights indexes, strength of organized labor, political and economic

TABLE 1
Irregular Changes in Government as a Proportion of All Major Government Change Events

	Successful Change Only		Successful and Unsuccessful Attempts	
	no.	%	no.	%
Australia	0:26	0.0	0:27	0.0
India	0:39	0.0	0:44	0.0
Switzerland	0:37	0.0	0:37	0.0
Kenya	0:22	0.0	1:23	4.3
Albania	0:12	0.0	2:14	14.3
Syria	12:82	14.6	25:119	21.0
China	5:30	16.7	8:34	23.5
Algeria	4:22	18.2	7:28	25.0
Argentina	8:35	22.9	23:52	44.2

discrimination, and potential separatism. It is not possible to deal with each of these in the present paper, however.

Some Comparisons

Not many irregular changes are attempted even in the most undemocratic countries. Change following legally and conventionally prescribed patterns is the norm. Hence, it is better to analyze the percentages of irregular changes to all changes and to renewals of executive power than to look only at the aggregate numbers. The more that popular demand is met by adequate response through the regular political process, the less likely will be crises of violent pressure. The greater the proportion of these crises to total change, the less likely are democratic norms suffused throughout the society.

Percentages for nine countries are reported in Table 1. Countries were chosen for geographical distribution and for political system type. Five of the countries had no irregular changes in government in the thirty-five years between 1948 and 1982. Three of these—Australia, India, Switzerland—are generally recognized as democratic countries. Four others—Syria, China, Algeria, Argentina—had a number of irregular changes and many additional unsuccessful attempts at the same during the thirty-five years. The proportion of irregular changes to all changes and renewals ranges from 14.6 percent to 22.9 percent. When unsuccessful attempts are included, the percentages are even higher. In systems that are undemocratic, violent pressure may in fact not produce the changes in governmental responsiveness that are sought, so that coups d'etat may become a pattern of political life.

Although Kenya and Albania had no irregular changes during the period under study, there were unsuccessful attempts for such change in each. Kenya can be perceived as a marginal case of democracy, but it is difficult to think of Albania as democratic in any sense. Absence of irregular change is a characteristic of democratic systems, but it may be true for other systems as well. There are bases for legitimacy other than democracy, although these are becoming more and more scarce in the modern world. Albania is a country in which traditionalism and ideology have combined to bolster a stable, if

TABLE 2
Government Adjustments

	Number	Adjustments/ Major Changes
Australia	48	1.846
India	113	2.897
Switzerland	15	.405
Kenya	23	1.045
Albania	24	2.000
Syria	67	.817
China	79	2.633
Algeria	29	1.318
Argentina	147	4.200

undemocratic, government. The number of regular changes and renewals of executive power is smaller for Kenya and much smaller for Albania than for any of the other seven countries. A truly democratic system must have frequent political challenges that take place within the context of a common set of rules.

Adjustments within the ruling structure may also be means by which governments may respond to popular demand. Unfortunately, they may also be ways to enhance undemocratic power. Minor power changes of this kind may reflect shifting coalitions among factions or parties, but similar changes in a military junta are more likely to be related to power struggles among unrepresentative elites. Adjustments, it turns out, are less clearly related to the degree of democracy within a system than are major government changes. Adjustments are evidence of responsiveness, but the question remains as to whom the response is made.

Table 2 presents the nine countries in the same order as in Table 1 and gives the number of adjustments along with the ratio of adjustments to total government change. There is a tendency for less democratic countries to have a higher ratio of adjustments to major changes, but this relationship is not a strong one. In order for this measure to be more useful in assessing the degree of democracy in a country, more information would have to be used.

The data thus far have been considered for the period as a whole. This makes sense in that democratic norms are subject primarily to slow growth or decline within a society. Governments may change relatively rapidly, but cultures do not. Nevertheless, secular shifts do take place and it is worth examining the experience of thirty-five years—as is done in Table 3—to identify what may be found there.

The three countries that had no attempted irregular change also had rather consistent patterns of regular change or renewals over time. Switzerland is the very model of consistency since it elects a new president of its Federal Council every year. Nevertheless, the parliamentary systems of India and Australia, with their variable lengths of times between elections, also demonstrate a consistency in regular change that differs from the less democratic countries.

Much of Kenya's change is concentrated in the years surrounding inde-

TABLE 3
Periodicity of Major Government Change 1948–1982

	1948	1949	1950	1951	1952	1953	1954	1955	1956	1957	1958	1959	1960	1961	1962	1963	1964	1965	1966	1967	1968	1969	1970	1971	1972	1973	1974	1975	1976	1977	1978	1979	1980	1981	1982
Australia																																			
Regular	1																		1	1	1			1	1		1	1		1					
Unsuccessful Regular																							1												
Renewals	1			1	1	1	1	1				2				2		2			1			1			1	1					1		
Irregular																																			
Unsuccessful Irregular																																			
India																																			
Regular						1									1		2		2	1		1	1				1			2		1	1		1
Unsuccessful Regular					2																									2					1
Renewals	1			2		1				4					1	1	1	4	3	4					1							1			
Irregular																																			
Unsuccessful Irregular																																			
Switzerland																																			
Regular	1	1	1	1	1	1	1	1	1	1	1	1	1	1	1	1	1	1	1	1	1	1	1	1	1	1	1	1	1	1	1	1	1	1	1
Unsuccessful Regular																																			
Renewals													1				1																		
Irregular																																			
Unsuccessful Irregular																																			
Kenya																																			
Regular					1								1	1		1	2	3	1			2								1					1
Unsuccessful Regular																																			
Renewals															1				1			1			1			2	1			1			
Irregular																																		1	
Unsuccessful Irregular																																			
Albania																																			
Regular	2				1	1									1				1															1	1
Unsuccessful Regular																																			
Renewals											1		1																	1					1
Irregular																																			
Unsuccessful Irregular						1		1																											
Syria																																			
Regular	1	3	3	5	1					4	3	1	2	1	1			5	3	4	3	2	2			1	2					1			
Unsuccessful Regular	4	1	1	9						2	1	3	1						1	1															
Renewals	2	2	2	2						1	2	2			1				1	1		2	1				1	2							
Irregular	3			2		1												1	1	1			1			1	1								
Unsuccessful Irregular				1			1	1			1							1	2	1	1	1						1				1			1

TABLE 3
(Continued)

	1948	1949	1950	1951	1952	1953	1954	1955	1956	1957	1958	1959	1960	1961	1962	1963	1964	1965	1966	1967	1968	1969	1970	1971	1972	1973	1974	1975	1976	1977	1978	1979	1980	1981	1982
China																																			
Regular	3	3										1								1								3		1			1	1	2
Unsuccessful Regular		1																																	
Renewals	1						1		1		1	1							1	1			1						1						
Irregular	1																				4														
Unsuccessful Irregular	1						1		1																										
Alberia																																			
Regular		1						1					1	2			1			1			3		1	1						1	2		
Unsuccessful Regular																							1	2											
Renewals													1																		1				1
Irregular																1			2				1												
Unsuccessful Irregular																			1	1				1											
Argentina																																			
Regular				1					1				1					2	2			2	1			1		3	1	2				5	3
Unsuccessful Regular					1													1																	
Renewals						1																										1			
Irregular					2											2				1			1	1					1						
Unsuccessful Irregular				1				2	1				1	1	4	1	1	1							1			1							

pendence. In this it follows the pattern of most sub-Saharan African countries. The one Kenyan attempt at irregular transfer of power came at the end of the period, again following a pattern set in much of the rest of the region. Albania's attempts at such transfer, on the other hand, came much earlier in the period. After that, change of any kind became scarce. The country reached greater stability in its undemocratic ways.

Three of the countries that experienced irregular changes—Syria, China, Algeria—had periods of time with relatively little change of any kind and other periods with a great deal of change. In Syria, there were forty-four regular changes of government up until 1966 and a dramatic reduction thereafter. This turnabout was true for irregular changes as well; i.e., irregular change was not replaced by regular change. Syria simply continued to be undemocratic in other ways. In China, several changes occurred before the great revolution in 1949, but thereafter change of any kind was rare until the late 1970s, with the exception of the Cultural Revolution. Change in China comes in fits and starts. In Algeria, there was a great reduction in both regular and irregular change after the French left in the mid-1960s. The struggle to gain self-government did not result in responsive government, if that is measured by the frequency of political challenges.

Argentina is an exception to this relationship of consistency of change and the presence of irregular government change. Regular changes and renewals were spread out relatively evenly over the thirty-five years. Irregular changes and attempts at irregular change also continued through much of the time with a concentration especially in the late 1950s and early 1960s. Argentina is a country that continues to display signs of both democracy and nondemocracy.

Data Quality

It is of primary importance that any data collection be replicable. First of all, this requires a clear statement of category definitions and of coding rules. Even with very extensive notes made by previous coders, however, the task of replication is sometimes difficult. Yet ambiguity, in either the coding procedures or the original sources, is only one of the problems in the collection of events data. We have tried to carry out the coding with clinical detachment and without undue intrusion of our own values, but complete objectivity is never possible for finite people. We can only hope that we have made our biases known and that we have kept them to a minimum.

The training of coders has received considerable attention. It was essential that the assistants approach the sources and the coding scheme with a common understanding. Even with stringent training, however, it is easy for coders to develop their own specific, implicit definitions and coding conventions. Minimizing this diversity requires constant managerial oversight, renewed substantive training, periodic testing, and willingness to discard data that do not meet the required standards.

Tests of inter-coder reliability were employed to check upon consistency of coding among coders and over time. Each coder coded events for common samples of countries and time periods. These samples were constructed to avoid periods of either high concentrations or absences of events. Samples had to include enough events to assess coder accuracy but not so many as to distort the workload. Results of these tests are reported in the second and the third editions of the *World Handbook*. (See Taylor and Hudson 1974: 392–412, and Taylor and Jodice 1983: vol. 2, 188–96.)

But coders, no matter how good they are, must rely upon the sources that are available. Ideally, of course, the distribution of events should be independent of the sources used, but that has never been the case. The source quality problem did not originate with quantitative analysis. Historians have always been at the mercy of what happened to be recorded and of artifacts that happened to have been left and found. Similarly, personal interviews, employed in much contemporary research, produce impressions and memories that cannot easily be checked and they cannot often be replicated. The implicit nature of fragmentary evidence makes it no less of a problem for scholarly work. Even if perfect sources are impossible, it is still our responsibility to choose sources that are as comprehensive in coverage and as unbiased in perspective as possible.

The first problem with mass media sources is the selection decisions made with regard to what is to be reported and to be published. The range of freedom for the press varies widely from country to country. Governments exercise censorship and editors may limit independent reporting on the basis of what they believe to be politically acceptable. Countries also attempt actively to influence reporting and there is some evidence that such attempts are successful. Beyond these politically motivated distortions are those due to limited resources. Even the largest news organizations cannot cover all the countries all of the time nor do they have space or time to include even all of the events that they know about. Moreover, the events that are reported and the facts about those events that are written are filtered through the particular values and understandings of the reporters on the scene.

Are the mass media then unusable? The choice may simply be these data or none at all. Yet the question remains. Can measures taken from the mass media be used for political analysis? There is now a good deal of evidence that the mass media, even the elite press, are particularly sensitive to spectacular events that occur in selected "interesting" sections of the world. Editors publish items that they believe will be of interest to their readers. Unfortunately, internal political events, especially in the countries of the developing world, are not considered to be of high interest by editors. Documentation on some of the reporting bias is reported by Taylor and Jodice (1983: 178–179).

Efforts were made to recognize and to deal with this bias by selecting supplementary sources for the coding effort. A consensus has grown up that *The New York Times* is the best single printed source for event data coding. But regionally specific secondary sources, which generally distill reporting from national newspapers, wire services, and government information agencies, have been shown to increase significantly the number of events reported and the amount of information for each event. Moreover, we have reason to believe that the additional information evens out some of the peaks and valleys of reporting in *The New York Times*. Further discussion of sources used for the data collection are reported by Taylor and Jodice (1983: 180–186).

More recently some experimental work has been done using the wire services directly. Through the use of NEXIS, an information retrieval system that includes a large number of wire services and news publications, we were able to examine several sources and compare them with regard to coverage of domestic political events. After some initial work, we concentrated on three wire services—the Associated Press, United Press International, and Reuters, and two newspapers—*The New York Times* and *The Washington Post*. These clearly had the most extensive worldwide coverage. To be sure, they are all American or British based and sources from other areas, including the Eastern countries or the Third World, would have provided additional perspective. They would have also added enormously to the cost of the work and would have provided very few additional events.

We found that the AP offered the most intensive and country-extensive articles. The UPI, on the other hand, was roughly equivalent to the AP with regard to countries covered, but it was lower on total volume and relevant articles. As our research progressed, the UPI began to report less and less relevant news. This was probably related to its increasing financial problems and its eventual bankruptcy. UPI remained the second most useful source (after the AP) for the period of our testing (1982–84), but Reuters became more and more useful during the period. Its volume and intensity of detail increased and its regular reporting was supplemented by in-depth articles on a wider variety of countries. It was often the sole source of reporting for some of the smaller countries throughout the period. Incidentally, as the UPI was facing growing financial difficulties, Reuters began for the first time to offer stock shares to the public.

Unlike the wire services, the newspapers were more limited by space. Therefore, they contained reports on fewer countries and included less detail. The *Times* included more relevant international events than the *Post*.

The use of these five sources together provide a much larger number of events per year than that reported in the second and third editions of the *World Handbook*. Indeed, it is greater by a magnitude of more than three! Even so, the coded events are still only a sample of all the relevant events that have actually taken place during the period under investigation. Moreover, we can expect that this sample is not a random one although we have no way of testing its degree of bias. Certainly in general, the larger the sample, the greater degree of confidence we can have in it. Hence, the more sources we use, the more comfortable we can be with our analyses. Like historians, then, we must take what we have and do the best we can do, but a little humility in stating the results would probably be helpful.

A new project proposed by Data Development in International Relations, to be conducted at the University of Maryland, will search for a more efficient way to do more exhaustive events coding by computer more directly from on-line wire services. The focus of this project is upon interactive events among countries, but the methodology might be beneficial to the coding of domestic events within countries.

A personal note might also be helpful here. The collection of political events data from mass media sources is extremely time-consumptive and expensive. Financial support has been sporadic and usually insufficient to do a proper job. What is needed is a long-term commitment in funding that would allow the development of careful, cumulative coding practices to produce the most comprehensive and comparable data set possible. Perhaps the most significant step in the assurance of data quality would be reliable long-term funding.

Whither?

Criticisms of *World Handbook* events indicators have included the argument that the relationships between the indicators and particular phenomena of interest to the scholar are complex. Without doubt, this is true. To some extent, this is inherently a problem in any general collection that attempts in some sense to be comprehensive, geographically and substantively, and to do so over a long period of time. The realities of the world change. Even more rapidly, however, the realities and understandings of the research world change. What we want to now and what we want to measure becomes ever more complex. This is indeed appropriate if we are to get further in our political analyses.

Even so, the *World Handbook* measures still have a role to play, but they must be conceived of as building blocks. Bollen (1986), for example, observes that the government sanctions indicators, i.e., actions taken by the authorities to neutralize, suppress, or eliminate a perceived threat to the security of the government, the regime, or the state itself, are not direct measures of political liberties. Fabricated espionage charges used to suppress legitimate opposition are sometimes confounded with real spying cases. Second, he says, there is a bias against the countries that have higher political liberties. As pointed out in the *World Handbook* itself, governments with generally repressive policies may not need to impose sanctions on occasional bases. They are already in place. Third, sanctions are more likely to be used when a government feels threatened. Bollen concludes that this indicator has a complex relationship to political liberties and must not be used without adjustment. This is true, but the adjustments are possible. Duvall and Shamir (1980), for example, have suggested the regression of sanctions on domestic violence to obtain residuals that would be measures of propensity to repression.

Stohl, Carleton, Lopez, and Samuels (1986) also criticize the events indicators on much the same grounds. The data, they also say, were collected "because of an underlying theoretical premise regarding the nature of anti-regime violence." *World Handbook* data have often been criticized for not reflecting other people's interests and research needs, but it is true that not enough attention was given to violence by the state. Interest in the profession in the late 1960s, when the indicators were first created, was directed more toward regime stability.

The focus was, therefore, more fully upon the legality of actions by the state than upon the justification for these actions. To some extent this focus was corrected somewhat by a concern for the "conventional" procedures thereby adding the dimension of legitimacy. Also to be fair to the *World Handbook*, the points made in the critiques were in fact stated in the handbooks themselves. It was not the intention of the authors that number crunchers use the data mindlessly. For this reason, a great deal of attention was devoted not only to discussions and estimations of data quality but also to reporting the sources. We perhaps naively expected the users to consult the original contexts of the event reports.

Stohl, *et al.*, suggest that statistical analysis must be informed by political analysis. They recognize that this is no small task but they rightly add that it is foolish to ignore. "If we are to capture the complexity of the concept adequately . . . we must bring political knowledge to bear in shaping our collection of information and measurement schemes. Such an approach may well lack statistical elegance, but it is necessary to insure that quantitative data retain validity and interpretable meaning." (Stohl, *et al.* 1986: 598)

That is more easily said than done. Much of the point in political measurement is to reduce the complexity for easier handling. The cost in the reduction, in measurement as in modeling, is to risk unreality. We must operate on some fine balance between the demands of possibility and of meaning.

The development of technology may be helpful to us in the task. The first few generations of computers encouraged us to turn everything into numbers. Their expanded capabilities give us greater opportunities for storing and retrieving more ambivalent information. We have experimented with the extensive inclusion of coder comment in our data bases. First of all, reliability was increased because it became much easier to tell whether or not the event had already been coded. The updating of an event, the addition of information about it, also became easier. Finally, nouns used to describe an event tell a story that numbers cannot.

Hence, the qualitative and quantitative can be joined. In commenting upon this procedure, one of our research assistants wrote eloquently of the greater quality of the new dataset, but he added, "What usage this will have to the user is unknown at this time." Indeed, the creation of strategies for using the more complex datasets is the next major challenge. But at least from the measurers' point of view, the events that do not fit the customary patterns will not be eliminated from the collection but will be available for a wider set of theoretical interests.

The system with which we have experimented can only be a way station. If legal and financial problems can be managed, it should be possible to include a significantly greater amount of text into the data files. This will at least make it easier for users to have access to the contexts of the events, but the complications of analysis will remain.

References

BOLLEN, KENNETH A.
1986   "Political rights and political liberties in nations: An evaluation of human rights measures, 1950 to 1984." *Human Rights Quarterly* 8 (November): 567–591.
DIAMOND, LARRY, SEYMOUR MARTIN LIPSET, AND JUAN LINZ
1986   "Developing and sustaining democratic government in the Third World." Paper prepared for delivery at the 1986 annual meeting of the American Political Science Association, August 28–31, Washington, D.C.
DUVALL, RAYMOND AND MICHAL SHAMIR
1980   "Indicators from errors: Cross-national, time-serial measures of the repressive disposition of governments." *Indicator Systems for Political, Economic, and Social Analysis* (ed.) Charles Lewis Taylor. Cambridge: Oelgeschlager, Gunn and Hain. 155–182.
LUTTWAK, EDWARD
1969   *Coup d'Etat: A Practical Handbook.* London: Penguin Books.
STOHL, MICHAEL, DAVID CARLETON, GEORGE LOPEZ, AND STEPHEN SAMUELS
1986   "State violation of human rights: Issues and problems of measurement." *Human Rights Quarterly* 8 (November): 592–605.

TAYLOR, CHARLES LEWIS AND MICHAEL C. HUDSON
    1972   *World Handbook of Political and Social Indicators: Second Edition*. New Haven: Yale University Press.
TAYLOR, CHARLES LEWIS AND DAVID A. JODICE
    1983   *World Handbook of Political and Social Indicators: Third Edition*. New Haven: Yale University Press.

9

Democracies and War

Richard L. Merritt and Dina A. Zinnes

The assumption, oft heard from classical writers such as Tocqueville and social scientists such as Quincy Wright, that democratic governments opt for peace rather than war, has not been adequately tested by empirical data. Alternative conceptualizations and measurement procedures have assessed both the independent and dependent variables in terms of a variety of multidimensional indices. The argument that régime type "causes" war-peace outcomes, more often asserted than explored, is not uniformly confirmed by empirical data. Previous writings moderate a direct linkage by emphasizing leadership as an intervening variable, or by introducing a measure of "society" that both influences and is influenced by régime type. More important but untested ideas trace war-peace outcomes not to régime type but to (1) the foreign policy process, which is similar across régime types, and (2) the economic structure of societies, especially the complexity of modern economies.

For two centuries and more statesmen and scientists have praised the value of democracy as a form of government. Democracy, they say, improves a society's standard of political life through popular and regular elections, open political parties, freedom of the press, and so forth. Democracies are also better able to meet certain needs, such as economic growth and equality.

Not the least of the virtues claimed for democracy is its potential for international peace. Alexis de Tocqueville saw Americans, enjoying their democracy in the 1830s, as "lovers of peace."[1] Less then a century later Woodrow

Richard L. Merritt, professor of political science and research professor in communications at the University of Illinois at Urbana-Champaign, has studied systematic international politics, with emphasis on political integration and postwar German politics. Besides articles in such journals as *World Politics, Comparative Politics*, and *Journal of Peace Research*, his writings include *Systematic Approaches to Comparative Politics* (1970), books on German public opinion, edited volumes on international and comparative politics, and, with Elizabeth C. Hanson, *Science, Politics, and International Conferences* (1989).

Dina A. Zinnes, Merriam Professor of Political Science at the University of Illinois at Urbana-Champaign, has focused her research on the construction, analysis, and empirical testing of mathematical models of international relations. Her research has appeared in *Journal of Conflict Resolution, International Studies Quarterly, World Politics*, and *American Political Science Review* among others. She has edited volumes devoted to, and written a survey of quantitative research in, international relations, *Contemporary Research in International Relations* (1976).

FIGURE 1
Régime Type and War Involvement: Correlational Analysis

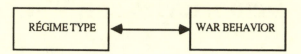

Wilson envisioned the same democracy having an "historic mission" to create "a peaceful international order based on world law" (Levin 1968: 4).[2] Another generation passed before Quincy Wright put such visions into social scientific terms. "Absolutistic states with geographically and functionally centralized governments under autocratic leadership," he wrote (Wright 1942: 847–848), "are likely to be most belligerent, while constitutional states with geographically and functionally federalized governments under democratic leadership are likely to be most peaceful."

Statements like Wright's led modern quantitative researchers to explore empirically the proposition linking types of régimes to international conflict. The results have been mixed. Different studies, often using distinct conceptualizations of both régime types and international conflicts, produced apparently conflicting results. The debate initiated by Wright a half century ago is still unresolved.

This paper evaluates the current status of the debate on linkages between régime types and international wars—or, as we shall call this complex of issues, the *régime-war nexus*. Figure 1 suggests a bidirectional linkage between régime type and war behavior. Our concern here, however, will be with research focusing on a single direction: that régime type influences war behavior rather than the other way around. In fact, of course, the opposite directionality is a common occurrence, well discussed in diplomatic histories. After World War I, for instance, their enthusiastic involvement coupled with their miserable military performance led to the governmental collapse of autocracies in Russia, Germany, and Austria, followed by their replacement with putative democracies. The reality, however, is that this régime-war directionality has not elicited data-based research. We can only point to it as an area for potential research.

Here we shall focus on efforts to understand how régime types influence war behavior. An initial section explores alternative conceptualizations and measurement procedures for assessing countries' governmental types—and more specifically democracy, since almost all the literature on the régime-war nexus stems from the analysts' interest in democracy's impact on war. Subsequent sections focus on war as the dependent variable, and the arguments about as well as the data used to explore linkages between régime type and war. A final section suggests some other ways to look at the régime-war nexus empirically. The intended result is not new research but rather an analysis about how we might conduct that research.

FIGURE 2
Democraticness Continuum

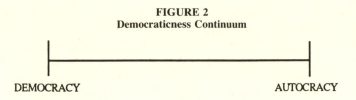

DEMOCRACY   AUTOCRACY

What Is the Independent Variable—Democracy?

If we are to link democracy to war or peace, then it is critical that we understand the meaning of democracy, that we understand what it is about this form of government that implies something about its foreign policy.[3] Our review of scholarly literature on the idea and reality of "democracy" found disarray. The term so familiar to us all, which we think we comprehend, disappears into the sand like a gentle shower in the desert as soon as we look for a generally acceptable operational definition. The reasons for this are several. One lies in the historical roots of democracy itself. What once occasioned only philosophic disputation about the behavior of ancient Greeks moved during the eighteenth century into the real—and very complex—world of politics. The term itself became a slogan to describe what people wanted in politics or to justify what they had; and scientists found the term convenient to use for referring to disparate phenomena and, eventually, quantitative measures.

Quantitative measures of democracy are by now quite diverse. They conceptualize democracy differently, select different indicators, and rely on different sources of data. Indeed, it is difficult to view the total collection of such measures as a contribution to an integrated font of cumulative, social-scientific knowledge about democracy. Since each individual measure is designed for specific research purposes, of course, its value rests on the freight it bears for that project. Particular measures are nevertheless targets of opportunity for researchers interested in other issues—and herein lie well-known analytic pitfalls. If, then, we wish to use existing measures of democracy to study the régime-war nexus, we must understand their various dimensions.

Global Indices

At first blush it seems a simple matter to rank all countries according to their degree of democracy. This rests on two assumptions. First, we must assume that all countries are more or less democratic. The key question, then, is a particular country's *degree of democraticness*. The most democratic countries may be located at one end of a democraticness continuum as *democracy* (or "polyarchy"). At the other end is the less specific concept of "undemocracies," such as nondemocratic, closed hegemonic, and authoritarian countries—or, to use a more generic term, *autocracy*. Thus democratic and autocratic states are assumed to be two ends of a single continuum (Figure 2).[4]

Second, we must assume that for a given year, or long time span, a standardized ranking from democratic to autocratic countries is possible. It may be based either on a single variable such as freedom of the press, or on a combination of variables such as freedom of the press, open elections, individual rights, and so forth. If such a global index can be constructed, it could then be correlated with an appropriate indicator of war to provide quick answers to our régime-war questions.

The most influential use of the global-index approach was in Dahl's (1971; cf. Dahl and Lindblom 1953; Dahl 1956) study of polyarchy, an "institutional arrangement" providing the best but nevertheless "imperfect approximation" of the ideal called democracy (p. 9n). For Dahl, the variables shaping a government's form are liberalization (or public contestation) and inclusiveness (or the people's right to participate in elections and office).[5] He argues that the polyarchy enjoys high and the closed hegemony low scores of both. Somewhere between the polyarchy and closed hegemony are the competitive oligarchy (high contestation but low participation) and inclusive hegemony (high participation but low contestation). Dahl then uses the two variables to develop a régime classification of 114 states in the mid-1960s.

Two important contributions have enriched Dahl's empirical approach. Bollen (1980: 372; cf. Bollen 1979, 1983, 1986, 1990; Bollen and Grandjean 1981; Bollen and Jackman 1985) defines "political democracy as the extent to which the political power of the elite is minimized and that of the nonelite is maximized." He interprets this to mean two concepts, each measured by means of three variables: political liberty (press freedom, freedom of group opposition, and government sanctions); and political sovereignty (fairness of elections, executive selection, and legislative selection). The final Political Democracy Index linearly transforms each of the six variables between 0 and 100. Bollen scores 113 countries in 1960 (from 11.9 points in Yemen to 100.0 in Luxembourg, Iceland, Australia, and New Zealand) and 123 countries in 1965 (from 5.2 points in Cuba to 100.0 in Iceland and New Zealand).

Coppedge and Reinicke (1990; cf. 1988) classified 170 states in c. 1985 on a Polyarchy Index based on Dahl's (1971) approach. They developed two scales. One, inclusiveness, measures suffrage—but, since almost all countries with elections also have universal adult suffrage, the variable is omitted from further discussion. The other, political contestation, uses a Guttmann scale to assign cumulative scores ranging from 0 to ten points on four variables: freedom and fair elections, freedom of expression, availability of alternative sources of information (or media pluralism), and freedom to form and join organizations. The most polyarchic countries, forty-one in number, score high on all four political contestation variables, and the twenty-seven least polyarchic countries score low on all of them.

Bollen's Political Democracy Index and Coppedge and Reinicke's Polyarchy Index are creative, general-purpose scales for measuring how democratic or polyarchic the world's countries are. They nevertheless raise some questions that require our attention. First, what do the democratic variables included in each index really measure? Many politicians and writers, especially outside the United States, argue that such characteristics as press freedom are meaningless for most of the world's people. A "true" democracy, in this view, provides its population with adequate food, employment, medical care, and the like.[6] In this view the measures cited here represent Western parochialism rather than international scientific research. Second, how interdependent are the individual variables that comprise the scales?[7] If the variables are highly interdependent, what is the meaning of an index that combines them? Third, is it reasonable to weight each variable equally when constructing the aggregate index?[8] Fourth, how different are the resulting indices? Correlating the Bollen index for 1965 and Coppedge and Reinicke index for c. 1985 produced an r^2 = 0.502 (Merritt and Zinnes 1988).

Yet another question concerns the "meaning" of the scaled scores, particularly those at the lower end of the democraticness continuum (Figure 2). The various autocratic régimes are in fact quite different. Coppedge and Reinicke's (1990: 66) lowest category (scale score 10) finds twenty-seven rather diverse countries, including Afghanistan, China, Mali, South Yemen, and the Soviet Union. Assuming that these countries can all be arrayed on a univariate continuum is highly questionable. The countries may indeed be ones in which "no meaningful elections are held, all organizations are banned or controlled by the government or official party, all public dissent is suppressed, and there is no public alternative to official information." The question, however, is whether these are the most relevant characteristics of autocracies for understanding their international behavior.

Special and Regional Indices

Various solutions to this problem have been offered. Some opted to investigate only those countries that are either highly democratic or highly autocratic. Others focused on a single region. Thus Powell (1982: 1) scaled twenty-nine "working political democracies" according to whether they enjoyed this status for a continuous, somewhat limited, or severely interrupted time span in 1958–76. Lijphart (1984: xiii) classified twenty-one countries with "majoritarian (or Westminster) and consensus . . . models of democracy," that is, those countries possessing political rights, civil liberties, and democratic durability. In contrast Dick (1974), looking at patterns for 1959 to 1968 in fifty-nine less developed countries (17 LDCs in Africa, 21 in America, 15 in Asia, and 6 in Europe), found thirteen competitive, nineteen semicompetitive, and twenty-seven authoritarian régimes. Somewhere in between the foci on high democracies and LDCs is Muller's (1988) scaling of fifty-five countries in terms of the impact due to the years of democracy enjoyed.[9]

These various studies pose a dilemma. Powell and Lijphart tell us much about the characteristics of countries traditionally considered to be highly democratic, Dick about the behavior of less developed countries, and Muller about a selected set of both rich and poor countries. None, however, says anything about the meaning of democracy itself. We cannot assume that differences and similarities among highly democratic states result from the characteristics of democracy or the idiosyncratic characteristics of the specialized nature of each sample (Przeworski and Teune 1970). The same is true regarding LDCs or countries providing UN statistics.

Typologies

Other approaches handle differences among nondemocracies by "typologizing" the countries—integrating evidence about democratic status with other indicators of régime characteristics. Stammer (1968: 162), describing how dictatorships "make allowance for the interaction of the cultural, social, political, and psychological factors," lists five ideal types: (1) despotic one-man rule, (2) elite-related rule, (3) oriental despotism, (4) totalitarian rule, and (5) constitutional dictatorship. Among Third World countries, Shils (1962), Levy (1966), Pye (1966), and others emphasize military rules, which they generally suggest are more creative than nonmilitary rules; O'Donnell (1973) cites political democracy and bureaucratic-authoritarianism as the keys to Latin American politics; and Sloan and Tedin (1987) use qualitative criteria on twenty Latin American countries for each year from 1960 to 1980 to find five régime types: democratic, bureaucratic-authoritarian, communist, traditional authoritarian, and transitional.

All this research has made explicit the multivariate nature of these types of political governments. In an attempt to capture this multivariate nature of governments, Huntington (1968: 80; cf. Huntington and Domínguez 1975) offers a sixfold matrix dividing types of governments according to three levels of political participation (low/traditional, medium/transitional, and high/modern) and two giving the ratio of institutionalization to participation (high/civic and low/prætorian). Each of Huntington's six types is distinct.[10] They cannot be collapsed meaningfully into a single index between 0 and 100. Berg-Schlosser (1984) divides forty-five Black African states into four régime types: polyarchy, socialist, authoritarian (or, following Dahl, hegemony), and military (or, following Huntington, "an unstable régime of the prætorian type").[11] The typological decisions are derived through "a 'handmade' factor analysis"[12] from judgments on eight issues such as party system, dominant bases of legitimacy, and scope of control.

By implication, these typologies raise an interesting point about the place of communist states in empirical studies of régime types. Analysts concerned primarily with democracy tend to ignore them while those with a broader focus on régimes do not.[13] In Western social-scientific research, however, both positions treat communist states as *sui generis*, somehow apart from a single index that runs from traditional democracies to autocracies. This suggests a new, dichotomous relationship (Figure 3). Two points must be added to this example of a communist type. First, what is true about communist states also occurs vis-à-vis other authoritarian and even democratic types of government:

FIGURE 3
Democracy, Autocracy, and Communism

	NONCOMMUNISM	COMMUNISM
DEMOCRACY	1	2
AUTOCRACY	3	4

FIGURE 4
Bivariate Dimensions of Régimes

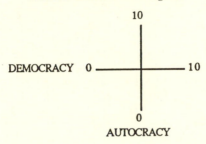

They do not necessarily fit into a single, univariate diagram. Second, some-times these distinctions reflect political sentiments rather than scientific anal-ysis and hence must be evaluated carefully.[14] In general, however, it suggests the importance of thinking about democracy in multivariate as well as uni-variate terms.

Multidimensional Indices

Gurr, Jaggers, and Moore (1990) provide a new way to categorize régime types. For 155 contemporary and historical countries during the 1800-1986 period, they developed "nine operational indicators of political authority pat-terns [based on] influence dimensions, the recruitment of chief executives, and aspects of . . . governmental structure" (p. 78). These are then combined into two 0 to 10 point scales, one for institutionalized democracy and another for institutionalized autocracy. A country may thus rank high on one and low on the other (Spain in 1978, which scored 9 on democracy and 0 on autocracy) or rank the same on both (Spain in 1878, which scored 5 points on both democracy and autocracy).

Gurr, Jaggers, and Moore's procedure shifts us from univariate to at least bivariate thinking about régime types. The two dimensions are characterized in Figure 4. And as we might expect, most of the data they report fall across the main diagonal.[15] A preliminary analysis characterizing the bivariate dimensions relies mainly on graphs that show 187 years of European and Latin American shifts in their levels of democracy and autocracy. But the procedure also opens the way to more sophisticated methodologies to analyze régime types.

What Is the Dependent Variable—War?

The concept of war is as problematic as the concept of democracy. Clausewitz's dictum that "war is nothing more than the continuation of politics by other means" illustrates the vagueness found in the literature. But definitions of war are flexible over time. Describing them in the traditional terms of international legal norms loses meaning in an era when countries attack one another first and provide law-like rationalizations afterwards, create Johnson or Brezhnev doctrines justifying a superstate's "right" to intervene in the domestic politics of its ally, or send paramilitary operations to destabilize foreign countries and foment civil war. Consider, for example, U.S. interventions into Guatemala in 1954, Cuba in 1961, Chile in 1973, Grenada in 1983, and Panama in 1989; or Soviet interventions into Czechoslovakia in 1948 and 1968, East Germany in 1953, Hungary and Poland in 1956, and Afghanistan in 1979. Was any—or each—of these events a war?

Webster's Seventh New Collegiate Dictionary defines war as "a state of usually open and declared armed hostile conflict between states or nations." While the breadth of this definition does not permit a distinction between post–World Cup street brawls among fans of rival national soccer teams on the one hand, and nuclear attacks aimed at national extermination on the other, it characterizes the ingredients needed for an adequate definition: (1) the identification of those entities that are legitimate actors regarding the behavior in question, namely states, and (2) the interactive behavior between those entities that qualifies as war, viz. "open and declared armed hostile conflict." Differences found in the literature revolve around differences in these two components.

One might expect no quarrel on the first point, the identification of the legitimate entities. That this is clearly not the case can be seen by contrasting the major datasets on war compiled over the past several decades by Wright, Richardson, and Small and Singer. The most glaring difference is between Richardson's dataset and those generated by Wright and Small and Singer. "From the psychological point of view," Richardson (1960: 6) wrote,

> A war, riot, and a murder, though differing in many important aspects . . . have at least this in common, that they are all manifestations of the instinct of aggressiveness. . . . There is thus a psychological justification for looking to see whether there is any statistical connection between war, riot, and murder.

Wars were therefore a subset of the more general class of *deadly quarrels*— "any quarrel which caused death to humans." So saying, the legitimate entities for Richardson were human individuals, groups of individuals, or groups of individuals organized into entities known as states.

Such a delineation was far too broad for either Wright or Singer and Small. These researchers required a more constrained delineation of the legitimate entities. Wright's characterization is somewhat less precise than that of Small and Singer. His list of wars "is intended to include all hostilities involving members of the family of nations," Wright (1942: 636) notes, and then specifies more explicitly those that qualify for the "family of nations." "Entities were to be regarded as participants" if they had "actual independence before or after the war rather than legal status under international law. . . ." (p. 637).

In contrast, Small and Singer (1982: 38–46) spend several pages grappling with the qualifying criteria. Their analysis of the problem leads them to propose that

> whether or not a national political entity qualifies as a member of the interstate system should be a function of two factors. First, was it large enough in population or other resources to play a moderately active role in world politics . . .? Second . . ., [was] the entity . . . sufficiently unencumbered by legal, military, economic, or political constraints to exercise a fair degree of sovereignty and independence[?] (pp. 39–40)

Using these criteria the authors then specify that entities, to qualify for statehood, must have a minimum population of 500,000 and legal international recognition through the existence of diplomatic missions from both Britain and France.[16]

Definitional differences across these datasets are equally severe with respect to the appropriate act or behavior that qualifies as a war. Indeed, as we have just seen, Richardson (1960: 6) eschews "war" in favor of a more generic label, "deadly quarrel," and defines the relevant act in general terms as "aggression" and in more specific terms as "death to humans" by humans as the result of a quarrel: "The term thus includes murders, banditries, mutinies, insurrections, and wars small and large; but it excludes accidents, and calamities such as earthquakes and tornadoes." Distinctions among deadly quarrels are expressed in terms of the numbers of humans dying because of the quarrel. To minimize measurement errors, the dataset reports magnitudes of deadly quarrels measured in logarithmic units.

Numbers of deaths are equally important for Small and Singer's (1982: 50) definition. A war is not counted as one until it leads "to at least 1,000 battle fatalities among all participating system members." Unlike Richardson's procedure, however, wars are not classified in terms of the number killed but rather by the attributes of the participating states, viz. whether the states qualify for membership in the "central or major power sub-system" (p. 51).

In contrast to both Richardson and Small and Singer, deaths are not a criterion Wright (1942: 636) used to identify the critical act. Rather, it is "the legal recognition of the warlike action, the scale of such action, and the importance of its legal and political consequences" that were used "in deciding whether a given incident was sufficiently important to include in a list of wars."

The "scale of such action" is defined as 50,000 troops. While Richardson classifies war in terms of deaths and Small and Singer in terms of the qualities of the participants, Wright (p. 641) discriminates among

> Balance of power war, in sense of a war among state members of the modern family of nations; . . . Civil war, in sense of war within a state member of the modern family of nations; . . . Defensive war, in sense of a war to defend modern cvilization against an alien culture; (and) . . . Imperial war, in sense of a war to expand modern civilization at the expense of an alien culture.

Even among researchers who have studied war scientifically, then, criteria for operationally measuring war differ significantly. And if one burrows more deeply into these tomes even more problems abound. What happens when armistices occur during a war? When hostilities begin anew, is it a new war or part of the old one? Should a state enter ongoing hostilities during their last week, is it considered a participant?

Research linking democracy or régime type to war is further compounded by differences in focus on the relevant attributes of war. Does régime type predict involvement in war or war initiation? Are the proponents of democracy arguing for the unlikelihood that democracies will initiate a war, or are they contending that democracies seldom participate in wars? Clearly an important difference exists. But the difficulty lies not simply in specifying what aspect of the dependent variable is under consideration. If initiation is the key, then it is necessary to establish yet a new set of criteria. If A sends B an ultimatum, and B responds by sending the Marines, is A or B the aggressor? If A sends B an ultimatum, B ignores it, A then amasses troops at B's border, and B, understanding from intelligence sources that A is planning an attack, launches a preemptive strike against A—which is the aggressor, which the victim? Still other complications involve multilateral wars. If A invades B's ally, C, and B rushes to C's defense, is B the aggressor or victim?

The point is that wars are complex phenomena. This is not to say that empirical measures of types of wars or aspects of wars cannot be developed, but rather that those generating or borrowing such measures must be careful in using them for scientific analysis.

Linkage Between Régime Type and War

Régime-War Nexus: Argument

Although statements like that quoted from Wright at the beginning of this paper are repeated in the régime-war nexus literature, one is hard-pressed to find the details of the argument leading to such statements. What precisely is it about a democracy that suggests it might be more peaceful? A search through some of the classic literature on democracy produced surprisingly meager results. Major proponents of democracy such as Tocqueville (1835/1958) and Bryce (1921) barely hint at the linkage between this governmental form and

FIGURE 5
Régime Type and War Frequency

WAR FREQUENCY

	YES	NO
DEMOCRACY	1	2
AUTOCRACY	3	4

RÉGIME TYPE

FIGURE 6
Location and Wars

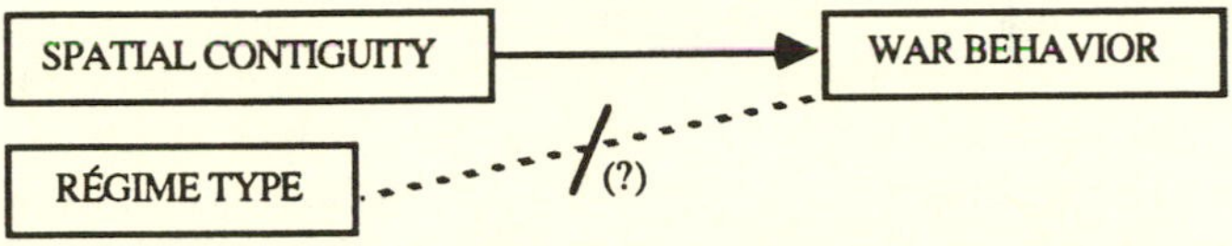

international conflict, although, as we saw earlier, Tocqueville clearly believes that democracy is a force for peace, and Woodrow Wilson saw it as the hope for "peaceful international order based on world law."

Wright's comment suggests a strong argument in favor of a democracy-peace linkage. In fact, however, the several pages he devoted to the question see Wright arguing all sides of it. As shown in Figure 5, he begins by contending that all cells are equally likely, that is, no relationship exists between régime and war. "Statistics," Wright (1942: 841) notes, "can hardly be invoked to show that democracies have been less often involved in war than autocracies." This position is consistent with the contention of Small and Singer (1976: 67). Neighbors, they say, are inclined to fight with each other irrespective of their forms of government, while distant countries are not inclined to do so.[17] Ignoring the question of whether or not the data reported by Small and Singer support their explanation,[18] the explanation itself has a serious limitation. It obviates any need to pay attention to régime types if what interests us is the outbreak of war. This is shown in Figure 6.

If statistically democracies are involved in as many wars as are autocracies, "it is probable," Wright speculates, that this is because democracies "were attacked by nondemocratic governments." But this is not the whole story. Wright now moves to cell 1 of Figure 5. Clearly, he observes, democracies themselves "have displayed some aggressive characteristics."

What is it about a democracy that might account for these aggressive tendencies? Wright provides several answers. First, democracies by their elective, representative nature are not capable of seeing beyond their own self—that is, national interest. "Democracies insist," he writes (pp. 843–845), that the government should be the servant of the state and the state should be the servant of the national society. . . . [Therefore] foreign policy, though it affects the people of other states, should conform to the opinion of the people only of one state. That opinion can neither be representative of all the interests involved nor be adequately informed of the changing circumstances of international politics. . . . Democratic statesmen are obliged to base their policies upon the opinion of the public . . . and to ignore . . . realistic dispatches of their diplomats or the resolutions of international bodies when these are in conflict with that opinion. Therefore, democracies, while usually theoretically against war, often fail to take measures, whether to balance power or to organize the world democratically, which might preserve the peace. Instead, they insist upon policies which, though consciously directed only to domestic ends, are in fact likely to lead to war. . . . [Thus] the tendency of democracy [is] to avow universal principles but to act only for national ends.

Accordingly, those in charge of a democractic state function much as do lobbyists in the U.S. Congress: They see their job to be representing their state and its interests. If these interests conflict with those of other states, the leaders of democratic states, knowing that they can be relieved of their office at the next election, push relentlessly for their own special interest. Like the gun, drug, automobile, or smoking lobbies the leaders of democracies are incapable of seeing the broader social picture. In the long run international peace, like a healthier, less fear-ridden society, is better for all. But the accomplishment of this goal requires the ability to sacrifice some short-term interests. Democracies are no more capable of this than are Congressional lobbies.

The problem, however, runs even more deeply. Wright argues that functioning effectively in international politics requires the ability to make threats and, more particularly, the ability to make credible threats. A player in the international arena must use threats easily and be willing to carry them through when necessary. But democracies are not capable of making credible threats:

Democracies normally require that important decisions be made only after wide participation. . . . They are, therefore, ill adapted to the successful use of threats and violence as instruments of foreign policy. Autocracies, on the other hand, are accustomed to ruling by authority at home and are able to make rapid decisions. . . . Consequently . . . democracies pitted against autocracies are at a disadvantage. They cannot make effective threats unless they really mean war; they can seldom convince either themselves or the potential enemy that they really do mean war; and they are always vulnerable to the dissensions of internal oppositions (p. 842).

Thus democracies are unable to avoid conflict and war.

Moreover, democracies are also unable to work toward peace: Democracies, in principle, oppose war, but have "shown little capacity to co-operate for peace through world-organization" (p. 845). The structural defects that cause democracies to stumble into conflict and war are also the basic problem that restricts any serious efforts toward world peace:

The incapacity of democracies to maintain peace [in a] balance of power [international system] arises from the fact that democracy cannot give foreign affairs priority over domestic affairs; that, with its party changes, it cannot pursue any foreign policy

FIGURE 7
Leadership Style and Wars

continuously; and that its procedures, designed for deliberation, prevent the rapid balancing operations essential to stability under the system. In an interdependent world, in which governments are related only by such a balance of power, democracies are not likely to survive.

The Greek tragedy is complete (p. 846):[19]

> Unable to work the balance of power and unwilling to build an effective international organization, democracies have tried to secure their interests by isolation and neutrality, but science has been against them. In the age of world trade, news, and radio, democratic people have been unable to avoid or to evade an interest in world-problems.

Having argued that (1) no difference may distinguish among régime types' propensity for war and (2) democracies carry within them the potential seeds for conflict and war, Wright comes full circle. Back to his belief in the potential good of democratic institutions, Wright proposes how and why democracies could be peaceful (p. 847–848). We are now in cells 2 and 3 of Figure 5:

> Democracy has inherent possibilities of being the more peaceful. . . . Autocrats . . . tend to be aggressive types of personality. . . . Democracies . . . tend to give leadership to personalities of a conciliatory type, to attach importance to respect for law, to oppose military preparation and war, and to value liberty, humanity, and welfare above power. . . . Absolutist states . . . under autocratic leadership are likely to be most belligerent, while constitutional states . . . under democratic leadership are likely to be most peaceful.

From this we can draw Wright's one clear argument linking democracy and peace:

> Since
>   • Democracy gives leadership to personalities of a conciliatory nature; and
>   • Conciliatory personalities do not make decisions for war.
> Therefore,
>   • Democracy does not cause war.

This argument may be seen graphically in Figure 7.

In more recent times Rummel has supplied two additional arguments. His purpose is empirically to examine the régime-war hypothesis, but before turning to the data and various statistical analyses he suggests the rationale for his efforts. Two rather different arguments result. The first concerns the cross-pressures concept of a free democratic society (Rummel 1983: 27–28):

> In libertarian states (those emphasizing individual freedom and civil liberties and the rights associated with a competitive and open election of leaders) exist multiple, often

conflicting, elites, whose interests are divergent and segmented, checked and balanced. . . . Political power is relatively decentralized and diffuse. . . . Libertarian
states comprise social fields in which the actions of groups and individuals respond to
many divergent and opposing social and psychological forces, . . . interlocking and
nested balances of power. . . . Such systems (like the free market) tend to be self-
regulating and to isolate and inhibit conflicts and violence when they occur. They tend
to encourage exchange, rather than coercive and violent situations, in conflict between
groups and individuals.

From this we can draw out the key ingredients that link democracies and
peace:

Since
  • Democracy embodies multiple interests;
  • Multiple interests lead to cross pressures;
  • Cross pressures permit no single coalition;
  • War requires a single coalition.
Therefore,
  • States without a single coalition do not cause wars.
Therefore,
  • Democracy does not cause war.

Rummel's second argument is somewhat different and rests on the assumed
dislike of the masses for blood and taxes:

Political elites are dependent on the support of a public unwilling to bear the cost in
taxes, property, and blood of foreign adventures and intervention. . . . The public
cannot be trusted to pay the price of foreign violence. . . . The essential diversity of
interests and values of free people must be overcome. . . . This is not true for states
whose political elites are unrestrained by a free press and contending centers of power
and which are unaccountable through free elections. . . . The freer the people of a
state, the more nonviolent its elite's expectations and perceptions, and the less likely
they are to commit *official* violence against other states.

From this we can outline the following argument:

Since
  • In a democracy, the people's preferences are basic for decision making;
  • The people's preferences are for no taxes and no spilling of blood;
  • War entails both taxes and spilling of blood.
Therefore,
  • Having no taxes and no spilling of blood means no war.
Therefore,
  • Democracy does not cause war.

Rummel's two arguments add a new dimension to régime-war studies. Something about a democratic society,[20] he says, forces its political régime to pay
attention to (a) multiple interests that lead to cross pressures and/or (b) popular perspectives decrying taxes and spilling of blood. That is, the society not
only chooses the régime type but also dictates what policies the régime will
carry out. And, of course, the effectiveness of the régime has a feedback

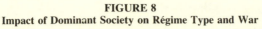

FIGURE 8
Impact of Dominant Society on Régime Type and War

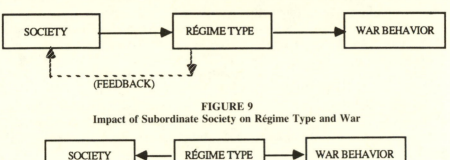

impact on the society, encouraging it to continue supporting the social norms. This relationship is described schematically in Figure 8.

Does this relationship hold only for democracies? Rummel does not address the issue of nondemocratic régimes. However, two answers to this question seem possible. First, let us assume that the "society" comprises the mass public. In this case, most definitions of autocratic governmental forms would deny to the masses any role to play in foreign-policy or other decisions. Thus the society either disappears from the schema shown in Figure 8 or else takes a subordinate position, as shown in Figure 9. As far as the régime-war nexus is concerned, the assumption of a subordinate society puts us back into the earlier task of correlational analysis (Figure 1).

But this assumption of the subordinate society may be irrelevant. Most definitions associate the "society" of the autocratic régime with its dominant elite. Even Hitler and Stalin had to pay attention to the top military, party, and bureaucratic officials. In such cases the régime and dominant elite both seek, if possible, to co-opt the masses through rewards for compliance to the dominant elite's social norms, or, if necessary, to suppress them. The success of either strategy removes the masses from the decision-making arena. The dominant elite thus functions as the system's society—or, consistent with the above schema, dominant society.

Whether the masses or elites comprise the dominant society, this line of argumentation moves our theoretic interest from the *régime → behavior* paradigm (Figure 1) to the *society → behavior* paradigm (Figure 8). It argues that the political régime simply carries out the society's wishes. But is this true? It is one thing for a political régime in general or governmental leaders in particular to accept the demands of the dominant society, but quite another to implement them. Consider for example President Kennedy's dismay during the Cuban missile crisis of October 1962, to learn that the Defense and State departments had not carried out his instruction well over a year earlier to remove U.S. missiles from Turkey. How does the foreign-policy process affect the régime-war linkage? We shall return to this question later.

The surprising and significant feature of the Wright and Rummel arguments is their peripheral linkage to the definitions of democracy or war reviewed earlier. Consider, for example, Bollen's definition of democracy in terms of press freedom, freedom of group opposition and government sanction, fairness of elections, and executive and legislative selection. To what extent do these definitional characteristics imply, as in Wright's argument, that conciliatory individuals will take leadership positions? Although potentially a more direct implication exists with Rummel's argument, it is still not entirely clear how Bollen's democratic characteristics fit with either the cross-pressures or blood-and-taxes argument. Presumably freedom of the press and fair elections produce the multiple interests and permit the masses to let their wishes concerning war be known. But these details are not given.

Equally serious is the proper interpretation of the dependent variable. First, it is not clear whether the arguments concern democracies getting involved in wars or initiating them, a rather important distinction. As Wright speculated, perhaps democracies get involved in wars because they are the targets of nondemocratic aggression. Second, as we have seen, wars have multiple characteristics and multiple interpretations. In which sense is it that nondemocracies are more prone to "war" than democracies? The fact that the hypotheses link democracies and the *absence* of war compounds the problem. One would be hard-pressed to point to a dataset of non-wars.

A final point concerning the three arguments is worth noting. In all three cases the arguments are in "monadic" form. In each case the linkage being postulated is between a democracy on the one hand and, on the other, its foreign policy behavior. In each case it is something about the internal democratic process that makes this type of régime less aggressive. Surprisingly, however, Rummel concludes his arguments by hypothesizing about the interaction between régime types. One of the three hypotheses he intends to test concerns war between democracies (Rummel 1983: 29):

> *Joint-Freedom Proposition:* Libertarian systems mutually preclude violence (violence will occur between states only if at least one is nonlibertarian).

Clearly nothing in the arguments to this point permits this deduction. Nevertheless, as we shall see below, this is the one hypothesis about which there is little disagreement. Perhaps somewhere embedded in the assumptions that make the proposition reasonable lies the key to the complete régime-war nexus argument. We shall return to this issue in the next section.

Régime-War Nexus: Empirical Research

Doubtless the most impressive effort to examine empirically the democracy-peace hypothesis is Rummel's. His initial paper (Rummel 1968) was sufficiently convincing in presenting the finding of *no relationship* between régime type and involvement in wars that the issue itself almost seemed dead. A subsequent replication and expansion (Weede 1971) verified the thrust of Rummel's earlier results. Some years later, Small and Singer (1976) added further evidence. As their central question, they ask (Small and Singer 1976: 55): "What has been the war experience of bourgeois democracies compared to the other states that have participated in international war from 1816 to 1965?" Using the war data from the Correlates of War project they find that bourgeois democracies are neither more nor less involved in wars than are other kinds of states. However much they may prefer peace to war, democracies are not averse to seizing arms if the circumstances are appropriate (p. 66).

But while others continued to provide evidence to question a relationship between democracy and interstate behavior, Rummel did an about-face. In a series of books and articles (Rummel 1976, 1979, 1981, 1983, 1984, 1985) he reviewed earlier data and presented new data that now strongly suggested that *libertarianism promotes peace*. "Libertarian countries" enjoy "democracy" in terms of the oft-listed "civil liberties and political rights," together with "classical liberal democracy" and its "free market" (1985: 426–428).[21] Rummel's (1983: 27) opening salvo examines "all reported international conflict for 1976 to 1980; and . . . a list of wars from 1816 to 1974, and of threats and use of force from 1945 to 1965." He now finds that "the more libertarian a state, the less its foreign violence" (p. 27).

Weede (1984: 649) responded to Rummel's (1983) report by using "various definitions of war and compilations of data for the 1960s and 1970s" to demonstrate "that democracy and war involvement are not consistently and significantly correlated with each other." Some possible association in the late 1970s cannot be verified because of the absence of complete data. Chan (1984: 617) attempted to reconcile the divergent findings by pointing out various differences in operational measures and research designs. However, when he "examines the proposition that political freedom promotes peace, as suggested by R. J. Rummel, in its monadic form," he finds that the proposition

> tends to be contradicted and unsupported, if we focus only on monadic relationships, if we refer to wars from a more distant past, if we include wars of an extrasystemic nature (i.e., colonial and imperialist wars) or if we assess political freedom cross-sectionally (i.e., comparing a country's political conditions with those of its contemporaries).

Undaunted by either Weede or Chan, and continuing his study of libertarian countries, Rummel (1985) reports evidence from new time periods. He continues to assert that "the more libertarian a state is the less it will be involved in foreign and domestic violence" (Rummel 1985: 419).

Throughout this time, however, and despite the conflicting results concerning democracy or libertarianism and peace, there emerges one finding on which all seem to agree. Beginning with his 1983 study, Rummel finds that "Libertarian states have no violence between themselves" (p. 27). This result is consistent with an observation made earlier by Small and Singer (1976: 67):

FIGURE 10
Régimes and War Involvement

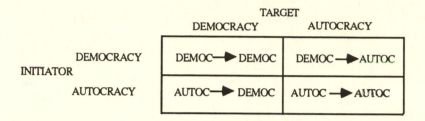

Through an examination of all wars from 1816 to 1965, they note that "bourgeois democracies . . . do not seem to fight against one another."[22] Despite his findings regarding the basic, monadic hypothesis relating democracy and war, Chan (1984: 617) also finds a significant difference between a monadic and a dyadic perspective: The relationship between freedom and peace "tends to be confirmed, if we focus only on dyadic relationships." These observations suggest the modified research design shown in Figure 10.

At least two interpretations of this intriguing piece of evidence are possible. The difficulty with all three studies is that the democracies-don't-fight-democracies fact is not put into some context. In effect, we do not know what the expected values should be for Figure 10. To take a trivial example, if only one democracy existed in the international system, the finding would clearly be meaningless. To take a slightly less extreme example, it could happen that, over the time period examined, only a few democracies emerge at its tail end. Even if the international system contains 100 states examined over 150 years, if only five democracies enter the system in the last two years the democracies-don't-fight-democracies observation is not particularly interesting. In short, one needs to weigh the democracies-don't-fight-democracies observation against the potential for dyads of this type to become involved in wars. As many researchers have lamented, it is necessary to contrast the incidence of war with the incidence of "no-war." Unfortunately, as many have found, this is not an easy task.

Another interpretation of the contrast between a monadic examination and a dyadic one nevertheless exists. The democracies-don't-fight-democracies observation tells us something about dyads. This is consistent with Most and Starr's (1989) note that the only legitimate approach to the study of war is at the dyadic level of analysis. Since it takes two to make a war, by definition, the only reasonable research design must be dyadic. Hence researchers at the level of the single nation-state will necessarily come up short. Why might this be the case? Suppose, as Wright argues, that democracies are led by individuals with conciliatory personalities. When two democracies engage in conflict, the conciliatory personalities of both countries permit a peaceful resolution of the conflict. The same outcome, however, will not occur if a democracy finds itself in conflict with a nondemocracy. Here conciliation meets hostility or aggression. Such encounters between democracies and nondemocracies produce violence and war. If the international system contains reasonable numbers of both democracies and nondemocracies, then a monadic correlation over nation-states and war could well be non-significant since sometimes democracies go to war (with nondemocracies) and sometimes they don't (with other democracies). What we have done is to collapse Figure 10 into the first cell of Figure 5 by combining the values in the top row of Figure 10.

Reconsidering the Régime-War Hypothesis

To this point we have explored the generally accepted but, as we have seen, poorly argued connection between democratic régimes and their potential for war. These arguments assume that a democracy's foreign-policy process differs from that of a nondemocracy. While democratic and nondemocratic régimes clearly have differing governing processes, we cannot conclude from this that the foreign-policy process—the decision-making system that determines war or peace—is also different.

Foreign-Policy Process

To the contrary, it can reasonably be argued that the foreign-policy processes of both régime types, democratic and nondemocratic, are quite similar: The foreign-policy elites who carry out the foreign policy of countries throughout the world use the same means such as diplomacy and protocol, control information, claim expertise and the need for secrecy, and are not particularly controlled by the dominant elite, including democratic representatives.

How can we assess this notion? Let us assume that an adequate empirical measure finds a democratic country, one that enjoys open elections, freedom of speech, and other democratic characteristics. How does this country function politically? Bryce's (1921, II: 368) classic study of *Modern Democracies* outlines the generally accepted pattern. What distinguishes a democracy from oligarchies, he tells us, is that its people determine the ends of politics; that is, what the society hopes to accomplish and how it intends to do so.[23] Citizens can do this in the domestic environment because they have ready access to events, historical understandings, current debates, legislative actions, and a host of other sources of information.

This closeness to politics, however, does not exist in the foreign-policy arena. Bryce points out that a country's citizenry has neither the deep understanding nor current information about foreign lands required to have a meaningful viewpoint. What is more, the country itself must frequently make rapid assessments about a foreign crisis and respond quickly to protect the national interest:

> The general principles which should guide and the spirit which should inspire a nation's

foreign policy are . . . too wide in scope, too grave in consequences, to be determined
by any authority lower than that of the people.

For this reason governments create foreign-policy establishments—foreign
offices, diplomatic envoys, intelligence agencies, and others—empowered to
trace what is occurring abroad, make recommendations to the head of state,
and, sometimes, implement the decisions:

> The relations of States to one another, varying from day to day as the circumstances
> which govern them vary, cannot be handled by large assemblies who are incessantly
> watching the foreign sky. Modern legislatures accordingly . . . have recognized that
> in foreign affairs the choice of Means must belong to a small body of experts, and
> have accordingly left to these persons all details, and the methods which diplomacy
> must employ in particular cases, allowing them a wide, possibly a too wide, discretion.

The democratic citizenry thus relinquishes *direct* control over foreign policy
to a foreign-policy elite, while retaining *indirect* control through such procedures as legislative oversight, parliamentary hearings, and legal action.

The linkage between citizen control and foreign-policy elite is critical for
our understanding of the democracy-war nexus. The foreign-policy elite has
a *mandate to know* what is happening overseas. This gives it a potential to
dominate both the flow of foreign information and the "official" interpretation
of that information. Even the freest, most objective press cannot effectively
offer news regarding foreign-policy issues that contradicts the official version;
and hard-nosed critics think twice before taking foreign-policy stances that
could lead to charges of disloyalty. The foreign-policy elite, it is believed,
embodies the experts who know how correctly to interpret the implications
of overseas events for national security. It is extremely difficult for others,
regardless of free press, open elections, and the like to put forth contrary
policies.

Further, the foreign-policy elite's *mandate to act* instructs it to carry out
policy decisions in a timely fashion. This mandate gives the foreign-policy
elite a license to manipulate decision making in favor of policies that the
citizens and their representatives might, if they had the information and opportunity to consider them, be unwilling to support. For example:

- Thomas Jefferson's abandonment of his democratic principles in 1803 to purchase
  Louisiana and in 1807–1809 to embargo U.S. exports (Tucker and Hendrickson
  1990);
- Anglo-French-Israeli invasion of Egypt in 1956;
- U.S. "Iran-Contra" scandal in the 1980s or invasion of Panama in 1989; and
- West Germany's supine support of a firm giving Libya the means to manufacture
  poison gas.

In such circumstances, democratic representatives may eventually investigate,
excoriate, and even punish those responsible for the wrong-headed policy.
But, given the mystique surrounding foreign-policy decision making, and given
official-secrets acts designed not only to facilitate this decision process but

FIGURE 11
Foreign-Policy Process as an Intervening Variable

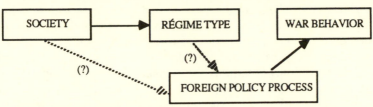

also to protect the foreign-policy elite, it is not surprising that such scrutiny usually comes about too late to bar the policy.[24]

The frequency with which democratic countries unleash foreign-policy actions before consulting popular representatives, and sometimes even after deliberately misleading them, makes us question the extent to which the foreign-policy process of democracies differs from that of autocracies. Furthermore, it should be observed, although the "oppressed masses" in autocracies do not enjoy the oversight functions of a democracy, they can, albeit sometimes at great cost, passively resist unacceptable policies. Thus popular resistance, plus the immense social and economic cost of carrying out the war, led the Soviet Union to withdraw its troops from Afghanistan in a manner reminiscent of the U.S. withdrawal from Vietnam a decade and a half earlier. Forty-four and a half years of authoritarian control did not deter the bulk of East Germans from following various forms of passive resistance, not the least of which being a willingness to "vote with their feet" by fleeing the German Democratic Republic. The oversight capacity of democratic societies is thus less than is often acknowledged while the impact of societies on nondemocratic régimes cannot be ignored.

Régime type is thus not a clear-cut indicator of the foreign-policy process. Sometimes democratic countries carry out their foreign-policy process in a remarkably undemocratic fashion. For example, a well-placed member of the U.S. foreign-policy elite could proudly report having lied to Congress, and the president who had appointed him could declare the man a national hero. Sometimes authoritarian states realize that they must bow to popular pressure. For example, the Polish government found that it could not function without dealing with the workers and their banned organization, Solidarity. The question, then, is one of gradation rather than absolutes—not whether or not a régime has "democratic controls" over its foreign-policy process, but rather the extent to which the régime systematically carries out such democratic controls. This suggests, as shown in Figure 11, that, while the foreign-policy process clearly determines a régime's behavior, the linkage between régime type and the foreign-policy process is less clearcut.

Economic Structure and Foreign Policy

Another independent variable that helps shape foreign policy, but has been largely ignored in the scientific literature, is economic modernity. The modern industrial or postindustrial state is a complex phenomenon. It requires integrated modes of production and distribution, access to foreign markets and sources of supply, efficient managers, a skilled labor force with growing competence in the information sector, independent trade unions, research and development, and a government-supported network of social welfare to cushion less competitive workers, the disabled, retirees, and others. Developing such a modern economy is both expensive and time-consuming.

Not surprisingly, countries that enjoy modern economies want to protect them—and the destructiveness of contemporary warfare is a serious threat to their survival. In earlier times, when the main costs of war were the national treasury, soldiers' lives, and property damage, a government might risk one if it could assure itself that victory was guaranteed and probable costs not overwhelming. Warfare is different nowadays. It challenges a complex economy's capacity to sustain its very existence. The economic cost that World War II visited upon European countries took them years, and in some instances decades, to recover. None of them wishes to embark on new wars that they can avoid. As a general principle, then, we might hypothesize that the more modern a country's economy, the more the country avoids involvement in wars. Governments find it difficult to undertake military action.

Then why have modern-economic countries caused wars anyway? We might think of U.S. soldiers sent to Vietnam and Panama, Soviet troops in Afghanistan, the Anglo-French-Israeli assault on Egypt, and so forth. The answer to the question doubtless lies only in part on conceptions of vital national interests that drive their political leaders. More significant are other circumstances. For one thing, the targeted countries were economically and militarily weaker. They seemed to promise the initiators a quick victory. For another thing, the conflict would be carried out overseas. While the home body might suffer somewhat in terms of both taxes and blood, it would not suffer devastation by direct military attacks. By contrast, wars pitting NATO and Warsaw Treaty countries would be neither quick, inexpensive, nor domestically painless. The Cold War was carefully—and successfully—calculated to avoid precisely that kind of disaster.

If the hypothesis linking economic structure to war behavior has any merit, it raises questions about the role of political régimes. First, how are political régimes and economic structures (or régimes) related to each other? Historically, in some countries they emerged roughly simultaneously, but in other countries one preceded the other and, indeed, may be said to have "caused" it.[25] Imperial Germany showed us that, by co-opting the mass of workers and preventing the emergence of an independent middle class, a feudal aristocracy could build massive industries and aggressive military establishments; but Germany's subsequent history demonstrated the fragility of such a modern economy unsupported by liberal democracy (Dahrendorf 1967). Recent events in Eastern Europe give renewed strength to the argument that the dominance of economic issues forces countries to reform their political régimes.

Second, do political or economic régimes (via the foreign-policy process)

FIGURE 12
Political and Economic Régimes and War Behavior

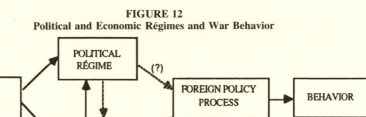

determine foreign-policy behaviors? A century ago most writers did not question the political régime's dominance. Such theorists as Karl Marx and Charles A. Beard (1913), however, convincingly argued that at least in some cases the economic tail wagged the political dog. Today, it appears increasingly that, while the political régime formally controls the foreign-policy process and hence prefigures war behavior, the economic régime is the driving force behind decisions made by the political régime. This postulated pattern of linkages, stressing the dominance of the economic régime, is described in Figure 12. But, it must be added, other patterns are conceivable. The point is that the idea of modernized economies is too important in basic decision making to be shunted aside from scientific consideration.[26]

The Next Step

Does a government's decision-making structure—régime—influence its international behavior, particularly its choice to go to war? The bits and pieces assembled here do not provide a sufficient basis for any definitive answer. At best, they point to areas that need attention.

Although the conceptual and operational definition of one form of government, democracy, has elicited extensive research, a similar analysis of other régime types is far from complete. It is not clear whether régime type is a unidimensional or multidimensional concept. The concept of war poses additional operational problems. Far more serious, however, is the argument, or lack thereof, that might link régime types and foreign-policy behaviors. Although noteworthy prejudices assume that democracies are inherently peaceful, the rationales explaining why this might be the case are extraordinarily simplistic and surprisingly unrelated to the conceptual and operational definitions of the basic variables, régime type and war.

Given the underdeveloped state of the argument linking régimes and war and peace behavior, it is not surprising that empirical analyses have arrived at conflicting conclusions. Although Chan has argued that the differences in findings are attributable to differences in research design, a potentially more promising approach is suggested by Most and Starr, who contend that war-related research must be dyadic. The monadic hypotheses linking régime and war must necessarily come up empty-handed. On the other hand, one might accept the conclusion that no relationship exists between régime type and war-and-peace behavior, and search for explanations that would make plausible such a conclusion.

We have suggested two such arguments. First, differences in régime type may have little or nothing to do with the foreign-policy process because the very nature of the foreign-policy process makes it elite-driven and closed to social inpute. The foreign policy process is the same across régime types. Decisions for war thus have little to do with régime type. A second argument postulates the importance of a third variable: the economic structure of societies. Democratic or nondemocratic, economically modernized societies have too much to lose to gamble on any serious war. It is not régime type but economic development that must be considered in seeking to understand the decision for war.

Research on the régime-war nexus is far from complete. The results to date have been intriguing, if frustrating. We hope that the present effort provides a basis for a next step in understanding what is an important issue for not only social scientific research but also peaceful international politics.

Notes

1. People in democratic societies, Tocqueville (1835/1958: 279) wrote, are not inclined to seek military glory: "The ever increasing numbers of men of property who are lovers of peace, the growth of personal wealth which war so rapidly consumes, the mildness of manners, the gentleness of heart, those tendencies to pity which are produced by the equality of conditions, that coolness of understanding which renders men comparatively insensible to the violent and poetical excitment of arms, all these causes concur to quench the military spirit."
2. As Wilson told Detroit businessmen in 1916, "You are Americans and are meant to carry liberty and justice and the principles of humanity wherever you go." (Levin 1968: 18).
3. A related question, not addressed here, is the way in which régime types at the *nation-state level* of analysis pursue policies aimed at democratizing the *international level*. Democratic internationalism focuses not only on issues of war and peace but also international legal norms, collective security arrangements, economic equality, free flow of individuals, and so forth.
4. Scientists have by now used this univariate linkage so frequently that it is accepted in the scholarly literature. Thus Sirowy and Inkeles' (1990) review of literature on the "effects of democracy" describes it primarily in terms of authoritarian vs. democratic models.
5. Dahl's efforts to measure the participation variable were not wholly successful, and later his students (Coppedge and Reinicke, 1990) essentially jettisoned it.
6. Some Western intellectuals share a part of this argument when they question the vaunted value of free (i.e., commercial) information, Tweedledum and Tweedledee as electoral candidates, and so forth.
7. Bollen (1980: 377) notes that correlations among the six political-democracy components are "relatively high" (average $p = .704$ in 1960 and average $p = .728$ in 1965); and Coppedge and Reinicke (1990: 56) state that the minimum coefficient of reproducibility is $+.900$ between the polyarchy-scale score and a country's ratings on one of the component variables.
8. Both Bollen's combined linear transformations and Coppedge and Reinicke's Guttmann scale assume the variables to be equal values. This procedure seems reasonable. But how confident can we be that press freedom and fair elections are equally critical for democracies or polyarchies?
9. Dick's authoritarian-nonauthoritarian régimes are defined in ways similar to the democratic-autocratic régimes of other writers. Muller narrows his sample by omitting countries not reporting economic data to standard United Nations or similar sources. Other studies (e.g. Kohli et al. 1986) focus on more specific regional areas.
10. These are Organic (traditional/civic—Ethiopia), Whig (transitional/civic—Chile), Participant (modern/civic—Soviet Union), Oligarchical (traditional/prætorian—Paraguay), Radical (transitional/prætorian—Egypt), and Mass (modern/prætorian—Argentina).

11. Although some boundaries may be fluid, Berg-Schlosser treats the four types as distinct.

12. Berg-Schlosser (1984: 128) does not describe this procedure, reporting solely that "A factor analysis proper, in the statistical sense of the term, was precluded by the fact that the n of cases was relatively small and the variance quite large and, even more important, that some of the variables only were of a nominal or ordinal nature."

13. The latter stance does not surprise socialist writers who see democracy embodying greater splendor than the bourgeois model allows.

14. In some U.S. circles it was popular beginning in roughly 1979 to see only three governmental types. Democratic and authoritarian régimes are of course noncommunist (hence, cells 1 and 3, respectively, on Figure 3). Communist countries are by definition antidemocratic (cell 4). Not only does this pose the intellectual problem of the missing cell (cell 2 in this case), but it also led to a foreign-policy perspective arguing that the United States had no justifiable position denying financial and military support to noncommunist régimes simply because they were authoritarian.

15. For thirty-nine European and Latin American countries in 1878, $r^2 = 0.579$; and for fifty-three such countries in 1978, $r^2 = 0.833$.

16. Small and Singer provide a list (Table 2.1, pp. 47–50) of those admitted to the status of statehood.

17. "The incidence of geographic contiguity between democratic nations is quite small. Thus if war is most likely between neighbors, and if bourgeois democracies have rarely been neighbors, this may well explain why they have rarely fought against one another" (p. 67).

18. Using war as the criterion for inclusion in the dataset, the research ignores a much larger set of situations, nonwars, in which war did not occur between each pair of countries. Spatial contiguity may have a bearing on the former phenomenon but we do not know what impact it has on the latter. (A world with an average of eighty countries engaged in bidirectional interactions [that is, from France to Germany as well as from Germany to France] over a 150-year period would have 150[80 × 79] = 984,000 dyadic relationships, very few of which did involve wars.) If our concern is to understand the circumstances in which wars occur, Small and Singer's limited sample provides no solid answer.

19. Wright's critique of democracy, penned after continental Europe's collapse before Germany's *Wehrmacht*, reflected a pessimism prevalent during those dark days among other writers and politicians — and, in a way, Adolf Hitler's (1925/1939: 387; cf. 584–587, 669–670 *et passim*) vision about the ineffectuality of democracies confronted by "the wonderful power and strength of the old Reich" with its "State authority."

20. *Webster's Seventh New Collegiate Dictionary* defines society as "an enduring and cooperative social group whose members have developed organized patterns of relationships through interaction with one another" (3a) and "a community, nation, or broad grouping of people having common traditions, institutions, and collective activities and interests" (3b).

21. "Libertarianism . . . is a structural variable — a particular cluster of political characteristics that should always be found together: free and open elections for top leaders, competitive party systems, freedom of speech and the press, freedom of groups to oppose government, individual rights and limited government, and so forth" (1985: 426).

22. Small and Singer (1976: 67) found only two "marginal exceptions" of "wars between such states" in 1816–1965: "an ephemeral republican France attacking an ephemeral republican Rome in 1849 and a rightward-drifting Finnish democracy joining Germany to attack Russia (and thus the [democratic] Allied Nations) in 1941." The criterion they used for their dataset is the *interstate war*. Adapting their data to account for *dyadic behaviors*, we find that their forty-nine wars (omitting the unclear war of Navarino Bay in 1827) comprise eleven dyadic wars carried out by democracies against democracies (with ten of these involving Finland's formal role in World War II as an aggressor against Great Britain, France, and the other Western democracies), twenty-five by democracies against autocracies, 111 by autocracies against democracies, and 167 by autocracies against autocracies.

23. "Ends, if not assumed as generally recognized, are and must be determined by the people through their representatives. Justice, the maintenance of public order, economy in expenditure are understood to be aims in every department while the particular objects for which money is to be spent and the modes of raising it are prescribed by statute" (Bryce 1921, II: 368).

24. Epstein (1962: 179) writes: "Coherence in foreign policy-making appears to require a functioning political model in which the elected executive authority is entrusted with the formulation of policy. . . . The only effective limits on this authority are then no more than those imposed by the very broadest strategic goals which a nation has in common and on which it is not consulted in any formal institutional way. That the public, attentive or otherwise, should be prepared to support governmental policy thus become but another task for government's leaders to accomplish."

25. The debate about this interaction is similar to studies focused on the linkage between political régime types and economic growth (cf. Sirowy and Inkeles 1990).
26. A related set of issues deals with the impact on war and peace of business cycles and Kondratieff long waves (cf. Hower and Zinnes 1989).

References

BEARD, CHARLES A.
    1913   *An Economic Interpretation of the Constitution of the United States.* New York: The Macmillan Company.
BERG-SCHLOSSER, DIRK
    1984   "African political systems: typology and performance." *Comparative Political Studies* 17,1 (April 1984): 121–151.
BOLLEN, KENNETH A.
    1979   "Political democracy and the timing of development." *American Sociological Review* 44,4 (August): 572–587.
    1980   "Issues in the comparative measurement of political democracy." *American Sociological Review* 45,3 (June): 370–390.
    1983   "World system position, dependency, and democracy: The cross-national evidence." *American Sociological Review* 48,4 (August): 468–479.
    1986   "Political rights and political liberties in nations: An evaluation of human rights measures, 1950–1984." *Human Rights Quarterly* 8,4 (November): 567–591.
    1990   "Political democracy: Conceptual and measurement traps." *Studies in Comparative International Development* 25,1 (Spring), 7–24.
BOLLEN, KENNETH A. and BURKE D. GRANDJEAN
    1981   "The dimension(s) of democracy: Further issues in the measurement and effects of political democracy." *American Sociological Review* 46,5 (October): 651–659.
BOLLEN, KENNETH A. and ROBERT W. JACKMAN
    1985   "Political democracy and the size of distribution of income." *American Sociological Review* 50,4 (August): 438–457.
BRYCE, JAMES (Viscount)
    1921   *Modern Democracies*, 2 vols. New York: The Macmillan Company.
CHAN, STEVE
    1984   "Mirror, mirror on the wall . . .: Are the freer countries more pacific?" *The Journal of Conflict Resolution* 28,4 (December): 617–648.
COPPEDGE, MICHAEL and WOLFGANG H. REINICKE
    1988   "A scale of polyarchy." In Raymond D. Gastil, ed., *Freedom in the World: Political Rights and Civil Liberties, 1787–1988.* Lanham, MD: University Press of America.
    1990   "Measuring polyarchy." *Studies in Comparative International Development* 25,1 (Spring): 51–72.
DAHL, ROBERT A.
    1956   *A Preface to Democratic Theory.* Chicago: University of Chicago Press.
    1971   *Polyarchy: Participation and Opposition.* New Haven and London: Yale University Press.
DAHL, ROBERT A. and CHARLES E. LINDBLOM
    1953   *Politics, Economics, and Welfare: Planning and Politico-Economic Systems Resolved into Basic Social Processes.* New York: Harper & Row.
DAHRENDORF, RALF
    1967   *Society and Democracy in Germany.* Garden City, NY: Doubleday & Co.
DICK, G. WILLIAM
    1974   "Authoritarian versus nonauthoritarian approaches to economic development." *Journal of Political Economy* 82,4 (July/August 1974): 817–827.
EPSTEIN, LEON D.
    1962   "Democracy and foreign policy." In William N. Chambers and Robert H. Salisbury, eds., *Democracy Today: Problems and Prospects.* New York: Collier Books.
GURR, TED ROBERT, KEITH JAGGERS and WILL H. MOORE
    1990   "The transformation of the Western state: the growth of democracy, autocracy, and state power since 1800." *Studies in Comparative International Development* 25,1 (Spring): 73–108.

HITLER, ADOLF
    1925/1939   *Mein Kampf.* Boston: Houghton Mifflin Co.
HOWER, GRETCHEN and DINA A. ZINNES
    1989   "International political conflict." In Joseph B. Gittler, ed., *The Annual Review of Conflict Knowledge and Conflict Resolution,* vol. 1. New York and London: Garland Publishing Inc.
HUNTINGTON, SAMUEL P.
    1968   *Political Order in Changing Societies.* New Haven and London: Yale University Press.
HUNTINGTON, SAMUEL P. and JORGE I. DOMÍNGUEZ
    1975   "Political development." In Fred I. Greenstein and Nelson W. Polsby, eds., *Handbook of Political Science,* vol. 3: *Macropolitical Theory.* Reading, MA: Addison-Wesley Publishing Co.
KOHLI, ATUL, MICHAEL F. ALTFELD, SAIDEH LOTFIAN and RUSSELL MARDON
    1984   "Inequality in the Third World: An assessment of competing explanations." *Comparative Political Studies* 17,3 (October): 283–318.
LEVIN, N. GORDON JR.
    1968   *Woodrow Wilson and World Politics: America's Response to War and Revolution.* New York: Oxford University Press.
LEVY, MARION J.
    1966   *Modernization and the Structure of Societies: A Setting for International Affairs.* Princeton, NJ: Princeton University Press.
LIJPHART, AREND
    1984   *Democracies: Patterns of Majoritarian and Consensus Government in Twenty-One Countries.* New Haven and London: Yale University Press.
MERRITT, RICHARD L. and DINA A. ZINNES
    1988   "Democracies and international conflict." Paper presented at the Conference on Measuring Democracy, Hoover Institution, Stanford, CA, 27–28 May.
MOST, BENJAMIN A. and HARVEY STARR
    1989   *Inquiry, Logic and International Politics.* Columbia: University of South Carolina Press.
MULLER, EDWARD N.
    1988   "Democracy, economic development, and income inequality." *American Sociological Review* 53,1 (February): 50–58.
O'DONNELL, GUILLERMO A.
    1973   *Modernization and Bureaucratic Authoritarianism: Studies in South American Politics.* Berkeley: University of California, Institute of International Affairs, Politics of Modernization Series, no. 9.
POWELL, G. BINGHAM, JR.
    1982   *Contemporary Democracies: Participation, Stability, and Violence.* Cambridge, MA, and London: Harvard University Press.
PRZEWORSKI, ADAM and HENRY TEUNE
    1970   *The Logic of Comparative Social Inquiry.* New York: John Wiley & Sons Inc.
PYE, LUCIAN W.
    1966   *Aspects of Political Development.* Boston, MA, and Toronto: Little, Brown and Company.
RICHARDSON, LEWIS F.
    1960   *Statistics of Deadly Quarrels.* Pittsburgh, PA: The Boxwood Press, and Chicago: Quadrangle Books.
RUMMEL, RUDOLF J.
    1968   "The relationship between national attributes and foreign conflict behavior." In J. David Singer, ed., *Quantitative International Politics: Insights and Evidence.* New York: The Free Press.
    1976   *Understanding Conflict and War,* vol. 2: *The Conflict Helix.* Beverly Hills, CA, and London: Sage Publications Inc.
    1979   *Understanding Conflict and War,* vol. 4: *War, Power, and Peace.* Beverly Hills, CA, and London: Sage Publications Inc.
    1981   *Understanding Conflict and War,* vol. 5: *The Just Peace.* Beverly Hills, CA, and London: Sage Publications Inc.
    1983   "Libertarianism and international violence." *The Journal of Conflict Resolution* 27,1 (March): 27–71.

1984   "Libertarianism, violence within states, and the polarity principle." *Comparative Politics* 16,4 (July): 443–462.
1985   "Libertarian propositions on violence within and between nations: A test against published research results." *The Journal of Conflict Resolution* 29,3 (September): 419–455.

SHILS, EDWARD
1962   *Political Development in the New States.* The Hague and Paris: Mouton Publishers.

SIROWY, LARRY and ALEX INKELES
1990   "The effects of democracy on economic growth and inequality: A review." *Studies in Comparative International Development* 25,1 (Spring): 126–157.

SLOAN, JOHN and KENT L. TEDIN
1987   "The consequences of regime type for public-policy outputs." *Comparative Political Studies* 20,1 (April): 98–124.

SMALL, MELVIN and J. DAVID SINGER
1976   "The war-proneness of democratic regimes, 1816–1965." *The Jerusalem Journal of International Relations* 1,4 (Summer): 50–69.
1982   *Resort to Arms: International and Civil Wars, 1816–1980.* Beverly Hills, CA, London, and New Delhi: Sage Publications Inc.

STAMMER, OTTO
1968   "Dictatorship." In David L. Sills, ed., *International Encyclopedia of the Social Sciences,* vol. 4. New York: The Macmillan Co. and The Free Press.

TOCQUEVILLE, ALEXIS DE
1835/1958   *Democracy in America,* 2 vols. New York: Alfred A. Knopf Inc.; Vintage Books Inc.

TUCKER, ROBERT W. and DAVID C. HENDRICKSON
1990   *Empire of Liberty: The Statecraft of Thomas Jefferson.* New York: Oxford University Press.

WEEDE, ERIC
1971   "Charakteristika von Nationen als Erklärungsgrundlage für das internationale Konfliktverhalten." In Rudolf Wildenmann, ed., *Sozialwissenschaftliches Jahrbuch für Politik,* vol. 2. München and Wien: Günter Olzog Verlag.
1984   "Democracy and war involvement." *The Journal of Conflict Resolution* 28,4 (December): 649–664.

WRIGHT, QUINCY
1942   *A Study of War.* Chicago: The University of Chicago Press.